About the Author

Den Dover never knew his father until the end of the wars in Europe and Burma. He lived halfway between Liverpool and Manchester under the bombers' airpaths. American soldiers and airmen were the heroes of his childhood years. Churchill was his hero and the saviour of Britain. Den resolved that he would follow Churchill by dedicating his life to caring and providing for the people by becoming a Member of Parliament.

Dedications

Ian Sellers and Elsie Whittington.

My mother and father to whom I owe everything.

Den Dover

The Road to Westminster

AUSTIN MACAULEY PUBLISHERS™

LONDON · CAMBRIDGE · NEW YORK · SHARJAH

A CIP catalogue record for this title is available from the British Library.

ISBN 9781398452138 (Paperback)
ISBN 9781398452145 (Hardback)
ISBN 9781398452169 (ePub e-book)

www.austinmacauley.com

First Published 2022
Austin Macauley Publishers Ltd
1 Canada Square
Canary Wharf
London
E14 5AA

Acknowledgements

Carrie Crowe (niece) and Amanda Dover (daughter).

How a Lancashire lad from humble beginnings took the long, tricky, hard and difficult road to achieve his ambition of becoming a Member of Parliament.

Chapter 1

Albert Dover was born in Warrington on 20 January 1906—half a mile from the Manchester Ship Canal which ran from the entrance to the Irish Sea in South Liverpool all the 40 miles to the Salford Docks, which were very close to the centre of Manchester. This inland waterway had been carved out of the underlying sandstone and clay layers by the 'navvies' in the middle of the 19th century. Those were pioneering days when much of the current infrastructure of roads, canals and waterways was installed by huge numbers of Irish immigrants who quickly trained their English counterparts to form a massive army of dedicated, hardworking, rugged and physically tough labourers who literally built the backbone of Victorian Britain.

The house where Albert was born was a small 19th-century terraced property typical of the huge estates of mass urban housing built near the centre of most cities and large towns in England at that time. These terraced homes were occupied by large families and were terribly overcrowded, with children and parents being squashed into the only four very small rooms—'two up, two down'—that were available. However, this was the only accommodation they could afford, and they were thankful and grateful for it.

Over the first half of the 20th century, huge numbers of up and coming young couples in such areas fought very hard indeed to escape from this dirty, downtown, down market, unsatisfactory urban squalor. They worked extremely hard to be able to afford to set up homes a few miles away from the densely populated towns and cities where the occupants of the factories, mills, shops, schools and businesses of all shapes and sizes had struggled for far too long, and had had to share the often heavy polluted air that breezed in from the Irish Sea to the west.

This regularly brought rainfall and fogs along the basin of the River Mersey that ran between Liverpool on the coast and Manchester nestling just to the west of the Pennine hills that form the central spine of England from north to south. The younger generations wanted fresh air, countryside and freedom—and they were willing to work damn hard to achieve a better quality of life for themselves and their families.

Albert's father had also been born in the town which was halfway between Liverpool and Manchester. Albert had attended the local school and then moved on to an apprenticeship with Metropolitan Vickers, a huge industrial engineering combine near the centre of Manchester. His single ambition since starting his schooling was to serve an apprenticeship with Metropolitan Vickers. Albert's days were extremely long. He would leave at 6 am to walk the twenty minutes to the railway station and wait on the cold, exposed open platform for the steam train that would transport him to within a few miles of the centre of the city of Manchester.

He knew the names of all the stations and every day he spent the whole journey reading the handwritten notes that he had taken during lessons on the vast array of detailed subjects that he was studying during his apprenticeship. He had thoroughly enjoyed his early schooling and had rapidly developed his natural aptitude for both mathematics and all the technical subjects such as electronics, physics, chemistry and geography contained in the apprenticeship syllabus. These were the essential building blocks that he needed to put in place if he was to achieve his one over-riding ambition which was to be selected to serve with hundreds of other boys at the enormous factory of Metropolitan Vickers in Manchester where the annual intake of three hundred boys would form the bedrock and the starting point of a five year apprenticeship which was second to none.

Albert had realised from an early age that he could match any of his contemporaries—not just in the educational field but in any of the physical skills such as cricket, football and fighting. Indeed he was renowned as a very able wrestler and boxer and spent as much time as his scholastic studies allowed at a small boxing club round the corner from his parents' home. In fact Albert never seemed to take a minute's rest during the whole of his waking life because he had so much boundless energy, and the desire to succeed in his chosen career as a so called 'mechanical engineer.' In Albert's book this meant that he wanted and needed to know everything possible about machinery and engines. He was totally fascinated by the world of new inventions which was expanding at a very fast rate—into aeroplanes, steam engines, calculating machines and motorcars.

For him the most interesting classes were those in which he learned about both the theory and the practical aspects of new subjects that had never been mentioned at all in his local school. He felt that his knowledge was expanding unbelievably quickly each week because there were so many different subject headings within each of the numerous specialist fields that were contained in the mechanical engineering apprenticeship syllabus.

He focussed his attention on every word spoken by the various lecturers and he wrote copious notes from the blackboard into a giant hard backed blue book of some 500 pages that he had picked out of a waste bin down one of the streets of central Warrington in the business area. Every night at home he worked at a makeshift table and looked over the twenty or so pages of notes that he had made that day. He found that by doing this he was able to understand every detail of what the various lecturers had covered each day.

The next morning he would go through in his mind, as he walked and travelled by train, all the notes he had digested the previous evening to ensure that he knew and understood them totally. He was determined to make a success of his apprenticeship with Metropolitan Vickers so that he could eventually apply for a job with one of the many large manufacturing firms near the centre of Warrington, his home town.

Albert had always been the one boy in his street who, from an early age, could take any toys, scooters and tricycles/bicycles to bits when they needed attention. He had a natural gift of being able to understand what needed to be done to any piece of equipment to restore it to full working condition. He soon discovered that his school and apprenticeship studies expanded his detailed working knowledge of equipment and toys enormously. He was delighted, but not totally surprised, that he had clearly chosen exactly the right type of apprenticeship to suit his interests and his needs.

His favourite classes were those where practical sessions were carried out in very large workshops with some massive machines. Working in pairs the two groups of around twenty apprentices were joined by very experienced workshop technicians who knew everything about the various machines and who explained to the apprentices how the various machines needed to be operated to achieve the various functions being carried out—safely and to very high standards of quality and precision. In this way, the whole class learned about the practical side of mechanical engineering in parallel with the theory being taught in the lectures.

Albert was amazed that the machinery allowed settings to such precise accuracies. He had not realised that blocks of metal were cut, rotated, milled and grinded on such huge machines that would fill any of the rooms in his house several times over—and yet the machine settings could be adjusted down to thousandths of an inch! Albert had a natural ability when he operated the numerous machines, probably because he was used to handling and mending all sorts of metal fixtures and moving parts when repairing his friends' equipment back in his own neighbourhood. He had a tremendous feeling of achievement, fulfilment, understanding and even gratitude—that he had somehow found his way into what was for him the perfect scenario, where he could learn more and more each day about what interested him most.

At the weekends Albert spent most of his time improving his football skills in the winter months and his cricket and swimming skills in the summer. There were no sports clubs or activities available to the apprentices at Metropolitan Vickers. Indeed it would have been impossible for any such leisure activities to have been fitted into the apprentice programmes which were so intense. However, Albert had noted that on the few open fields surrounding the huge factory complex there were several football pitches and even a small number of pavilions. His football and cricket skills were improved season by season by joining in with ad hoc teams put together by slightly older boys than Albert himself.

Usually, there were no real goalposts or wickets, merely coats slung down and cardboard boxes or crates used to add reality to the proceedings. This in no way detracted from the importance of these matches. Indeed, every sort of cup final or test match was played out on the few open fields within walking distance of the boys' homes. These matches were fought just as intensely as the real professional games, as each boy assumed the mantle of their favourite players and/or heroes of the time.

After several years of playing football and cricket in these makeshift games, Albert often wandered over to join a slightly older group of boys playing rugby. All of the boys had witnessed the growing popularity and professionalism of the game of rugby that was played every Saturday afternoon by all the major town teams—not just in Lancashire but also across the border in Yorkshire (where the standard was, by definition, inferior to that in Lancashire).

In those days not one of the boys playing rugby was aware of the existence of a parallel, but different, code of rugby named Rugby Union instead of what they were playing—Rugby League. Furthermore none of the thousands of boys learning and playing Rugby League in Lancashire and Yorkshire were even aware that there were such establishments as public schools where some of the richest and smartest boys in England were busy honing their skills in Rugby Union—with just as much enthusiasm for their game as the working class lads of Lancashire and Yorkshire had for their code of the game.

Albert knew that he was one of the most travelled boys in the whole area because of his daily railway journeys from Warrington to Manchester. However, his whole world was contained in an area of some forty miles (Liverpool to Manchester) by five miles (the distance across the Mersey river basin). He was more than happy to devote all his efforts to his studies, his sport and his family. He had an older brother Tom who was happy to work every day of the week in the family business selling groceries, supplies and newspapers at a corner shop by one of the huge swing bridges on the Manchester Ship Canal. Tom was a pleasant enough lad but Albert had far more ambition and abilities, and he was going to aim for the top—rather than be content with serving in a small local shop.

Chapter 2

At the end of his five-year apprenticeship, Albert Dover had completed what was, at that time, the best form of industrial skilled training in one of the leading technical and academic countries in the world. He had been trained by some of the most highly qualified technicians and industrial engineers—and in the most advanced apprenticeship training facilities with one of the top half-dozen world-renowned firms.

Throughout the rigorous course, Albert had always been in the top ten apprentices in all the course work, the testing practical examinations and the highly technical written examination papers. He had also mixed very well indeed with the wide spectrum of apprentices from very disparate family backgrounds. Albert was very competitive but he also had a very warm, friendly manner. He had been playing both football and cricket for local league teams in the Warrington area and had, to his surprise, already played on the first class Metropolitan Vickers football and cricket pitches against teams that represented the firm in the recently formed local leagues.

It seemed ironic that he had served his lengthy apprenticeship without once playing sport for his own sponsoring firm. He had convinced himself that he could not efficiently and effectively divide his very high level mental and physical abilities and energies between sport and academic studies. He decided that he needed to focus more specifically and closely on one or the other. Albert decided that to get on in both his career and sporting activities he would have to make whatever sacrifices were necessary in order to achieve the success he so craved for. He wanted to show that he was someone to be reckoned with—and someone who could rise to the highest levels in whatever fields he decided to compete in.

He realised that he had come from a very ordinary family background, but he saw this as a distinct advantage because people would not have too high an expectation of him. He could therefore often be overlooked and/or under-rated. He considered that this might well benefit him in future because he would never be seen as a natural competitor and people would not be jealous of his success, but join with him in celebrating any of his future achievements.

*****

After he successfully completed his apprenticeship with top grades, Albert spent his first two years working for the large soap and detergent firm of Crosfields, near Warrington railway station. He was delighted to be able to enjoy a mixture of technical and manual tasks. He was always the first to volunteer to work overtime because he realised that he wanted to marry early and start a family as soon as possible. He had few memories of the 1914 to 1918 war because this was over before he started his apprenticeship. However, he was only too well aware that everyone was talking about the near certainty that there would be another war 'in the next few years.' Albert was not a keen follower of political events but he did realise that he needed to find a wife, buy a home and start a family before any such second war began—otherwise he would never keep his head above water or succeed in his life's ambitions.

Every Saturday night Albert's mates went to the Parr Hall in the centre of Warrington. This was a huge meeting hall where plays, pantomimes and local meetings took place on a very regular basis. However, his mates had only one thing in mind every Saturday night. They wanted to meet the most beautiful girls in town and impress them with their dancing skills—even if they hadn't a clue about the seemingly very large number of complicated and different dances that they would be expected to perform.

Albert had noticed that two of his girl cousins often boasted to both his and their parents about their dancing skills and also their abilities to attract the most handsome young men. He decided that he would team up with them and one of his male cousins and they would all four head off to the Parr Hall each Saturday night. To his dismay, the two girls were very reluctant indeed to lose their independence and their freedom. Albert even wondered if they were all talk and no action. Were they just bluffing, or were they as talented as they imagined and boasted of being? There was only one sure way of finding out.

Albert and his cousin Fred discussed their plan of action and what concessions they were willing to make. They were unwilling to attend any dancing lessons in advance because this was unheard of for males. After all, it was only sissy girls who needed to learn about dancing before venturing onto the dance floor wasn't it? They also debated at length whether or not they would be asked, or would indeed be willing, to pay for the entrance tickets for the two girl cousins.

They decided that they needed to discuss the whole subject with the two mothers of the girls concerned for several reasons. First they could not possibly broach the subject with any of their uncles, particularly because they had no idea if any of them knew anything at all about dancing. Secondly they did not want to show themselves up to their mothers as girl chasers and thirdly they reckoned that the two girls' mothers might welcome the approach and see it as a way of having someone in the family keeping a friendly eye on their daughters, and on the boys that they were mixing with every weekend.

Albert and Fred decided they would try out their plan with one of the mothers concerned, provided they could arrange to do it when both the girls would be safely out of the way. This took some time to arrange but the plan worked well with the first mother being very keen and reassured by the fact that her daughter would in effect have a chaperone, or two, who would report to her on all relevant matters. Unfortunately the other mother thought that they both 'had the cheek of old Nick'—despite their assurances and their heartfelt pleadings.

After a few weeks of reflection Albert and Fred decided that, in the spirit of 'nothing ventured, nothing gained' they should proceed with the one willing mother—provided she swore to cooperate with them in total confidence and never to discuss the matter with the other mother, or either of the two girls. Finally the two boys agreed that they would have to take the two girls along as their guests, provided they could split from them once they were inside. This was mainly to avoid having to pay for any of the girls' drinks or food—and also because they had enough courage in their abilities to attract other girls, particularly once they had learned how to dance at least a few of the complicated dance routines.

The two boys joined up with the two girl cousins in fear and trepidation on their first ever Saturday night outing. It was of all things the biggest dance event of the year, namely the New Year's Eve Ball! The one thing going round in their minds was the saying 'Nothing ventured, nothing gained.' They realised how awkward they would seem and how out of place. It would certainly be a night to remember—hopefully for some good reasons, and not for any disasters that might occur. The two boys spent most of the first hour trying to look at ease whilst taking in the general ambience and aura of the dance hall itself, which was buzzing with activity and filled with hundreds of young boys and girls in their teens and twenties.

Albert and Fred were most impressed by the band, the musicians and the singers. However, they steeled themselves for their first ever steps on the dance floor, under the close supervision and attention of their two girl guides, who had already impressed them both by their dancing skills with several of the local boys. The girls had also shown that they were natural mixers by the way they stood and chatted with so many boys at the various bars and the way they glided across the dance floor with so many different partners.

Albert, Fred and the two girls eventually ventured onto the dance floor. The girls took control as best they could, as they had often had to do exactly that with many of the boys at the Parr Hall. It turned out that large numbers of the boys at the Hall had learned how to dance by courtesy of the excellent on-the-job training provided by these two girls. Nevertheless it was a nightmare for both Albert and Fred as they stumbled around, regularly almost bringing down their girl cousins, and others, as well as themselves.

There were long periods when Albert and Fred decided to sit out the dances, or retire to one of the bars. As the time on the clock approached the finishing time of midnight—the bewitching hour—the whole mood in the dance hall changed. The lights were lowered gradually and the hall was in semi-darkness for a slow waltz. This stirred both the boys into choosing the most attractive couple of girls they could find, and asking them if they would care to dance.

For both Albert and Fred, time stood still for the first time in their lives. They experienced for the first time ever the wonderful, relaxing feeling of waltzing romantically round a dance floor together with hundreds of others—and being spellbound by the beauty, the peace and the wonder of it all.

Finally the lights were turned up and the National Anthem was played to a rapt audience of dancers who stood to attention and then applauded with much enthusiasm the band, its leader and all the staff for the wonderful evening they had been privileged to spend together.

This was an evening that both Albert and Fred would remember for the rest of their lives. They both met their future wives that evening and for them it was the beginning of a lifelong love of dancing and the joy and freedom that dancing brought into their lives.

Life is a series of opportunities and they realised how very fortunate they had been that night to have been able to be introduced to such a wonderful pastime as dancing—and to meet their life partners, and the mothers of their children.

What an evening it had been!

Chapter 3

Emma Kirk had five sisters and three brothers. She was born, along with the rest of her siblings in their 'two up, two down' terraced house only a few hundred yards from the very centre of Warrington. She had jet black hair and was a real 'corker' as the local lads called any of the local girls who were beautiful. She was as happy as the day was long. In her mind she lived in a wonderful neighbourhood with extremely friendly and helpful people. The fact that there were rows and rows of terraced housing for several blocks around her home was a distinct advantage in Emma's opinion because it meant that there were plenty of playmates and school chums literally on her doorstep.

Emma and her brothers and sisters shared one of the two upstairs bedrooms while her Mum and Dad shared the other with whichever of the children were either being reared and/or nursed through an illness at that time. There was no running hot water in the house but all the children bathed each week in the front room in a tin bath that would hold two or three of them at a time until all were as clean as a whistle and had had their hair washed. All the water was heated up to bath temperature in the outhouse under the corrugated sheeting roof. This was where all the clothing would be laundered on a Monday morning and then hung out to dry, on the washing line, across the back yard.

On the right hand side of the back yard was the one outside toilet that was used by all the family and any visitors/playmates who came to the house. This toilet was nicknamed the 'privy' and consisted of a large wooden board with a one foot diameter hole near the front and in the middle. Old newspapers were used as the toilet paper and these were kept on a couple of sharp nails on the side walls so that they could be reached by hand by both children and adults using the facility.

When children visited the house for the first time they checked out the 'privy' and were always intrigued by how clean it was kept and the fact that all the wastes were efficiently disposed of, with the help of water that was flushed down the privy from the side by pulling a chain with a hard rubber grip within easy reach of the privy users.

*****

Although their home at 54 Sutton Street was almost certainly classified by the council's housing officials as the worst type of housing stock, Emma and all her family considered that they were well housed, and they were certainly all very house proud. Every week Emma's mother would not just scrub the stone front step but wash the whole pavement in front of the house—as did all the other householders. All the front windows would be cleaned on a Monday morning by sitting on the windowsill and hanging out of the window with the cleaning rags. This same ritual was carried out throughout the whole of the terraced housing areas of Lancashire and the northern towns. It was a mark of respect for the housing that the families were privileged to live in. Local pride meant that there were even regular ad hoc competitions to see who could keep the tidiest housing judged by its external appearance.

All the Kirk children attended the local school which was within a ten minute walk from their home. Nearly four hundred children between the ages of five and eleven attended the school and were taught in classes of around fifty children. Class discipline was extremely important and all the teachers were very strict indeed. They stood no nonsense and soon identified and isolated any troublemakers—often using the threat of sending any offenders to the head teacher's study for special treatment.

Although several children in each class would often have their knuckles rapped with a ruler or their bottoms smacked with a heavy book, this was fully accepted by the children, their parents and their schoolmates as being a fair and justifiable treatment to ensure that bullies, pranksters and disobedient children were made an example of. The other children were only too keen to get on with their studies and behave as well as they possibly could, rather than risk punishment and shame on their family names.

*****

Emma worked hard at school and loved both 'doing sums' and writing essays. She often worked in one or other of the corner shops within easy

20

walking distance of her home, particularly when there were school holidays. Some shopkeepers refused to pay for the helping hand given by children, on the basis that they were offering the children a training opportunity. However, several were only too willing to pay a small amount for the part-time assistance of local children. Indeed they often found that new customers were introduced to their shops because the children helping out were keen to show off to their friends that they had acquired a part-time job.

When Emma was approaching the age of eleven she was keen to move on to a school that would give her a more specialised education so that she would be better able to find suitable employment. However, places at these so-called secondary schools were fiercely fought for and she made the mistake of opting to start work in a local clock manufacturing firm. The one advantage was that it was just round the corner from her home. However, the only job that was available to a school leaver such as Emma was wrapping and packing the clocks for despatch to the customers. She thoroughly enjoyed her work but after a few years she realised that it was a job with no future.

Most of the working girls at the factory spent much of their time talking to their work colleagues about their latest boyfriend and about their evenings out. Emma listened to all this gossip but never joined in. It was clear that she was living quite a sheltered way of life, and could well remain a spinster for the rest of her days. The thought of this filled her with dread but she also accepted that she was often needed at home with so many brothers and sisters needing nursing and/or attention from their older siblings—particularly when their mother was suffering badly from a very bad chest and a 'hacking' cough which was painful to listen to in their small house.

Emma was a very determined young lady and she set herself the goal of finding herself a boyfriend who would rescue her from her present surroundings and make sure that she lived happily ever after. If all the female film stars could find the right person, so could she. However, she realised that it would not be easy for her, particularly because there were no handsome potential boyfriends within her part of town—nor indeed in the town centre which she ascertained when she was taken shopping by her mother and/or one or more of her older sisters.

Eventually Emma came up with a plan. She had listened intently for far too long to her work colleagues boasting about their handsome boyfriends, their wonderful evenings out at the cinema and their amazing exploits at the Parr

Hall—which they swore blind was the most famous dance hall in the whole of the country. It was time for Emma to summon up sufficient courage to dip her toes in the water and venture out into the big wide world.

She decided that she needed to express her interest in joining some of the girls on a night out to the Parr Hall. She knew she had no idea about dancing but she reasoned that none of the girls had been any more experienced when they first went along to the dance hall. In addition she had fallen in love with the film stars who so often swept round the ballrooms so gracefully that she was smitten by the thought of dancing with a partner herself!

Emma started to chat with a few of the more sensible girls, asking them what it was like at the Parr Hall. Eventually one of them came out straight and asked her if she would be interested in coming along one Saturday evening. Emma could hardly believe her luck and started counting down not just the days but even the hours before the agreed meeting time of 7 pm on the coming Saturday night. The meeting place was to be the front of the Ritz cinema by the bridge over the River Mersey. This was Emma's favourite cinema and she felt quite at home when Saturday evening came. She had not mentioned to any of her sisters what she was doing or where she was going. However, they all suspected where she was off to. They had never known her take such care of her appearance, nor to iron her one and only smart dress so many times that week.

Finally, Saturday night arrived and she was so excited when all her best friends from the clock factory turned up. By half past seven, they were seated inside the Parr Hall on the front row of wooden chairs surrounding the dance floor. The band was already playing their music, but fairly quietly. They were, as always, using the first hour or so as a substitute for their lack of practice time spent during the week.

Emma felt so exposed and lonely although she was surrounded by the girls from work. One or two of them pulled her onto the dance floor and helped her with her faltering steps until, after an hour or more, she started to get into the swing of things. That is as far as she got for the first few weeks but she thoroughly enjoyed the sheer release and pleasure that it gave her to be able to move around the dance floor with a partner—albeit one or other of her colleagues from the factory!

Over the next few months, Emma gradually grew in confidence and was able to practice the various dance steps at home or out on the nearby fields. She picked up the courage to dance with several boys and was delighted when she realised that it was the boys who were supposed to lead the dancing—although some of them had no idea at all!

Eventually, Emma grew in confidence and by the time of the first ever New Year's Eve Ball she was one of the most accomplished dancers at the Parr Hall. It was at that ball that she met her first ever heartthrob and she would never forget the magical moment when she was able to accompany him onto the dance floor—even though she had to lead him in the dancing. She realised he had hardly ever danced before but she was willing to be patient and teach him all that she knew.

However, she was so captivated that she forgot to ask him his name, or to arrange to keep in touch with him. She was going to have to be patient because of her own stupidity. No matter, she thought, because he did seem he would be worth the wait!

Chapter 4

Albert kept pestering his mate Fred about when they would be spending another night out dancing at the Parr Hall. Albert had been studying the local newspapers and had examined very closely indeed the two photographs of the New Year's Eve dance that had been held there. There was no way that the beautiful dark haired girl he had met that night was on either of the photographs, and he had a very good photographic memory. Anyway he would never forget her sparkling eyes which gave her a mischievous look which he adored so much. Albert started to study the local newspapers in the main Warrington library and he discovered that there were Saturday night dances at the Parr Hall every week. All he had to do was persuade Fred to come along with him. It seemed to him that all the boys and girls who went dancing were always with a group of friends, apart from a few pairs of boys.

Initially, Albert accepted Fred's word that he was required to work a great deal of overtime to meet the very high workloads in the factory where he worked. After several weeks however he lost patience and had a long chat one day with his mate. Far from working overtime Fred had lost his job and had not dared to tell Albert. He had no money at all to go living it up at the Parr Hall and he apologised to Albert, who fully understood how distraught his pal was.

After a long period of discussion, Albert and Fred devised a plan. Albert would pay for Fred to attend the Parr Hall with him until he found suitable employment, after which he would repay Albert as soon as possible. Albert was so sorry that his closest friend had not confided in him about losing his job, but he realised that it was a matter of pride for Fred, as well as being a huge embarrassment for him when out with friends and former work colleagues.

Both of the boys were very keen indeed to meet the two girls who had made such a huge impression on them the first time they had been to the dance hall. They had both shown their naivety and innocence by not making any arrangements with their dance partners. Perhaps the girls, who were obviously far more experienced than they, had not been impressed at all by the two boys– and were thankful and grateful that no further arrangements had been made on that first night. Albert, who was always a deep thinker, worried that the keenness of the two boys was completely at odds with the total lack of the girls' interest in them. If so, he realised it might be extremely difficult to rekindle any sparks of interest that there may have been in the hearts and minds of the girls.

*****

It was mid-February before Albert and Fred headed off together again for their second expedition to the Parr Hall. They had had to deal with much joking and poking of fun from their brothers, sisters and parents about venturing forth on something that they had never heard of before, namely St Valentine's Day. At least they were slightly prepared for the night in question, as they had quizzed all their friends and relations about this special day, what it meant to the girls and what was the best way of handling the whole situation.

Albert and Fred planned to arrive just after nine o'clock because they reasoned that, by then, they would be able to merge into the crowd instead of showing their embarrassment and inexperience if they were too clearly visible to the gaze of others when the dance hall was only partly full. They had dressed in their smartest clothes and had spent most of the afternoon in each other's company—cutting their hair, parting it with more care than they had ever shown before and talking nonstop through the sequence of how they were going to impress the two girls, and hopefully, get themselves 'hitched up' as their friends called it.

Approaching the front entrance of the dance hall they suddenly both had a terrible thought. What if the two girls did not arrive that night? Worse than that 'What if they are there and they totally ignore us—or even worse—are already hitched up to two boyfriends?' Albert spoke for both of them when he said that they must be mad to be so badly prepared for what they sincerely hoped and prayed could be the start of two wonderful romances.

They did not have to wait long because, as soon as they walked into the main dance hall, having combed their hair for the hundredth time that day, the two girls whom they had come to see were already on the dance floor and dancing in pairs with a group of more than a dozen other girls of around their same age. Albert and Fred were afraid that they were going to be ignored and that it might prove to be extremely difficult to gain the attention of the two girls they were targeting.

The two lads decided that they needed to be patient and wait for the big group of girls to break up, if indeed they ever did! Their patience was rewarded eventually when the band took a short break. Without hesitation Albert and Fred made a direct bee line for the two girls—pouncing on the long awaited opportunity that had opened up before their eyes.

Albert went up to his target, shook her by the hand and at that same moment introduced himself and said how lovely it was to meet her again after all the intervening weeks. Her reply was immediate, but not entirely unexpected.

'We were wondering what had happened to you two. We thought we must have scared you off on that night. New Year's Eve, wasn't it?'

'Yes it was,' said Albert as though he was in full control of the situation, even though his stomach seemed to be revolving on its bearings. 'We thoroughly enjoyed that evening and it is such a pleasure to meet you again.' He waited for the response he did not want to hear, but at least it was delivered in a quizzical manner rather than what could have been a nasty tone.

'We were wondering what had happened to you both, and we thought you were just like all the rest of the boys here, just after a good time.'

'No, no, no,' said Albert. 'We have been wanting to come each week but my friend Fred had some bad news and things have only just improved. In fact this is the very first time we have been out all year'—being conscious that it was only six weeks into the year as he spoke.

Out of the corner of his eye, Albert could see that Fred was making some progress with the other girl so he decided that it would be polite and sensible to spread the risk and join forces with the other two. This worked well and before long they were sitting with the two girls at a small round table with just the four seats. Now comes the hardest part, thought Albert. How on earth do I manage to get up on the dance floor and start dancing without losing this gorgeous girl who has never been out of my thoughts since the night I met her. He decided that it was time for boldness and bravery—and time he showed the girls that he was a man of substance and a force to be reckoned with.

He politely but encouragingly asked his girl to dance and, guess what, she accepted with good grace. They both rose gently from their chairs. She took him by the hand and led him onto the dance floor. The only problem he had was that he had no idea what the dance was, and he dare not ask! However, to his amazement, it did not seem to matter at all. Clearly his partner knew what the dance was and had guided large numbers of male novices around this same dance floor. Albert was able to relax on the dance floor for the first time in his life and...slowly but surely...he was wishing to himself that the dance would last for ever.

The pair glided round the floor several times until the band finished playing that particular dance. Instead of feeling awkward Albert waited on the floor and spoke softly to the girl. He felt at ease, relaxed, and as though he was an experienced dancer whereas he was an absolute novice. He realised that the girl was so experienced on the dance floor that she was able to cope with complete novices—just like a true professional.

After a few more dances, the band took a further break so Albert returned to the table, holding the girl's hand as gently as he could. They sat down at the table and it was only then that Albert realised that Fred had managed to get on just as well with his partner—and they too returned to the table. Albert and Fred were delighted that the other girls had melted away into the background and they realised that this was probably part of a carefully constructed plan by all the girls to give themselves quality time with the boys of their choice, if that was what they wanted.

The whole evening had gone really well and the two boys made sure that they obtained the contact details for the girls. They were not going to make the same mistake that they had made on New Year's Eve!

Albert and Fred became regulars at the Parr Hall and soon became the boyfriends of the two girls they had fallen in love with on their first visit to the dance hall. After six months of courtship during which Fred had been taken on by one of the best employers in town, the two boys and their two girlfriends had become quite famous locally—and such a good advertisement for the power and ability of the Parr Hall to bring couples together—thus helping to build the whole community in Warrington while peacetime prevailed.

Chapter 5

Albert and Emma were married one very sunny Saturday morning in August 1929 at Warrington Parish church which is easily visible for a ten mile radius because of the height of its spire. The best man was Albert's brother Tom and Emma was given away by her father who was a veteran of the Boer war in South Africa and also of the trench warfare in the first year of the 1914 to 1918 so called First World War. Tom was a stout man with a ruddy complexion and nearly six foot in height.

Emma's father was a complete contrast. He looked very smart indeed and had a carefully trimmed moustache that was showing traces of grey. He was just below five foot in height and was very slim but bristling with muscles and sinews. He had clearly been a formidable opponent in some of the worst fighting in both Africa and Europe. He was a very proud man and had every right to be. After all, he had one of the most beautiful daughters in the world, who was marrying a very handsome young man of both sporting and business renown—and he still had three more daughters and two sons to see safely married off before he could even think of slowing down.

Although Emma had worked since leaving school in the packaging department of the local clock manufacturers her father rated her as the brightest and best of all the children and families he had known. First she was beautiful in a refined way. Secondly, she always seemed to know how to handle any situation, when others often panicked. Thirdly, she always took the lead but somehow she was completely modest and never expected any acknowledgment for the results of her efforts in the three areas of her life—family, factory and the local neighbourhood.

Emma was so proud of her husband Albert who had been her boyfriend and fiancé for eight months ever since they had met that golden New Year's Eve at the Parr Hall (only a mile from where they were being married). Albert had served his apprenticeship with Metropolitan Vickers and had worked ever since for Crosfields—the very large soap and detergents manufacturer with two thousand workers in their factory, situated by the main railway station and on the banks of the River Mersey half a mile from the centre of Warrington.

Albert was a specialist in factory machinery and installations, and there were always parts of the factory complex being re-engineered to meet the ever changing needs of the market for toiletries and the booming cosmetics markets. Not content with being the top technical expert in the Crosfields complex, Albert let it be no secret that his aim was to reach the top and be the Works Manager at Crosfields one day—and the sooner the better. Albert had also been captain of both the First XI football and cricket teams for Crosfields for the last few years. This showed him at his very best, as a leader of the team who was determined to make sure that each team was highly successful—and also that he capitalised on the talent available to him. He was often the first to spot an up and coming cricket or football player—and had seen several progress to county cricket or league football.

In addition to all his other talents, Albert had been a very successful featherweight boxer and a distance swimmer of distinction. He was a professional boxer in his teens and had won many medals and championship belts at the renowned Liverpool Stadium boxing arena. The prize money came in very handy before he had been promoted up the Crosfields ladder. Albert had also twice won the annual three mile swimming race across Douglas Bay in the Isle of Man from Onchan Head at the north of the bay to the finishing line at the Head near the main port.

*****

Albert and Emma were a model couple. After two years of living in digs and sharing facilities with others, they moved to a one-bedroom flat in one of the huge areas of blocks of terraced housing near to where both their families had been raised. With the increasing industrialisation of the town of Warrington they often discussed the need to buy one of the new semi-detached houses being built—especially to the south of the town, near the village of Stockton Heath. This village featured a picturesque high street and had the distinction of having two huge swing bridges half a mile apart on the Manchester Ship Canal.

When the very large ships travelled eastwards towards Manchester along the Canal, the two swing bridges had to be opened up by huge mechanical cogs while the road traffic was prevented from crossing either of the bridges for a twenty minute period, often several times a day. The other advantage of moving to Stockton Heath was that there was a local tennis club where Albert and Emma could pair up when playing mixed doubles, and also spend relaxing warm summer evenings in the company of many of their equally ambitious and successful friends.

After a further year, Emma found an ideal 19th-century terraced house on the southern bank of the Canal and persuaded Albert that they should buy this and then move into one of the new semi-detached houses a few hundred yards further away from the canal—if and when they could safely afford to do so. The extra space would be needed if by then they were blessed with any children.

*****

Sure enough Emma was expecting their first child within a year of moving into their terraced house at Stockton Heath. They were both so excited and looked forward to family life as all expectant parents do. Unfortunately there were complications and Emma miscarried their first child. The whole process was a time of worry, concern, fatigue and disappointment. Nevertheless they both perked up when they discovered that Emma was pregnant again within a few months. However, their hopes were yet again dashed and the process of nature took its toll, both babies being girls.

After two years of uncertainty, Emma was delighted to be informed that she was pregnant again and this time the specialists were more confident than ever before that the baby would go the full term. Their son Alan was born on October 6th 1933 and soon showed that he was a likely footballer with all the kicking he did before emerging absolutely on time. Immediately Albert and Emma put the deposit on one of the new houses a few hundred yards up the hill from the canal. After losing two girls they were anxious to have another two children if at all possible.

The only risk to their happiness seemed to be the possibility of another major war in Europe. The chances of this taking place were increasing by all accounts. Albert and Emma were avid listeners to the radio and soaked up all the comment on political and international matters. It seemed such a tragedy that the radio brought them so many hours of tearful laughter with a very wide variety of famous comedians whilst at the same time bringing them increasingly dour hints and portents of future warfare.

Albert realised that he would have to enlist for the army because he would be a natural candidate for the Royal Electrical and Mechanical Engineers—the so called REME. All his schooling, apprenticeship and industrial experience meant that he would soon be promoted to a senior ranking if war broke out.

Fortunately, Albert had been promoted to within one step of becoming Works Manager at Crosfields before the war came. This meant that he would be fast-tracked into the army and also receive an assurance from his employer that a suitable job for his talents and experience would be made available to him at the end of the war—if at all possible. In those desperate days the only thing that motivated people was the survival of their country in the face of the German threat. Nobody gave any thought to their future prospects—they wanted to do what was best for their country. Men and women with some of the best personal and employment prospects had to take a blind step into the unknown, sign up and hope that fate and God would deal with them in the most appropriate way.

The old saying that 'all's fair in love and war' was very pertinent. Emma's personal motto had been to live every day to the full and this was now to be tested to the hilt. Many people would crack under the strain, but for others, the coming war would be their making.

It was certainly a funny old world in which to be rearing children, but Albert and Emma tried yet again for a brother or sister for Alan. No sooner had they been blessed with their second boy—Densmore, born at their new semi-detached house at 26 Walton Heath Road, Stockton Heath, on 4 April 1938—than the storms of war could be heard rumbling around the continent of Europe. Everyone heard that Poland was likely to be drawn into the conflict first but this was only seen as delaying the all-out war that was anticipated. The only hope was the famous visit by the British Prime Minister, Neville Chamberlain, to Munich where he thought, completely wrongly, that he had come to a sensible agreement.

However, he had not understood or accepted that it was impossible to reach a sensible agreement with a tyrant, never mind see a deal carried through to completion. The British Prime Minister was humbled, weakened and proved entirely wrong in his assessment of the prospects of peace or war—and Poland was occupied by a foreign force within weeks.

Albert was kept informed about what training and preparation he needed to undergo. Crosfields gave him carte blanche to spend any time on army duties that was required so that the country could be best prepared for what seemed to be the inevitable. Nevertheless Albert was surprised to receive an early call up and to be sent to France to assess its machinery, weaponry, transport and maintenance facilities, and how these could be matched with the best that Britain had—all to serve the best interests of the Western Allies.

Albert was not aware before he arrived in France that there was yet another front that was likely to open up if war came. This would be well away from Europe and would centre on the jungles of Burma. The reason was that Japan was likely to enter the war at an early stage and British engineers and soldiers would be needed to prevent the Japanese invasion which was confidently forecast—but never spoken about. One result of his early posting was that Albert was not aware that another son was on his way—one that he was not going to see until the war was totally at an end—if, and only if, he was still alive. These were very difficult times for all those families with mothers and fathers away in the war.

However, it made everyone thankful for the blessings and happiness they had already benefited from in their lives. It also concentrated their minds and hearts on getting on with their day to day duties, deepening their spiritual faith and looking forward to the possibility of peace and goodwill after the heartbreak and tragedy of warfare had ended.

What a trying time this was for all concerned. Those that lived through it all were changed for the rest of their lives—mentally, physically and emotionally. Those who perished would never know what they missed. Those who were split from their families, friends, and partners would be changed irrevocably. No-one could ever have foreseen the eventual improvements in everyday life brought about by the technical advances resulting from the war. However, in the late 1930s, there was nobody at all who wanted the war to take place. It may have been necessary to stem the over-ambitious plans and greed of certain tyrants.

It seemed then, as it seems now, too high a price to pay for freedom. It is such a tragedy that so many new and disparate nations or civilisations have mushroomed over recent years with the ambition to impose their ill-will on the world they have come to hate. Surely we should all have learned our lessons years ago and acted accordingly.

Chapter 6

Emma gave birth to her third son, Keith, on 21 January 1940 in a small nursing home by the River Mersey only half a mile from the town centre of Warrington. Her husband had been posted out to France just before she was confirmed as pregnant in June 1939. The next few months were very difficult for her because she now had to feed, clothe and shelter two young babies—and also make sure that six-year-old Alan made a solid start to his schooling at the Stockton Heath local school, fortunately only a ten-minute walk from their home on a direct line towards the village centre where Emma and the three lads did all their shopping and also visited the local library to keep in touch with local events.

It was wonderful having running hot water and a small garden around the front, side and rear of their home. The boys always ate round a two foot diameter circular wooden table positioned strategically in the very small kitchen between the side door, the gas cooker, the sink and the two doors—one to the hall and the other to the so called 'dining room' which looked out through a French window to the rear garden. There was a large expandable oak table in one corner of the dining room but this was only ever used for a very special, extremely rare occasion—such as a birthday party or the visit of an uncle and/or aunt and their children. The front room downstairs was always 'kept for best'—in other words it was kept in pristine condition, but never used at all. In the words of their mother 'it was always kept for a special visitor' but such a person never materialised throughout their eleven year occupation of the house.

The only regular visitor to their home was Uncle John who was one of Emma's older brothers. He lived with his wife and their two very young boys in the village of Padgate, on the far side of Warrington from Stockton Heath. Uncle John worked for a very large construction company, Monks, that was very busy indeed building armaments and aircraft factories—and carrying out preparatory levelling works to the north west of Warrington on the direct road between Liverpool to the west and Manchester to the east. Local rumours were spreading that an enormous area of land around the tiny village of Burtonwood had been earmarked for the construction of a massive airfield 'in case the Americans were ever persuaded to join the war against the Germans.'

All men and women in special occupations were told that they had to continue to work in their present positions for the next few years—and that they would be excused from having to enrol into the armed forces. One of Emma's brothers in law had been working in a large aircraft manufacturing firm near Manchester for several years and he too was not required to enlist for the armed services. These two close relations of their mother, John and Jack, were to act as substitute fathers for the three sons of Albert and Emma—and very close relationships were developed between the three families involved— John and his wife Elsie having two boys and Jack and his wife Florence one daughter, Hilary.

Uncle John would do most of their gardening. He would ride on his Raleigh bicycle all the five miles from Padgate to Stockton Heath every fortnight with a manual Ransome lawnmower balanced precariously on his handlebars! Every few months Emma and the three boys would travel by bus on a Sunday to Padgate to visit Uncle John's house—and to pay their respects to their deceased relations at the huge Warrington cemetery which they passed on the way.

In all, there were around six uncles, four aunts and fifteen cousins of the three boys. Every Christmas time, there was a huge party at one or other of their several homes close to the centre of Warrington. There were party games right through the evening—with two card games being highlights of the evening. One was called Newmarket and involved placing real money bets on cards, leading to much excitement as the game approached its climax and the winners emerged with embarrassed grins and what seemed like loads of money. The other was Chase the Ace where the thrills and dangers of being stuck with an Ace of one of the card suits were some of the highlights and nightmares of the year.

The main enjoyment however was for all concerned to know that they were part of a very happy large family which stuck together, played together and were, in their own way, fighting the war against the Germans in their own homes, schools and localities. Every major party ended with the much loved

Hokey-Kokey—with the roof of the house nearly being lifted off by the loud music, raucous singing and noises of dancing.

At the local school Alan, Den and Keith were in different years but would often walk to and from the school together. All the teachers were very strict indeed and kept a very tight discipline at all times. There was more than a four years age difference between Alan and Den, but less than two years between Den and Keith. Alan and Den attended a nursery school for nearly two years before starting their main schooling at the age of five. This gave them both a flying start in the fundamentals of arithmetic and reading—and also helped them to mix at an early stage with large numbers of children of their own age. By the time Keith started at the main school Alan had begun his final year or two at the school.

Emma had shown a very keen interest in the education of her three boys, and if she had been born a few decades later she would most certainly have become a school manager or governor. She developed strong personal links with some of the teaching staff and even invited them to join her at local whist drives or evenings of the card game Bridge at her home. The three boys often saw Miss Saltmarsh, the headmistress, playing bridge in their home together with another dozen or so teachers and/or parents. Den was once on the point of mentioning this to one or two parents until his mother hushed him up and said he must 'never mention the fact that Miss Saltmarsh often played bridge at their home on Saturday evenings.'

Den could not see what the problem was but realised, after due consideration and discussions with Alan, that anyone hearing about the bridge playing at their home might be jealous and think that it was inappropriate for the headmistress to spend so much time at one home. However, what it spelled out loud and clear to Den was that the three boys had a mother who was quite a wheeler dealer who was clever and smart enough to build close links with important people.

It was not very long after these incidents that Alan was put forward as a potential pupil at the very prestigious Manchester Grammar School which had the most stringent entrance examinations of all. Indeed no pupils had ever, to that date, progressed from the Stockton Heath school to Manchester Grammar School! However, Miss Saltmarsh was of the firm view that Alan Dover was about to be the first.

Chapter 7

Life for the three boys throughout the war years was idyllic. Their mother was very loving and attentive but she could rule with a rod of iron when necessary. They were only too well aware at all times that there was a war on. They also accepted that there were shortages of all kinds of items, but they realised that this was because of the need for everyone to economise, to pull together and to do whatever they could to help to win the war.

If their usual or favourite foods were not available, they all knew that they had to change to something else. If they did not have the usual size of helpings, they knew that economies were having to be made by their mother. Everyone was in the same situation, but nobody ever complained.

The three boys loved attending the local school. There were so many friendships that they formed, in the main with the boys, but occasionally with one or other of the girls. After all, they had several girl cousins whom they met from time to time and they had been able to form stable, understanding friendships with the girls at their local school along the lines they had pioneered with their female cousins.

It came as a surprise to the three boys whenever they came across a particularly bright girl. This took some getting used to until they all came to see it as an extra challenge or hurdle to be overcome. They could all honestly say that the teachers were marvellous at being scrupulously fair with all the pupils in their classes, without any favours. However, Den had a major problem in one particular year. A new teacher, Mrs Bott, arrived and her own daughter was in the particular class for which she was the class mistress. Up till then Den had always been top in most of the main subjects in the term examinations, and top overall at the end of each year. All the markings and rankings in each class were very carefully reported in great detail on the written reports prepared and signed by all the teachers involved in teaching the children in each class—and these reports were taken home at the end of each term and year by the individual pupils.

Den soon realised that Elizabeth, the daughter of his new class mistress, Mrs Bott, was both very bright and very sharp. She was the only one who could rival him in the early Monday morning mental arithmetic lessons that her mother held. This was Den's favourite lesson of all and he was so pleased it was held at the very start of the week—both to wake some pupils up and also to give an early challenge to the keenest. Elizabeth took longer to display her skills in the other subjects, but clearly, she was a force to be reckoned with. Actually, Den did not mind and wondered whether he had been sufficiently tested by his classmates before her arrival. What he did know was that he was going to have to use all his concentration, intelligence and knowledge to see off her challenge.

At the end of the Christmas and Easter terms, he noted that he was not obtaining as many first placings in various subjects but put this down to other classmates getting to grips with the various subjects—and demonstrating their knowledge and skills in the various end of term examinations. However, he was in for a very big shock indeed at the end of the school year. He had worked extremely hard throughout the whole academic year and in all the subjects. Even though at the end of the year he obtained extremely high marks in all the subjects, and was awarded 591 marks out of 600 overall, he was distraught to discover that his final placing in the class was second, yes second. He wondered if there had been a mistake but he had no way of finding out who had beaten him and ended up as the top pupil of the year.

On the last day of term, there was a farewell gathering for their class teacher Mrs Bott who was leaving to go and live well away from the Warrington area. At the ceremony Miss Saltmarsh, the headmistress, delivered a speech full of praise about how well Mrs Bott had fitted in and the contribution she had made to the whole school. Den would have been the first to say how thoroughly she had deserved the adulation afforded to her—until Miss Saltmarsh ended her speech by saying what a joy it had been to have Mrs Bott's daughter, Elizabeth, as a pupil at the school—and how well she had done to end up as the top pupil in that class, with an overall mark of 594 marks out of 600.

Den was gobsmacked and totally dumbfounded. After recovering his thoughts, he wondered whether or not there had been any favouritism shown to

Elizabeth by her mother and/or other teachers. Den never mentioned his concerns to anyone but the whole episode taught him two lessons. First never take anything for granted and secondly always be slightly suspicious of other peoples' motives—even if your first inclination may be to trust everyone.

These two lessons were to remain in Den's mind throughout his whole education and career.

Chapter 8

Life during the war in Warrington and the surrounding villages was very different from the period between the two World Wars. First there were very few men between the ages of seventeen and the late thirties. Second there was an invasion of girl and boy evacuees who were sent out from the centres of large cities to live with local families in 'safer areas.' This was a very disturbing experience, not just for the evacuees but for all the members of the families to whom they were allocated. A girl called Brenda, aged about eight years, arrived at the Dover household with a small case one day all the way from London and took up residence for two weeks. There was little information made available to the three brothers, even after she left—leaving a mystery in their minds, which none of them ever raised with their mother. It could have been that the authorities thought it inappropriate for a young girl to be housed with three boys, but nobody ever explained what had happened.

Church attendances increased during the war and the popularity of the radio as a means of entertainment and information gathering boomed. Children of all ages and beliefs were encouraged to attend Sunday school and to listen to the radio as much as they could—to further their education and to make them realise the need to be kept informed about what was happening, and of any new important information, advice and/or instructions. There were hardly any cars on the roads but there were bicycles everywhere. There were very few telephones indeed and hardly any policemen in the villages and the surrounding areas.

Every night there was a complete blackout with cars not being allowed to travel with lights, and all house windows had to be blacked out with a cheap form of roller blinds. Every evening the local warden would travel on foot or bicycle (with no lights) around the whole area. If he spotted any house lights that were showing he would knock loudly on the house door and give very stern and strict instructions about the need for total blackouts—to protect the whole neighbourhood.

Black or silver corrugated metal sheets were issued to most homes to be used to form a tiny bomb shelter for the house occupants. However, these were only some six foot long, four foot wide and four foot high. They barely afforded any protection at all to the families they were issued to. All householders were exhorted to make sure that they had a very large, sturdy and strong table in their dining room under which most of the residents were able to huddle together whenever there was a siren and/or warning of an air attack.

Warrington was exactly halfway between the major port of Liverpool and the inland industrial city of Manchester, forty miles to the east. Regular bombing sorties were made by the very large, noisy German bombers along this corridor and all these aircraft flew both westward and eastward directly over the line of the Manchester Ship Canal—in other words within two hundred yards of the Dover family home.

It took some time to achieve an efficient routine whenever there was an air raid siren. This was a very regular occurrence often by day but mainly at night time. At the local school there were special arrangements with regular air raid drills involving all the children and staff. In the school playground there were four large underground bomb shelters into which all the children and the whole teaching staff could fit. Lessons were often abandoned due to day time air raids and all the children were escorted by their teachers to these underground shelters. Nobody was allowed out of the shelters and back into the daylight until the all-clear siren had been sounded.

There was a marked contrast between the noise level and the amount of chatter between the children following the initial air raid siren and the all clear being sounded. The first event was marked by the pitter-patter of footsteps without any voices. The all clear was a noisy, boisterous affair with the chattering of hundreds of voices full of energy and relief that yet another air raid had been survived.

The network of local canals in Lancashire and Yorkshire is a major feature of the local landscape. Many of these were built by Lord Bridgewater in the second half of the nineteenth century. He was an extremely rich and powerful landowner who built the network of canals to permit the safe and efficient transportation of goods such as coal, timber and textiles to be undertaken. This worked well before the need for an even larger network of roads than had been built since the invention of the petrol engine motorcars and lorries. Lord Bridgewater had expanded his empire enormously during his lifetime and he was a wonderful benefactor to the public in general and a fine example of a responsible and far sighted businessman to all the employers and entrepreneurs who followed in his footsteps.

During both the immediate pre-war years and also the world war years, the volume of traffic up and down the Manchester Ship Canal had soared. In addition, all the factories in and around Manchester had easy access to the Canal and they all made use of the very large warehouses built alongside it. Many of the thousands of ships forming the food and ammunition convoys across the Atlantic Ocean to North America and back began their voyages from the Manchester Ship Canal.

Following the entry of the United States of America into the Second World War, an enormous airbase was indeed built at Burtonwood a few miles to the North West of Warrington. This brought a huge number of American servicemen into the Warrington area. They had their living quarters on the airbase but they were allowed to spend their leisure time between their duty rotas off the base. All the young local lads in the Warrington area were soon able to distinguish between the American and British trucks, jeeps and reconnaissance cars. Even tanks would appear on the roads surrounding the Dover home. Within an hour crowds of several hundred boys would gather to wave at and cheer all the troops on board the various vehicles. These were really exciting times for the local neighbourhood and did wonders for British American relations.

As the war progressed the first ever American ships sailed up the Manchester Ship Canal towards Manchester. The two swing bridges were turned through a right angle in what seemed to be both a salute and a greeting to the Yankees. Word soon spread along the whole length of the Canal when one of the American ships was due to travel up it. All the local lads were mobilised within an hour and they ran and/or cycled to the most westward part of the canal that was open to them. On days such as these families would use all the bicycles and tricycles available to form a very large, irregular army of boys—including even a few girls—who would greet the Americans as soon as they were in sight. Families like the Dovers with only one bicycle between the three of them would take it in turns running amongst the fleet of bikes.

The five mile stretch of the canal from the hamlet of Moore to the west right up to the Latchford Locks to the east was a very happy play area for the thousands of local boys and girls on such occasions because they all knew what the additional attractions were. They wanted to show their sincere appreciation to the American troops for being their buddies, mates, friends and even saviours. However, they greeted them with such loud cheers and shouts, even more, because of what the troops brought for them on every occasion.

The local children had never even seen a real banana before hundreds of them were thrown overboard for them by the American sailors and soldiers. They had never experienced the unbelievable taste and flavour of American chewing gum. They had never seen such beautiful packaging for items such as the chewing gum—and they would never, ever forget the ecstasy and sheer joy that was generated by the visits of the Yankees to their very own streets, alongside the canal, where they had been reared before and during the early dark and desperate days of the Second World War.

What a marvellous impression the American soldiers, sailors and airmen made on the British children during the war years. Friendships and romances blossomed and Warrington was, despite its sometimes dirty, downtrodden appearance surely one of the best places to be. They were exciting and stimulating times and lasting impressions were made on both the British and American folk who were privileged to be there to witness it all.

Chapter 9

All the three Dover boys were christened as Church of England at St Thomas's Parish Church in Stockton Heath. All the rest of the Dover and Kirk family members still lived in and around the centre of Warrington. The three Dover boys all attended the local primary school in Stockton Heath and they all considered that they had been born in the county of Lancashire. However, decades later Den discovered to his amazement and disbelief that their local school, only a few hundred yards from their home, was a Cheshire County Council school and indeed the whole of Stockton Heath was in Cheshire from well before their births! The truth was uncovered when Den had to produce his birth certificate when renewing his passport. This showed that the local Registry office for Stockton Heath was in Cheshire. It also proved that the house where he was born and the school where he was educated up to the age of eight years were also in the County of Cheshire!

The three boys were very regular attendees at the St Thomas's Sunday school and enjoyed learning as much as possible about the Christian faith, the Bible, Jesus and all His disciples, the miracles and other biblical events of at least two thousand years ago. They also had Religious Knowledge as one of their subjects at school and the two different education streams were mutually supportive.

Many of their school friends travelled in from the west and south of Stockton Heath—on foot or on their bikes. Alan became very friendly with a bunch of older boys from Walton, a lovely but very small village to the south west of the school about two miles away. Alan was invited by these friends to attend their Sunday school and church of St John's—and to become a member of the church choir. This was a real honour and appealed to Alan who had been having piano lessons and, with his mathematical mind, had been very attracted to studying music. He also had a wonderful tenor singing voice.

Den and Keith soon followed Alan to the St John's church and Sunday school at Walton. All three became core members of the Sunday school and took part in the various church ceremonies. The Autumn Harvest Festivals were amazing because so much fruit and other food items were taken into the church on the Saturday, used to decorate the Sunday school and the church that evening and then distributed to the local poor, ill and frail villagers of Walton on the Sunday evening or within a few days thereafter.

Hallowe'en was celebrated by huge marrows and turnips being scoured out and placed on tables and window sills with lit candles placed inside them. There was always a Christmas show during which Alan would sing a solo and all the three boys would join in with the rest of the children in a mini-pantomime or a concert with around twenty different acts—all documented on a printed programme containing their names. Was this going to be the start of a stage career for any of them?

All this community activity in a small village environment was like a new world to the Dover boys. Every bonfire night they played a very active part in building the bonfire, lighting it and joining in with gusto when the fireworks were set off and potatoes and chestnuts roasted around the perimeter of the bonfire. There were songs and choruses sung round the bonfire year after year, and particularly when the end of the war arrived—at long last. Everyone stayed round the glowing embers of the bonfire until three o'clock in the morning. They were all so thrilled that they could finally celebrate as a community the ending of such a long war which had changed their lives in so many ways.

*****

Looking back over all the years at Warrington and Walton, it always seemed that the weather was sunny, the air fresh, the grass green and dry, the trees full of fruit and everyone had a greeting for everybody else—plus a smile on their face. There was a very strict timetable for school days but at the weekends and during the holidays the three Dover boys would set off to meet their friends and they would often spend the whole day playing football, cricket and rounders on a large field half a mile from their home. This was nicknamed the 'donkey field'—no doubt after an earlier occupant of the field in question. This was perfect for all types of games, and there were even several trees that were ideal for tree climbing.

Once in a while, there would be a minor accident but the girls and boys knew that, whenever they were climbing the trees, they had to be careful at all times. Some of the resourceful older boys had very helpfully hammered nails into some of the trunks and branches of the trees at strategic positions to encourage, rather than deter the climbers.

The bus services into and beyond Warrington were reliable and reasonably frequent. The three boys and their mother would sometimes walk the two miles into Warrington to call on their numerous relatives. However, it was much more the case that they travelled by bus into the centre of Warrington, and then walked the remainder of the journey to the homes of their grandparents, uncles, aunts, cousins or even to non-family friends.

There was a certain ritual about these visits but the boys thoroughly enjoyed them. It was exciting and interesting to see where and how other people lived and coped. It was wonderful to meet new friends at times such as these. It was exciting if they had to celebrate a birthday, a new birth, a christening or any other important occasion. Often all the aunts, uncles and cousins would gather together—particularly at a wedding. The Dover and Kirk family empire always seemed to be growing. There was always so much chit chat about the various friends and relations that they needed to catch up on. Much of this was discussed by the older family members while the younger ones went outside to run, to skip, to play hide and seek and a wide variety of other games that they had learned together in the back alleys between the parallel terraces of houses.

There were always certain routines at these family gatherings. In the first the younger children would be given money and required to visit the local corner shop to buy one bottle of lemonade and an ice-cream for themselves, and sometimes for the tea to follow. At every such afternoon tea there was a wonderful spread of food and the tablecloths, china and cutlery almost sparkled with cleanliness. Afterwards the second ritual of playing games of all kinds would take place. These occasions were some of the rare times when the otherwise redundant "front room" was used to maximum benefit. At Christmas times a third ritual would be carried out. They would always celebrate Christmas at one of the houses where there was a piano so that carols and songs could be sung, and also dances such as the Hokey-Kokey could be performed—to the enormous pleasure of all those present.

At weekends and during the long summer holidays Alan and his friends from Walton would often meet at the local Post Office which was run by the mother of one of the boys, Peter Gleave. All of their bikes would be left in the back yard and/or the garden and they would wander off down the country lane to the hamlet of Moore to go train spotting. The boys would be armed with notebooks, pencils and a sandwich lunch that had been prepared by their mothers.

Moore was immediately alongside the main London Midland and Scottish railway lines which ran all the way from London up to the north of Scotland. The 'LMS line', as it was nicknamed, was one of the fastest in the country and most of the new models of streamline locomotives were soon put into service on this line to give them a thorough testing. The boys had specially printed books for train spotters in which there were full details of all the new 'streaks' as the boys called them. The wheel combinations of all the steam engine locomotives were given in these books and also the unique number of the particular locomotive. When the boys spotted a locomotive on its way towards them they would shout out what it was, which way it was heading and which of the pair of 'up' and 'down' lines it was running on. Between them all they would record the name of the locomotive, if any, its identification number and any of its defining features.

There needed to be at least four boys in the group for a thorough job to be carried out. Four pencils would be poised at all times and even when there were no trains in sight all the talking would be about train spotting matters. It was one of the most popular hobbies of that time. The best informed members of the group would be the bearers of the latest information on the rolling stock and which new engines were heading their way in the next few days. All the boys knew the key three numbers for the locomotives off by heart. Fast passenger engines would be 4-6-2, indicating that there was a four wheel bogey at the front, six huge driving wheels and two wheels at the rear under the driver's platform. The most usual wheel configuration for a slow shunting engine would be either 0-6-0 or 2-4-2.

Every time an engine passed them the boys underlined the unique locomotive number in their books to show that they had successfully 'spotted' that particular steam engine. The boys felt privileged and fortunate to live so close to the main LMS line. They were even more thrilled if, for whatever reason, one of the engines decided to slow down, and possibly stop, within a hundred yards or so of their chosen perches on the railway fences and/or banks that were situated on the north and south sides of the road from Moore that led down the hill to a railway level crossing on the goods line half a mile to the west. This linked the chemical plants and mines in Cheshire (the largest source of salt in Britain) with the factories in Warrington and further afield.

One outstanding landmark at Moore was the huge red brick water reservoir on the top of a nearby hill at Acton. This not only supplied all the local houses and factories with water, but it also fed water into every one of the railway engines that flew past Moore and Warrington at all hours of the day and night! While the uninitiated would never know how this was possible, all the train spotters knew about the complete technology involved—and they were never happier than when they were asked to explain to their families and friends how the engines were able to be refilled with water without even slowing down!

Alongside the four main railway lines there were smaller water towers which were kept 'topped up' by gravity from the main reservoir at Acton. In between the two rails on each of the four main lines, two heading south and two heading north, there was a long metal trough about two foot wide that was also kept 'topped up' to half its six inch height with fresh water from these small water towers. When the railway locomotives were approaching these water filling troughs the driver and his mate would lower a rubber scoop down from below the locomotive—thus allowing the water in the trough to be scooped up into the reservoir situated close to the coal-fired engine. The furnace at the rear of the main locomotive would be kept literally at white heat because the coal stored in the large tender behind the engine, on its own wheels, was almost continuously shovelled by the engine driver and his mate into the furnace itself from the two man driver's platform.

One day when Alan and Den were walking over the footbridge to the less used pair of north and south lines they were amazed to hear the screeching of brakes coming from a goods train that was slowing down near the troughs. To their amazement one of the men dismounted from the driver's platform and started walking along the side of the rails towards them.

'Don't worry lads, I'm just going to collect our breakfast. Do you want to come with me?'

Wow, what an invitation! Without any further ado they walked with him along a path behind the fence to the railway land, across a field and straight into the rear kitchen of a small farm. The farmer's wife had a hot cup of tea ready for the driver's mate and she quickly poured out two more cups for the boys. She filled up the metal flask that the mate was carrying and passed him the breakfast food for the two men—including two freshly laid, and boiled eggs.

When they returned to where the train had stopped the driver's mate asked them if they wanted to see what they did in the engine cab. They literally jumped at the chance but only just managed, with some difficulty, to mount the high steel steps up to the driver's platform. Then came the enormous thrill of standing on the platform alongside the driver and his mate! All the dials were explained to them, they were allowed to shovel some of the coal into the white hot furnace and they were even given a short ride back to the footbridge where they had crossed the line half an hour before.

Alan and Den took some time to recover from their shock at what had happened, and of course their train spotting pals took some convincing that they were not having their legs pulled. Alan and Den thought it was marvellous that there was such friendliness between the train crew and the local inhabitants of Moore. They returned with fresh vigour to their train spotting duties—and much enjoyed relating their story to their mother and brother Keith when they returned home for their tea later that day.

Chapter 10

As the oldest brother, Alan had the difficult role of arbitrating between Den and Keith, showing his seniority and asserting his authority. One day he was aided and abetted beautifully by his mother when he most needed it. Alan and his Walton mates had decided that they would all go on a bike ride to Pick Mere, a natural scenic small lake nearly twenty miles to the south of Warrington. As the anticipated date drew near, Den kept pestering Alan and demanding that he was both old enough and sensible enough to undertake the journey, even though his bike was much smaller than all the others, and even though he was nearly five years younger than all of them.

Alan explained the situation to their mother but Den persisted right up to the day in question. He was determined to have his way—perhaps to try to show to all the boys involved that he was old enough to be treated as one of their inner circle. Eventually the day arrived and, to his surprise and delight, Den was allowed to ride off with Alan towards the village of Moore where they had all planned to meet up before setting off on the bike ride.

When they arrived at the Post Office Peter's mother, the post mistress, gave them all a cold refreshing drink, checked that they all had enough food and clothing and then went into the back yard to show Den what her gardener was doing. The gardener was building a new hen run and also had to cut the rear lawn and clear up the leaves and fallen apples. The gardener asked Den if he could help him with the leaves and soon the two of them were very busy indeed. He then offered to let Den try out his new hand mower. Den had often helped Uncle John from Padgate cut the small lawns at their house in Stockton Heath. He was certainly interested in trying out the new lawn mower and really enjoyed himself.

After an hour of Den helping the gardener Mrs Gleave asked if they wanted a cold drink, and they certainly needed one. Den was very pleased with himself because he was the only one who was asked if he wanted to try the new lawn mower. He even managed to cut the lawn in reasonably straight lines in the next hour or so. He then suddenly wondered to himself where all the other boys were.

'Wherever they are,' he reasoned, 'they cannot be enjoying themselves more than I am.'

After the gardener had finished all his work he had a word with Mrs Gleave and came up to Den with both his own bike and Den's in his hands.

'Well young lad, let's take you back home. Your mother told me you always like to have your tea outside in the summer when it is a hot, sunny day.'

Without any more ado the pair of them mounted their bikes and waved goodbye to Mrs Gleave at the front gate. It was only then that Den realised that his older brother Alan and his mates had gone off on their bike ride without him.

There was no way he was going to complain. He had had a marvellous day in the garden with the gardener, who accompanied him right up to his own front door and explained how very helpful he had been, and how well he had coped with the new lawn mower.

Den knew that he had been set up and that they were probably all in on the plan. When Alan eventually arrived at home after the bike ride he was totally exhausted. Everyone, including Den, concluded that there was no way he could ever have ridden his much smaller bike all the way to Pick Mere and back!

*****

Many of the residents of Warrington never travelled more than a mile or two from their homes. There were hardly any families with their own cars and everyone was very busy getting on with their lives. Den and his family were in effect confined to an area of some five miles radius, if that. He often looked down what he knew was the road to Chester, the county town of Cheshire, from the main road junction at Walton where his church, his Sunday school and many of his friends were. There was a very new concrete bridge that had been built over the Bridgewater canal at that point and the main road to the west and south rose to the top of the camber on the bridge. For all he knew that was the end of the world in that direction. He often wondered whether he would ever go further than that bridge in the rest of his life.

51

There were very few cars owned by ordinary members of the public during the war. It was just before the end of the war in 1945 when Den and his two brothers had their first ride in a car. A new family had moved into the semi-detached house opposite. Mr Austin seemed to have a business of his own and was away much of the time. At the weekends he would take his wife and two young boys out in the car—usually to Warrington on the Saturdays and to the local countryside on Sundays. After they had lived opposite for a year Mr Austin called round one Sunday lunchtime and asked if the three Dover boys would like to join them for an afternoon picnic at Ackers Spit which was a very small natural lake only a mile or two from their home. Mr Austin took his family first and then returned for the three Dover brothers. Alan rode in the front. Den and Keith rode on the rear bench seat. It really was a luxury treat for them all. They waved at all the people that they passed and marvelled at how smooth the ride was, and how quickly the car moved. In a few minutes they were at their destination and helping to lay out the teacloth on the grass and all the plates, small sandwiches and cakes.

When they returned home they very excitedly related all their views on the journey and the picnic to their mother. Needless to say they went out playing with all their usual friends, and the Austin boys, for the next two hours before going in, having a joint bath and heading off to bed. What an exciting day they had had, and it was so unexpected. The Austin and Dover boys had become the best of friends even though they never again enjoyed the luxury of another journey in Mr Austin's car. He was just too busy, and anyway the Dover boys did not want to rise above their station. They knew where they fitted into the local neighbourhood, and the last thing they wanted was to be mocked for being snobs!

Holidays were a complete non-event for the Dover family until the end of the war. Their mother took them to Fleetwood and across the Irish Sea to the Isle of Man for a seven day holiday that coincided with Victory in Europe Day. This was a hot, sunny day on Tuesday 5 May 1945 and the promenade at Douglas was packed with thousands of local people and holidaymakers. The whole of Douglas Bay was literally crowded with all shapes and sizes of ships—as far as the eye could see. During the war all boys played a game called Battleships and Cruisers on sheets of squared paper. Each of the two or three contestants would start with their own fleet of two battleships, three cruisers, four destroyers and five submarines. The aim of the game was to sink the whole fleet of your opponents before they sank yours. They had seen numerous film newsreels at the local cinemas in Warrington and were easily able to identify all the different types of British warships, some of the American and most of the German ships too.

That day the three Dover boys and their mother realised that they were witnessing the most important event of their lives. The war in Europe had been fiercely fought—on land, in the air and at sea. For far too long families across the whole of Europe and even further afield had experienced the fear and dread of attacks of all kinds by enemy forces. Finally the day had come when warfare across Europe had ceased. There was of course still fierce fighting in several other countries involved in the Second World War. In particular the Dover boys were only too well aware that their father was still battling it out in the steamy, humid and hot Burmese jungle against some of the most vicious and skilful Japanese fighters who had fought might and mane against the British army. They had even built railways across that vast country using their British army prisoners of war for the strenuous work involved, in the most trying weather conditions, including torrential rainstorms and blistering hot sunshine.

The Dover family had seen some of the frightening films and photographs of the Belsen prisoners who had died in Germany in their hundreds of thousands through lack of food and nutrition. They had not yet seen any similar film footage of the prisoners in Burma who had been treated just as badly by the Japanese army forces. They just hoped and prayed that their father would be able to return home in the not too distant future. They did not realise that Victory in Japan would be celebrated only three months later. What historic times!

Chapter 11

Mrs Dover promised to take her three boys for another break that year. They pestered her for weeks and insisted that it would have to be to the Isle of Man again. Wouldn't it be marvellous if they were able to celebrate Victory in Japan Day when they were over on the island?

One evening during their school holidays the boys were told they would have to be up much earlier the next day than ever before. They were only too happy to agree and they all went off to bed really early, chattering excitedly about what they would be doing on their holiday, and how much they were going to enjoy it.

Extremely early the next morning the three boys and their mother had to walk the two miles to Warrington station. There were no buses so early in the morning and, even though they knew there were such vehicles as taxis, they knew that they were very expensive indeed and not on the agenda for families such as theirs. Alan noticed that they walked to a different railway station in Warrington than the one they travelled through for their recent holiday. Instead of going to Bank Quay station on the main north to south LMS line, they went to the station that linked with lines for Liverpool to the west and Manchester to the east. Alan also noticed that they headed off in the direction of Liverpool. He also knew that it was on the coast and that in years gone by ships with holiday makers had regularly departed for the Isle of Man, and even for Dublin and Belfast in Ireland.

When they left the station in Liverpool they walked through a large network of cobbled streets in the early morning mist which rolled off the Irish Sea. They turned one of the corners and got the biggest surprise of their lives. Out of the rolling mist, and walking in the opposite direction to theirs, appeared on the pavement opposite a large man—the like of whom they had never before seen. It was a black face which they saw and they blinked their eyes several times, wondering if the mist was playing tricks with their eyesight. No, it was definitely a man with a black face. Their mother wondered what they were staring at. She had often seen and met coloured people before—mainly in Liverpool but sometimes even in Manchester. She explained to the boys that Liverpool had people from a very large number of countries living there, because of all the foreign trade and business that went through the very famous Port of Liverpool.

After a half hour walk through the back streets of Liverpool they arrived at another railway station and climbed up several lots of metal steps until they reached the two platforms. Trains were travelling in both directions and their mother ushered them into one of the carriages of a train that had just pulled in. She urged them to sit at the far side of the carriage and she pointed out to them the amazing scene of huge ships that were berthed in a series of large docks pointing away from the line of the railway they were travelling on.

To the amazement of the boys the train stopped every few minutes at about a dozen stations—all overlooking different groups of docks. In most of the docks there were large passenger boats but there were also huge cargo boats with weird flags on them and words in foreign languages. The boys had also spotted some British naval ships—in particular three destroyers in the same dock, and two cruisers in another dock.

The boys were so excited that they had no idea of how far they had travelled on this overhead railway. They could see on the land side—away from the docks side—buses, lorries and a few cars travelling around the central roads of Liverpool. They became disorientated and soon were asked by their mother to get off the train, walk along a very large platform and board a different type of train to the ones they were used to seeing. This train had no discernible engine at the front but it was soon travelling across wide open green fields and at quite a speed, much faster than the overhead train.

After about fifteen stops at very similar stations the train reached the terminus. The boys realised that they had reached the end of the line. The terminus station was very similar to the ones at both Fleetwood and Douglas, on the Isle of Man. All the three boys assumed that they had arrived at the Isle of Man and were soon asking their mother to take them to the promenade to see the Douglas Bay beach which they knew so well, and loved playing on.

Their mother did indeed take them through a busy shopping area, just like Douglas—the capital of the Isle of Man. She also took them up and down the promenade and eventually onto a golden sandy beach. They played for hours in the sunshine, had some fish and chips and built several sandcastles. Something seemed different. When they asked where Mrs Ewison's hotel (their landlady in Douglas) was, their mother pointed way down the coast and seemed surprised that they had asked the question. Den made a complete mental picture of the view that their mother had pointed out, and decided he would store the image in his brain—until he could find some supporting information to verify his mother's assertion.

When the sun was starting to go down in the sky their mother gathered together all their clobber and packed it away in the small suitcase they had brought with them that day. The boys were all very tired, because of the very early start they had made that day. Mrs Dover did extremely well to get the boys back to the station and to retrace their journey all the way back to their home in Stockton Heath. The boys were literally half asleep all the way. They were unusually quiet, but the truth was that they were totally exhausted. They all slept on the three train journeys and however they managed to board the bus at Bank Quay station in Warrington was a miracle. This bus took them within a few minutes of their home and they all dropped off to sleep in their beds and never woke till midday the next day.

Somehow they had managed to complete the double by celebrating Victory in Japan day at the seaside on another hot sunny day, Wednesday 15 August 1945—just as they had celebrated Victory in Europe in Douglas three months earlier. However, it was many years before they realised that they had not crossed the Irish Sea to the Isle of Man that day. What they had done however was to visit and fall in love with Southport, the seaside resort which was, over the coming years, to be of significant importance to all three of them in so many ways.

There were three memorable occurrences that confirmed to them that the war was finally over. The first was when it was announced that one of the destroyers used in the war would be sailing up the Manchester Ship Canal and berthing at Naylor's Wharf, only half a mile from the Dovers' home, for a whole week. Den was so delighted with this news that he had picked up from the weekly Warrington Guardian newspaper that he decided he should write a letter to his own teacher, in his best copper plate 'real writing' setting out all the information about this historic visit. The headmistress, Miss Saltmarsh, was most impressed and announced this visit the very next day during the morning assembly. She urged all the pupils to ask their parents to take them along to Naylor's Wharf during the week that the ship was berthed there. Needless to say, huge crowds visited the destroyer and the navy described it as one of the most well attended displays that they had ever held.

A few weeks later, to everyone's astonishment, it was announced in the same newspaper that a real German U boat would be passing along the Manchester Ship Canal on its way to Manchester docks. The precise date and time had been set, and the whole school was given a half day off to view this historic event. All those who lined the banks of the canal for a close look were amazed because the German captain of the submarine led all the members of the crew out of the conning tower, onto the top of the hull, and lined them up so that they could salute and wave a big 'hello' to the hundreds of families that had come along. Den was surprised that, instead of feeling angry at the crew for having fought against the British and other navies, he felt really sorry for them! He realised how humiliated they must have felt, even though they put on such a convincing show of friendliness. Den thought perhaps that, like everyone else, they must have felt so relieved and thankful that the war was finally over.

The third occurrence took place the following summer in one of the Liverpool docks where several of the British warships were lined up and the public were allowed to board them and view not just the open decks but 'go below' to have a look at the accommodation and the engine rooms. Everyone was delighted at this opportunity and the whole occasion received a great deal of publicity.

The Dover boys knew most of the physical details of the various ships on display in view of their keen interest in not just details of army life, but also of the air force and navy, which had all been covered so extensively throughout the war in the filmed newsreels and in all the major daily newspapers.

Chapter 12

It seemed a very long time indeed to the Dover family before they were able to welcome home Albert Dover, the head of the household and father of the three boys. They had no prior warning of his arrival, even if their mother did. Den was wakened in the middle of the night by his mother and a man talking in the rear bedroom that he shared with his mother. The next moment he was aware of a very unshaven face and chin being rubbed against his own face. He could not believe that at long last, and after an interval of six years, he was for the first time in his life aware that this was his father who had been overseas fighting in the War.

He heard his father whisper the question 'Do you know who I am? It's your Dad. I'm back for good'- accompanied by another scrubbing of his face in the dark.

The next morning the whole family gathered together in the back room downstairs. Den spent much of that morning sitting on his father's lap—and feeling so relieved, and so proud of his Dad. He wanted to ask all sorts of questions of his father but his mother cautioned him.

'Your Dad is very tired indeed and he will tell you all about it over the next few days.' With that said, the three boys went back to their normal routine of having breakfast, getting their toys out, doing homework and reading the latest comics.

*****

It took several months before the boys totally accepted that their father was really home to stay. Initially he was posted by the Army down to Devon in the far southwest of England to deal with problems involving the repair and maintenance of the British tanks and their transport vehicles. The army had decreed that these facilities had to be restored to prime condition in case any further hostilities sprang up throughout the numerous countries that had been affected by the Second World War. Fortunately a more local workplace became available to their father. This was a large facility—again to do with tanks and their transportation—in the village of Burscough, only twenty miles due north of their home in Stockton Heath.

Their father thoroughly enjoyed his position of the rank of Major in the Royal Electrical and Mechanical Engineers. He had been promoted to that rank on his posting to Burma and he had been totally responsible for all the plant, transport, tanks and machinery in a large part of that country. However, as the months after the end of the war sped by, he was keen to settle into a civilian job where there were good prospects of promotion—ideally in a production factory environment—and possibly in the soap and detergents field that he had known, loved and experienced at Crosfields in Warrington.

In the short term he toyed with the idea of buying and operating a garage that would offer a couple of cars for hire and/or chauffeur service—thus underpinning all the basic facilities for the repair, servicing and fuelling of cars. His first possibility was at Leigh, a few miles north of Warrington, but this was badly situated and he wondered if it was better to be on the fringe of a large city where there would be scope for expanding the business. After inspecting several possibilities he set his mind on a chauffeur/servicing/repairing/fuelling garage business in the suburb of Liverpool called Bootle, six miles due north of the city centre.

Albert Dover did all the financial calculations time after time, and weighed up whether a move to a much larger conurbation would be acceptable and/or desirable to his wife Emma. He also thought long and hard about what the effects of such a change of home, environment and education would be on his three sons. The two younger ones were both doing very well at the Stockton Heath School and his older son Alan was already in his third year at Manchester Grammar school. Alan had been coping very well indeed with the twenty mile rail journeys into and out of Manchester for almost three years. Would a further twenty miles, each way and every day, plus the journey from Bootle into and out of Liverpool, prove too much of a burden for Alan, and start to affect his studies and performance at school?

It was not an easy decision to take and there were two further considerations. First Albert would have to pay out all the money he had acquired for such an opportunity as this, and there would be hardly any margin for errors or downturns in the market. Secondly, by all the accounts of the teachers at Stockton Heath School his second son Den was almost as bright as Alan, and he was highly likely to also pass the extremely difficult examinations to earn entry to Manchester Grammar School. This meant that there would be two lots of heavy travel costs for the boys and also two monthly school fees to be paid.

Albert was conscious that his wife's favourite saying had always been 'You have to speculate to accumulate.' Albert and Emma were also conscious that one of their favourite resorts for weekends away, or even day trips, was Southport which was a lovely seaside resort with the motto 'Come to Sunny Southport.' Albert had heard on the local gossip grapevine that large numbers of successful businessmen from Manchester, Warrington and Liverpool had begun a very popular trend of selling up their businesses and retiring to Southport. Indeed many had moved to that town and decided it was worth their time and effort to travel each day to their businesses from Southport for the last decade or more of their business lives.

At this very time Albert was approached by his former employers who wanted him to consider taking over as Works Manager of the whole Warrington Crosfields factory. Albert was very pleased about this approach because that had been his one declared aim in life for many years—particularly when he was literally fighting for his life in the Burmese jungle. He would often visualise what it would be like to return to Warrington, to be hailed as a war hero and immediately awarded the top job at Crosfields. However, Albert had grown to realise that both in life and in a career, timing was everything. Rather than the offer from Crosfields attracting him, he found that it concentrated his mind on what he and his family really wanted and needed at that time.

Emma was the first to know that he had made up his mind and his bank manager in Warrington was the second to know. The boys were never really informed until preparations for moving house had begun. They all thought it would be very exciting but they were always so busy studying at school, doing huge amounts of homework and playing as much sport as they could fit in. They did travel by car once to Bootle to take some suitcases of clothes to their new home, but they only had a very quick look around the garage and the office which was situated along one side of the house. During their brief visit they did not pick up the fact that there was a large treacle manufacturing works right in front of their new home. Thankfully this was hidden by an enormously high and long dark blue brick wall. On the far side of the treacle factory they were told that the Leeds to Liverpool canal ran on its way down from Leeds, a huge city in Yorkshire, all the eighty miles to its opening into the Irish Sea within a mile or two of Bootle.

A week later they had successfully moved into their home in Bootle. Den and Keith started to attend the local St George's Church of England Primary school which was very closely situated to what was one of the largest Church of England churches in the whole area. Alan had to catch a very early bus each morning into the centre of Liverpool from the bus stop in Stanley Road, just round the corner from their garage and home. He then caught a train from one of the main line Liverpool stations that stopped at Warrington station halfway along its forty mile journey to Manchester Central Station.

*****

Albert Dover was delighted that he had managed to own and run his own garage business so soon after leaving the army. He vowed to work day and night to ensure its success. Fred Harris was already in place as the chauffeur and was a qualified mechanic. There was also a trainee mechanic and Albert soon assessed them both as being entirely suitable for his needs. After all they had both already worked in the business for several years. There were two cars in the business that were hired out for special occasions; one was an old style straight up and down Rolls Royce and the other was a Vauxhall with a smart streamlined body. These were vehicles that the business could be proud of and regular bookings indicated that there was a strong demand for such a service. Fred often spent half his time on chauffeuring duties.

Although the garage was only open five days a week and on Saturday mornings there was always plenty of repair, servicing and maintenance work to be carried out at the weekends. Alan became quite proficient on checking, servicing and maintaining the large number of customers' cars that had all their upkeep work carried out at the Merton Garage, Merton Grove, Bootle, Liverpool. It was a reliable business with a good reputation—and a new owner with a distinguished war record!

There were two fuel pumps for cars and one for lorries. The location of the garage was ideal because Stanley Road passed right through the centre of Bootle and was the main spine road running between the centre of Liverpool and Southport, twenty miles to the north along the coast. Albert decided that he would build up the business as efficiently and effectively as possible and then sell up and buy a house in Southport, ideally after obtaining a job in works management at Manchester. He had heard about the huge new Trafford Park industrial area where major American firms were setting up their British headquarters and main factories. One of them was Procter and Gamble who also had a major factory complex in Newcastle-upon-Tyne two hundred miles north up the east coast of England.

Albert resolved to keep up to date with developments in the mechanical engineering, production management and works management fields. He bought and read all the latest British and American journals, attended many seminars and was in touch with all the recruiting agencies and the major firms that he was targeting for his next move up the industrial ladder.

Chapter 13

After two years of building up the garage business Albert Dover was able to look carefully at the last few years of the annual accounts that showed a sharp increase in the turnover as soon as he had taken over the business. He had continued with the same accountants that the previous owner had used, and he had insisted that they were to be completely consistent in the records, returns, forecasts and accounts used for the business so that he would easily be able to check all the expenditure, see where changes in methods of operation needed to be made, and ensure that there were no wasted monies. He ran a very tight ship and was used to very detailed and accurate accounting and recording procedures as they were employed in the British army.

Albert could hardly believe how well the business was performing and he was well aware that now every family was keen to own their own car, and experience the mobility that had been denied to them by the lengthy war. He showed the results to Emma and discussed with her what their options were. He knew he had a craving to return to large scale factory production facilities and he was willing to travel a long distance each day—as he had done when he served his apprenticeship with Metropolitan Vickers in Manchester. Albert and Emma spent many hours discussing the various options open to them, and they were both keen and determined not to disturb the education prospects for their three sons.

Albert kept his eyes and ears open for any really good prospects and prepared his first ever Curriculum Vitae on the outdated basic typewriter in the garage office. As he did so he realised how far behind the latest technologies his current office procedures were. There was an old fashioned, handheld, trumpet shaped telephone receiver that had to be rested in a circular hanger on the office wall. Furthermore all the telephone calls had to be made via an operator at the local telephone exchange. All the gadgets and procedures compared very unfavourably with newer businesses and premises that he had to visit regularly in the course of his business dealings. He needed and wanted to make real progress personally and business-wise in the second half of the twentieth century.

After a few months Albert read about the huge new factory facilities that the large American soap and detergents firm, Procter and Gamble, were having designed and built just to the north east of the centre of Newcastle-upon-Tyne. They had previously set up a large plant on the Trafford Park industrial estate in Manchester—not very far from the Old Trafford Lancashire County Cricket club ground which was one of the most well-known Test Match venues in the world.

Interviews were being held at the Trafford Park factory of Procter and Gamble. All those interested were asked to send in their CVs and a covering letter explaining what they thought they could offer to the firm, and why they wanted to work for Procter and Gamble in particular. Albert spent a whole week, plus the weekend, preparing his application and posted it off before the closing date. Emma had checked it out in great detail and had also read all she could about the firm, as set out in its brochures and copies of Newsletters that they had sent out to all applicants.

Albert was delighted to receive an early acknowledgment of his application plus an invitation to attend an interview at the Trafford Park factory. He decided to drive over to Manchester in the next few days, on a working day, to gauge the size and nature of the plant well before he attended the interview. It was absolutely vast. It was several times larger than the complete facilities of Crosfields at Warrington. He was overawed, but not surprised, because all the Americans he had ever met and worked with seemed to take great pride in boasting about the size of so many American landmarks and places.

He realised that the American firm could offer him a fantastic opportunity to widen his own knowledge and, at the same time, experience what it was like to work for one of the largest employers in the world. He was very excited about the possibility and could hardly wait for the interview. When it arrived he was most impressed by the cleanliness and the efficiency of the reception area and the interviewing arrangements that had been made. First, all the interviewees attended a film about the history of Procter and Gamble, its worldwide locations, its products, its markets, its achievements and its aims for the future. After some of these sessions questions were invited from the potential employees. Albert decided that 'fortune might favour the brave' so he

64

delivered his one question in a clear, meaningful voice while trying to sound confident and keenly interested. 'How many employees are there currently at Manchester and Newcastle-upon-Tyne and what growth is expected over ten years? Will future employees be required to work at both locations during their career with the Company?'

Albert was very impressed by the huge increases expected in the number of employees, and noted that they would be very keen to recruit people who devoted themselves to the Company, and who would also be willing to work at both locations. At his first interview there were three Company representatives present and one of them said how impressed they had been by Albert's question. They pointed out that, because he was married with a family of three boys they assumed that he would only be willing to work for them at the Manchester factory. Albert was quick to point out that he had had to work overseas throughout the whole period of the war. He would be very willing and indeed keen to work at both locations, in line with the Company's requirements. He emphasised that he was also very keen indeed to learn as much as possible about the whole range of the Company's operations.

Albert was convinced that this verbal exchange at his interview, and his question at the main gathering, had first of all made sure that he had been noticed and secondly had convinced them that they need have no doubts whatsoever about his interest in, and future loyalty to, the Company.

On his return home he reported on the events of the day to his wife. She asked him if they had enquired about when he could start with the Company. He said that they had put that question to him, but they said they realised that he would need some time to sell his business. However, Albert then admitted to Emma that he had already received two written offers for the firm he had built up over the last few years. The offers were both pitched at an acceptable level and from two trusted sources. The proceeds would enable him to sell the business quickly, buy a house in Southport and allow him to work primarily in Manchester, or even travel home at weekends from Newcastle-upon-Tyne if they wanted him to work up there. Albert had even checked the times and costs of the various trains from Southport to Manchester that would suit him for travel to work in Manchester—and Alan, plus Den also if he gained entry to Manchester Grammar School, for their school timetable.

After anxiously waiting for news in the post Albert was pleased to receive a written invitation to spend a whole day looking round the Manchester plant, and the following day visiting the Newcastle plant. Albert was so excited and resolved immediately to fully concentrate on finding out all he could about the two plants, so that he could convince the Procter and Gamble personnel that his experiences and knowledge in their fields of activity were second to none. Meanwhile he would have off the record chats with his solicitor, his accountant and his bank manager to make absolutely certain that the sale price for his business would be achieved, that it represented fair value to the two interested buyers, and that with the proceeds of the sale he would be able to buy a suitable property in Southport. He also made a mental note that their future home would need to be very close to a railway station that was convenient for travel to Manchester.

Over the next few weeks Albert burned the midnight oil every night. He knew he had come through some very dangerous and challenging times during his life, but he was aware that the next month or two would be crucial. They would determine whether or not he could successfully make the major move to a large employer of world renown. In addition he had to ensure that his wife and family would be able to settle down in a new location. He was so keen on ensuring that he made a real success of the wonderful opportunity that seemed to be opening up for them all.

Chapter 14

Albert Dover had managed the train journey from Southport to Salford station, two miles short of Manchester, with ease. The train had departed on time from St Luke's station, a mile out of Southport and only a five minute walk from his home. It also arrived on time after the forty mile journey which took only three quarters of an hour. He now had to catch the correct bus to Trafford Park and he was delighted that there was a bus going there every five minutes from the bus stop directly outside the Salford station exit.

After the twenty minute bus journey he alighted and headed off towards the Procter and Gamble factory only a few minutes away. He walked up to the security gates with pride and announced himself as Albert Dover, the new Assistant Works Manager. The security guard asked him to wait in the small office by the gate for someone to come and collect him. It was a familiar routine that he knew well from his many years at Crosfields in Warrington.

A young lady arrived to take him to the Administration Office where she said they would complete all the paperwork that was necessary for a new employee. This only took a few minutes and the same lady then took him to meet the Head of Personnel. He checked that all the paperwork had been completed and then said he wanted to talk with Albert for a few minutes before handing him over to the Personal Secretary to the Works Manager whom he would be meeting that morning. The Head of Personnel said that Albert would have seen most of the various facilities on the Trafford Park site when he had visited both the Manchester and Newcastle sites as part of the selection process.

The Personal Secretary had an office immediately adjacent to the Works Manager, Mr Arnie Shelby, who was an American and had steered all the early negotiations and plans, the design work, and the construction and fitting out of the plant to a highly successful conclusion. This included all the very intensive and extensive testing of all the production machines, the mechanical handling equipment, the cranes, the boilers, the mixing vats and the packaging machinery. This was truly a massive new factory and was built to all the latest and highest specifications and standards. Mr Shelby must indeed be very proud of what he had achieved.

The Works Manager offered a very strong handshake to Albert and, in the customary American style, he made him feel totally at home from the outset. Over coffee and biscuits the Works Manager explained to his brand new Assistant the role that he wished him to play. He said he needed to pass over to Albert the day to day effective and efficient running and management of all the on-site employees, and all the facilities they had at their disposal. He emphasised that this process would take some time, but he wanted it done very thoroughly indeed.

Mr Shelby explained that he wanted to, and needed to, return to the States in the next few years because he had spent far too many years globetrotting around the world for Procter and Gamble and far too little time with his wife and family of two boys and two girls who would be heading off in the next ten years to various universities, either anywhere in the States or even further afield. He was genuinely impressed by Albert's distinguished career in the British Army and amazed to learn that he had never seen his three sons for a period of six years. It was very clear indeed to Mr Shelby that Albert had carried out very important industrial jobs in his civilian life before the war and that he had had a very responsible job as a major in charge of the REME operations in the south east of France and then for five years in a huge area of Burma, during his war service. All these roles made him ideal for the position of Assistant Works Manager at the Trafford Park plant. Albert was to be his right hand man at all times. There was a workforce of a thousand to be managed, there were also important production targets to be hit and, at all times, the financial targets had to be achieved. Furthermore not only had the weekly, monthly, quarterly and annual spending levels to be adhered to, but also the production targets had to be achieved, if the plant was to be profitable and a showpiece for the future expansion of Procter and Gamble into other territories throughout the world.

After their introductory chat Mr Shelby said that he wanted Albert to spend the whole of his first two days meeting all the heads of departments and going round their various areas so that he could discuss with them on a one to one basis all the procedures, machinery, automation, electronic controls and safety measures that were being employed. After that he wanted his Assistant to spend the next two days in each of the service departments so that they could explain to him what they were each doing to help the various departments of the plant perform to their maximum capabilities. All of these services were crucial to the success of the whole operation and they included personnel, administration, communications, publicity, community relations, production control, planning, costing and bonus, work study, maintenance, fire, medical, finance and accounts, catering and public health.

On the Friday Mr Shelby wished to spend the whole day with Albert so that he could hear what his first impressions were, and what positive changes and/or improvements he thought could or should be considered. He said he would also need to know what Albert's impressions of the various managers, foremen and staff had been—and what were the differences he had discovered between the latest American industrial philosophy and that of the British industrial and military methods he had experienced prior to his appointment with Procter and Gamble.

It was certainly going to be a hectic week for Albert and he was so thankful that his family had almost completed their move into their three bedroom house in Southport. He was relieved that Den and Keith had already begun their education at St Philip's Church of England Junior School ten minutes' walk from their home, and that Alan was already travelling to Manchester Grammar School just as easily from Southport as he had managed from Warrington for two years and Bootle for two years.

More important than anything else Albert knew that Emma was very happy in their new home and was looking forward to exploring Southport and all its features. It was a wonderful place to live in and to bring up a family. There were several golf courses including both the Birkdale and Hillside courses where the British Open Golf championship had been held several times. There was a large open-air swimming pool, several tennis clubs, many cricket clubs, football clubs, badminton leagues and table-tennis leagues. In short Southport was not only a sunny place but it was a sportsman's paradise and a great town for a family of three active boys to grow up in.

*****

Albert could hardly wait to arrive at the factory each day that week. He knew from his wide experience of very many production and engineering operations what were the important features, and indicators, of an efficient and effective industrial operation. In the various departments of his new employer he examined every single operation and observed the attitudes and actions of all the employees. Over the years he had realised that one key and easy measure was to count how many of any group of ten operatives were focusing on their job, looking intelligent and interested in what they were doing, performing their tasks with a positive attitude, and had happiness written on their faces. These spot checks in the numerous parts of the factory were instantly logged into the Assistant Manager's brain—and sometimes jotted down in the small pocket notebook he had with him at all times. He knew that he would be able to retrieve and review these counts during any short break times he had at the factory, on his train journey from Victoria Station, Manchester back to Southport—and most importantly of all—back in his makeshift office at home each evening. His rigorous routine of spending every evening going through everything he had done, seen, heard and recorded that day had been developed during the years of his apprenticeship at Metropolitan Vickers. During his army service he had made enormous use of a standard issue typewriter not just to help him record all the necessary records for the army documentation, but to make notes on the lessons he had learned each day—whether technical, practical, mental, psychological or managerial.

When the Works Manager had set out his programme for the first week Albert's initial reaction and resolution was to burn the midnight oil that week and put in typewritten form all his impressions. These would be used by him in the numerous review and discussion periods inserted into his programme. They would form the basis on which he would produce a summary of his recommendations and conclusions which he would discuss with Mr Shelby at the end of the week.

Albert was a great believer in graphical representations to show trends in performance when plotted against a daily, weekly or monthly (four weeks) time frame. He considered that every key feature of plant or labour output could be measured in numerical terms—and that time bar charts showing all the key operations were invaluable. First they imposed a rigorous, challenging but essential need to quantify these various key activities. Secondly by plotting the changing values on a time frame the upward or downward trends could be identified at the earliest possible time—allowing effective actions to be taken to reverse any unacceptable trends.

Albert had been taught in his early days in an industrial arena that all people needed to do was to work hard. He soon realised that the really important thing was to work effectively and to be able to quantify your performance to ensure that you were on track to achieve your aims. This philosophy was the whole basis of production control. First produce a plan showing the sequence of the various activities to be carried out. Next put this onto a time bar chart and finally—and most importantly—record clearly what progress had been made each day, each week or each month. This final operation had to be done rigorously, accurately and truthfully.

By the regular and thorough use of production control charts all the managers, foremen and individual workers could be involved in the processes and sequences that would be adopted. They would also see what a particular workshop or department was trying to achieve. Furthermore everyone would be involved, and thereby motivated. All this effort had the enormous benefit of welding together all personnel in a particular area of the factory so that they came to both think and work better together. All who were involved would play their part and work together as a team. In Albert's view the sum total of the efforts of all the individuals in a team always fell short of the overall performance of a team that played and cooperated together. Teamwork was everything.

Albert drew up notional charts for the key operations in each part of the factory and included accurate quantities and/or financial values that he obtained from the appropriate people. They wondered what the Assistant Works Manager was trying to achieve but they were extremely cooperative in answering all of his numerous, sometimes very detailed questions, to the best of their ability.

He did not need to use his time bar chart system for the various service departments. He did explain to them however what he had been doing when he spent his two days in the numerous production areas. He was pleased that, as back up services to the general management throughout the factory, they were eager to agree with Albert on his overall aim of making sure everyone in the numerous production areas pulled together as one team. Even at the very advanced Trafford Park site there was much time and attention needed to motivate the workforce, thereby ensuring that everyone was pulling together and that the overall performance of the plant would be improved. The Trafford Park plant was an ideal factory to ensure that the best mixture of Anglo American ideas, methods, practices and controls were employed. By achieving better coordination, teamwork, control and supervision the individual, team and total outputs would be raised to their highest possible levels. This would bring financial benefits to all concerned—provided performance related pay deals could be negotiated, introduced and implemented fairly.

Albert realised that he had to ensure that Mr Shelby and his current team of heads of departments, foremen and managers did not think he had little or no right to come in and turn their whole operation upside down. One of his earliest lessons and firmest resolves in life had been never to rock the boat but to help the whole crew steer the boat into calmer waters where better progress could be made, thereby ensuring that the race could be won.

Each night Albert bounced his ideas off Emma, who had an inborn ability to pick up new ideas, ensure that they were soundly based and acceptable to all those involved—and that they were certain to lead to improvements. Emma 'role played' as the Works Manager to make certain that Albert had everything covered before he presented his ideas to Mr Shelby. In doing this she realised that she needed to be diplomatic in the way she advised Albert that he must in no way upset any of the existing employees, and in particular Mr Shelby who had clearly played a major part in ensuring that Albert, and no-one else, was the successful candidate and the one who was selected as his Assistant.

Eventually Albert found himself in Mr Shelby's office for the whole of the Friday. He began by saying that he had been most impressed by all the management, foremen, operatives, heads of departments and all those in the services operations. Albert was extremely impressed that Mr Shelby had clearly put together an excellent team in a very short period and they had, together, achieved acceptable performance levels and financial results. However, as Albert went round the whole Trafford Park plant he said he had detected some changes that should be considered and which he wanted to talk through with Mr Shelby. His whole aim was to improve liaison, bring in more planning and monitoring of performance, introduce an incentive scheme for all the employees, and retrain some of the staff in each department so that they would be the ones to help bring in the changes needed. He emphasised that these changes should only be embarked upon when a cost benefit analysis had clearly shown that they would be to the overall benefit of the Company and also to all the employees.

Mr Shelby posed many searching questions throughout this man to man, head to head encounter. At the end he said 'Young man, I am now totally convinced that I made the correct recommendation to the Main Board. You have identified exactly what we now need to do to make this one of the best plants that Procter and Gamble has anywhere in the world.'

Mr Shelby continued 'I am most impressed by the methods you have used throughout your industrial and army career. Some of the top world experts in management theory and in particular the American Peter Drucker, have been researching the best ways of improving the performance of individuals in the workplace—and the overall efficiency and effectiveness of the management and control procedures being used throughout the world. They have not yet reached their conclusions but I don't suppose you have even heard of Peter Drucker, have you?'

'No, I have not' said Albert.

'In that case you have developed your own practical ways of maximising the performance and output of a plant or workforce. That does you a lot of credit because in life you will find it is often very lonely, hard and soul-destroying to be ploughing a lone furrow when everyone round you has given you up as a misguided loner or a nutcase. Well done indeed. You need to get yourself fully accepted by the whole workforce on site, both blue and white collar. You need to create exactly the right impression by always keeping your door open, by listening to all their problems, by showing you are very fair minded—but at the same time willing to be as hard as nails when problems arise, as they most certainly will.'

'Anyway that is enough for today and this week. I am certain that we can work together for many years to come. You have a great future ahead of you with this Company. Meanwhile I want you to know that my door will indeed be open at all times to you. I realise that you like to work with as little supervision as possible. That is not a weakness, it is a great strength.'

'It is a great privilege and a pleasure to have you working for us. I wish you every success in your future career with this great Company. We are already among the list of the best companies in the world. You can help us stay up there with the rest, and also help us to show them the mud on our boots when they fail to keep up with us.'

Albert enjoyed his journey home that evening and decided that he needed an early night, but only after he had taken his whole family out for their first sample of Southport's dining facilities.

Chapter 15

Over his first few months as Assistant Works Manager at the Trafford Park plant Albert explored every corner of every department to ensure that he was fully aware of all the facilities that he was responsible for. He always spent the first hour of each day circulating through the whole area, never by the same route or sequence. He did this to check that everything was up and running as soon as possible, and because he did not want to visit a particular department at the same time. He needed to know that at all times in that first hour—and indeed throughout the whole day—the numerous activities were being performed efficiently and effectively.

Every few minutes during his factory tours he would stop and have a word with each shop foreman or supervisor. His opening phrase would usually be 'How are things going?' and this always elicited a different response but one which gave him in a minute or two a snapshot view of what was going well, or badly. Albert would follow up with a question such as 'So what can be done to make sure that we can improve any of the equipment, machinery or methods, to increase our output and reduce our costs?'

These short exchanges built up confidence between Albert and his workforce. This was a two way process, with Albert getting to know all the individuals better—and the workforce coming to realise that the Assistant Works Manager was very easy to communicate with, was interested in their opinions and was keen to improve every single aspect of the workplace. It was abundantly clear that both Albert and his individual workers had exactly the same aims—namely to make Procter and Gamble the most productive and efficient business operation ever. This pride in the job, eagerness to succeed and to be the best was very much in line with the philosophy and methodology of the armed forces during the Second World War. This esprit de corps at Procter and Gamble was engendered by the shared feelings of pride and loyalty which united all the members of the factory workforce from the day that Albert arrived at the plant.

Albert hated to waste time at formal meetings but some were essential. However, he was very keen indeed on short troubleshooting and pep-talk get-togethers. These would often be held on the actual shop floor to minimise any disturbance to the natural rhythm and pace of work. Albert had played league football for Stockport County and also rugby league for Swinton. He likened these brief meetings in the factory to the pep-talks he would give to his football and rugby colleagues playing under his captaincy. In both the work and sport environments these chats were very effective in concentrating mind and body on achieving aims as quickly and effectively as possible. The timeframe in these two sports was measured in terms of an hour or so. In the workplace however the results would show over a longer period.

Albert spent a great deal of time and effort discussing the various productivity measures being used, agreeing and making improvements to these wherever he thought they needed changing. He always wanted to see the maximum possible use of graphs to show the actual number of items produced compared to the number that was required to be produced in the same time period—both plotted against a horizontal timeframe. He instilled in everyone the need to produce this same information on a daily, weekly and monthly (four weekly) basis—so that early upward or downward trends could be spotted and effective action taken at the appropriate time.

It was not long before the results of Albert's methods and actions were clearly visible. Most of the production graphs in each workshop showed upward trends—to the delight of Mr Shelby—who had noticed from the financial figures that turnovers had improved across the whole factory. Furthermore there was more production bonus being paid out to the workers across the whole plant. There was a real buzz about the whole place and Mr Shelby was keen for Albert to speak at a forthcoming one day conference of all the United Kingdom Board of Directors, to be held at the renowned Midland Hotel, only two minutes from the Town Hall Square in Manchester.

This speech went down very well indeed and there were lively discussions at the end. Albert was a natural speaker and motivator. These were two characteristics of Albert that made him more than acceptable to his American employers. The new plans to expand the Newcastle-upon-Tyne plant were discussed at the one day conference, with a first class visual presentation and a model in a glass covered table top display. Albert was stunned by the size of the expansion proposed, but he was very aware that several very well-known household and beauty products were so popular that additional production facilities were urgently needed to meet the volumes of demand for these mainstream items.

A week after the Manchester conference Mr Shelby told him that Procter and Gamble had been giving thought to Albert being involved in the execution of the Newcastle expansion programme. He asked Albert if he would be interested and whether this would be acceptable to his wife. He was not surprised by Albert's eagerness, nor by the strong assurance given by Albert that his wife Emma would be totally supportive. She was so happy about Albert being employed by the Company and would never stand in the way of his progress in the firm.

Albert was asked to arrange to spend a whole week up in Newcastle to meet all the design team and the proposed contractors, suppliers and subcontractors. He realised that he would have to ensure that everything was running really smoothly and efficiently at the Manchester plant if he was to be able to concentrate his full attention to preparing for this week, and adding value to the whole process—with a clear mind. Meanwhile he resolved to read all the documents that Mr Shelby had retained about the construction and commissioning of the Manchester plant at Trafford Park. After all Mr Shelby had been in total charge of that operation, and would have learned many important lessons.

Chapter 16

Albert remembered his earlier visit to Newcastle-upon Tyne and admired the seven bridges over the River Tyne as his train slowed down before entering the main station. He took a taxi to the factory, as instructed, and arrived before the assembly time of midday on the Monday. On the way across the city he noted how poor some of the areas appeared to be. He was conscious that the Jarrow marches had hailed from only a few miles away, and he recalled the resolution of the thousands of men who had marched all the 400 miles to London to highlight the need for more jobs for their area. Clearly they had been experiencing poverty in their local villages. What they had done was to make their mark in a quiet and dignified manner. Consciences had been pricked and some action had been taken by successive governments over the intervening years to help to alleviate conditions in some of the worst areas.

Albert noticed the suburb of Jesmond which was only a couple of miles short of the factory. It was there that he would be spending four nights at a small hotel. It was called the Jesmond Dene hotel and it was painted in white, causing it to stand out from its surroundings. The area of Jesmond was quite picturesque and he looked forward to examining the area on foot over the next few days. Meanwhile he needed to keep his wits about him because there was a whole series of meetings that were planned for the week.

The assembly room was the venue for a brief lunch which was very welcome after his long journey. Around the walls of this large room there were twelve glass topped models of the proposed factory, showing larger scale versions of key areas and also of the huge vats, the largest items of machinery, and an even larger scale model of some of the automatic German designed and manufactured metallic rolling tracks used for the rapid and effective distribution of bottles, cans, boxes and finished products between one workshop and the next.

Albert reckoned that most of what he saw represented the next generation of machinery and mechanical handling equipment to the items he had been accustomed to. He waited with bated breath the opportunity to hear detailed descriptions of all this new gadgetry.

Introductions were made over the lunch and short speeches were delivered by one of the Procter and Gamble directors, the Newcastle Works Manager, the head of the design team and the Project Manager. His remit was to take control of all the design, construction and commissioning operations, and ensure that the whole new development was completed on time and within the financial budget. Finally Albert had come across somebody who might be even busier than he would be over the next two years!

The whole afternoon was taken up with explanations of the models that were situated around the perimeter of the room—using slide projectors to illustrate the older versions of the numerous items and also the new versions. In every case there was a more streamlined look and it was clear that far fewer workers would be required throughout the whole new plant. In addition the throughput figures that were envisaged were stunning—being well above any of the rates achieved to date on the kind of machinery Albert was used to in Manchester.

One of the most interesting talks that evening was by one of the top market research experts. He explained in great detail, again using slide projectors, the very exhaustive market research that had been carried out, not just in America but in major countries such as Australia, Canada, England, France, Italy and Germany. It was abundantly clear that P&G's products were extremely popular in the advanced world and that soaps, detergents, cleaning products and beauty products had growth rates far above most other consumer products—even outpacing the current very high growth rates for cars, bicycles and motorbikes. All the market research statistics had shown conclusively that the Newcastle factory had to be enlarged or redeveloped. Modernisation and extensions would be quite costly but, more importantly, they would not be able to meet the much higher levels of consumer demands. It had been 'blindingly obvious' that the only solution available to the Company was to build an entirely new plant on and near to the existing site, using some additional land owned by the Company. The existing plant and machinery would have to be kept running as long as possible until its output was replaced and exceeded by the new developments.

Albert was so impressed by all that he heard and could not believe his luck in being chosen to be part of the Development Team. His job was going to be providing advice on the numerous items of plant, machinery and mechanical handling facilities. He would have to liaise with the mechanical, electrical and heating/ventilation/air conditioning consultants, designers and contractors. It was clear to him that after the first few months of being involved in the Development he would need to be based in Newcastle most of each week right up to and slightly beyond the actual completion date of all the Development work. This did not concern him because he had, in a sense, brought this upon himself by posing his question at the end of his selection process for employment with the Company. He had asked then whether some staff would be required to work at both the Manchester and Newcastle sites. It now looked as though he was prescient. What he knew for certain was that he was thrilled at the opportunity to prove yet again his skills, application and suitability for another challenging role with the Company.

The remainder of the week was stimulating and allowed Albert to be briefed in detail on the new items of plant—and particularly the new metal framed conveyor systems using row upon row of shiny metal rollers, typically about four feet long and having a diameter of around three inches. This whole system had been conceived, designed, built and tested by German engineers throughout the Second World War period. The initial usage envisaged was in the aircraft, motorcar and tank industries. At the end of the war the Germans realised the enormous potential for their system in the non-military fields, and since then they had swept the world with it. Albert had kept in touch with these developments through his own market research and network of academic and industrial experts.

He was also able to be brought up to date with the latest heating, mixing and casting techniques and was highly impressed by the advances in all the manufacturing and handling processes to be employed in the new Development. At the end of the week there was a final debriefing meeting and he was able to bring all those present up to date with the latest methods of production control that he had introduced at the Old Trafford plant—involving his bar chart and graphical forms of planning and control. He was able to report on the increases in output and financial performance achieved by using these techniques. It was clear to all those present that Albert was at the leading edge of production control methods. It was also evident, judging by the high degree of interest shown, that they were intending to use Albert's new production control techniques during the design, construction and commissioning phases of the new Development project.

Chapter 17

For the next few months Albert was able to concentrate on all aspects of his work at the Old Trafford plant, without any diversions away from his base. He had received a very impressive written and illustrated report on the week of briefings about the Newcastle-upon-Tyne Development. Mr Shelby had asked him many questions about various aspects of the new plant up in the North East of England. He was keen to pass onto Albert as many of the benefits of his own experiences that he could. He was very proud of Albert, whom he viewed as his protégé.

The period before Albert's full time involvement up in Newcastle was a very good opportunity for bonding with his whole family, including occasional visits on Sunday afternoons to call on one or more of the numerous aunts and uncles in Warrington. His three boys had wonderful memories of their wartime upbringing in that town and did not want to lose any of the precious, and very close, links that they had forged with their cousins.

At long last Albert was sent details of his posting to the Newcastle site where the Company expected him to work full time for the six months before excavation of the new site was to be started. This would enable him to build up his personal links with the design and construction team before the redevelopment work began in earnest. The importance of those six months to the overall success of the redevelopment had been emphasised by the numerous consultants and contractors whom he had met during his week in Newcastle. It was agreed that a decision would soon have to be made on what percentage of his time that Albert would and should spend in Newcastle each week while the remainder of the redevelopment work was carried out. He realised that all the weeks he spent up there would be time very well spent, because he would be totally au fait with all the plant, machinery and equipment that he would be asked to take control of—if and when he was appointed to the permanent workforce up in Newcastle.

The Manchester plant had their best ever production and financial results in the final six months before Albert set off for Newcastle. By then all the three boys had settled down really well at their schools and had become used to seeing their father only from 7 pm each evening and at the weekends. Each weekday he set off walking to the railway station in Southport to catch the 7 am train to Manchester, returning home on the 6 pm train out of Victoria station, Manchester. The weekends were devoted to the family. They were all mad keen on sports and Alan was already in the top cricket and football teams at Manchester Grammar School, meaning that he had to travel not just five days a week to Manchester from Southport (an eighty mile round trip) but often six days a week!

Den and Keith at that stage were still at the St Philip's Junior School and too young to play representative sport. However, Den had a regular date with his Dad every Saturday afternoon at 3 pm when Southport Association Football Club played Third Division League football only ten minutes away from their home. One year they even progressed in the Football Association Cup games, the FA Cup, and came up against a First Division side. The only downside was that once every two or three weeks when there was no league match they would have to watch Southport Reserves against a non-league side, when the standard of the game was much lower.

One Saturday there was one of the non-league teams playing Southport Reserves at the Haig Avenue ground. There were no seats for the spectators in those days, except for some two hundred seats for the Season Ticket holders and a handful of Directors directly above the changing rooms in the West Stand. Albert and his son Den were surrounded by quite a crowd that day—all of whom had travelled by coach to the seaside to support their local team, Chorley. This was an old-fashioned town where coal mining and textile mills had been in abundance, thereby creating the wealth for many famous local rich families—and providing badly needed jobs for the honest hard-working folk of Chorley and the surrounding villages at the foot of the Pennine range of hills, and only fifteen miles from Southport across very fertile fields of farming land where crops, cattle and sheep all flourished.

The tightly knit contingent from Chorley was very vociferous. All the time they kept on bawling out 'Come on Charley. Come on Charley—you can do it.'

Even when Southport Reserves were two goals up, the chant went on 'Come on Charley. Keep it up. Come on Charley—show 'em what you can do.'

Den had looked very carefully at all the visiting players to identify who this star player Charlie was. None of the players listed in the programme for the match was listed as a Charlie, and Den was totally mystified. At the end of what turned out to be a tremendously close affair Chorley scored two late goals and all their fans were elated. As the fans boarded the line of coaches to take a tour of the town before returning home, they kept up the incessant chant 'Well done Charley. Good old Charley. Good old Charley. Well done lads.'

Only during their walk home was the mystery solved. Albert explained to Den that there was no player called Charley in the Chorley team. The ecstatic fans were merely shouting their team's name with a strong Lancashire accent. Chorley was in effect being translated by their accent to 'Charrrley.' Den so often recalled that day when he realised for the very first time how strong was the Lancashire accent when spoken by a true Lancastrian, born and bred in the mill towns of Lancashire where the first ever spinning mill and machinery was invented by Arkwright—only a few miles to the south east of Chorley. That town was one day going to play a major part in Den's life—but he was far too young to know or understand what the future would hold for him.

Chapter 18

For his first six months in Newcastle, Albert decided that he wanted to stay in lodgings in Jesmond on the main road through that part of Newcastle-upon-Tyne. He would travel home to Southport most weekends and he would spend most of his waking time hard at work at the factory. He loved walking and wanted to minimise his travelling time each weekday. The huge advantage was that the new site was only a brisk thirty minute walk each day for him. This would refresh him for the day ahead and also help him to wind down on the return walk in the evenings. The catering at the factory was excellent; he resolved that he would have a lunch there every day and a light breakfast in his lodgings each morning to 'set him up for the day.' He did not want to bog himself down with too much food, he had sworn that he was never going to smoke in his life and he only drank alcohol in moderation—when there was something to celebrate.

There was a special Redevelopment site office established using temporary buildings that were unloaded in large units from long low loaders, and positioned on the area at the front of the new factory complex that was going to be created. Indeed when the two storey temporary office accommodation was removed from the site the only operation left to be carried out would be the final turfing of the whole surrounding area to form the landscaping on the approach to the front entrance of the new plant.

There were several deep basements to be excavated and surrounded by interlocking steel sheet piling. These areas would contain the power station for the new complex, the silos containing most of the raw materials in granular form plus the very large circular, cylindrical and rectangular tanks in which the innumerable liquids and granular materials needed for the production processes were to be stored. Albert was most impressed by the soil mechanics experts in the team who had taken all the necessary soil, clay and rock samples over the whole site and then advised on and designed the most cost effective foundations for the whole redevelopment. The piling experts were very experienced in using steam or diesel powered hammers to drive the interlocking steel sheet piles into the banks along the adjacent River Tyne. The P&G site was only eight miles from the east coast at Tynemouth and an enormous number of factories had been set up along both the north and south banks of the Tyne. These stretched from the Newcastle city centre right out to North Shields and South Shields—the twin towns, one on the north bank and one on the south bank—that had been established near to the main entrance from the North Sea into the River Tyne.

Albert was used to liaising with the Royal Engineers—that branch of the British army that built bridges, dams and other engineering features required by the fighting soldiers to assist in their attack and defence roles. He was always impressed by the very high professional standards of the Royal Engineers who would have been proud of the external experts on soils and foundations who had been appointed for the Redevelopment project.

The maximum amount of prefabrication had been designed into the new complex. This had the twin advantages of speed and economy. A time and cost comparison of both a structural steelwork and a reinforced concrete frame for the whole development had been undertaken by the structural engineers and quantity surveyors appointed by Procter and Gamble. This had shown that structural steelwork would be faster and also cheaper. A similar comparison between having a gas, solid fuel or oil fired heating and energy source for the complex was also carried out, with oil emerging as the winner. For all these three energy sources the main factors of reliability of supply, cleanliness and price were very carefully examined—particularly considering that the area was surrounded by coal mines, and the miners were a very strong lobbying force indeed up in the North East.

Chapter 19

One Saturday morning Albert, Emma and their three sons walked into the town centre of Southport. They were passing by the main railway station in Chapel Street when they saw an enormous crowd spilling out of the station and halfway across the road.

'What is going on?' said Albert to a man who was quietly and efficiently controlling the crowd, urging them to keep on the pavements to ensure their safety.

'It's Mr Hudson, our Member of Parliament, who is due to arrive any minute now on Platform 1' replied the man. 'He always attracts a crowd when he is in the town.'

'How often does he come here?' shouted Alan to the same man.

'Three or four times a year, and he stays here in Southport for a few days each time.' By way of explanation the man went on to say 'He is always so very busy up in London working on our behalf. We're lucky to see him in Southport as often as we do.'

The Dover family tried to weave their way towards Platform 1 and succeeded in reaching the barrier gate where incoming and outgoing tickets were checked and/or collected by a ticket inspector. The eyes of the three boys nearly popped out of their sockets. 'Look at that, they've rolled out a huge red carpet along the platform and it must be Mr Hudson who is walking towards us on it.'

Den saw a white haired, smartly dressed man walking in a small group comprising three smartly dressed ladies and two men in dark grey suits. Suddenly the station porters opened up a folding gate across the end of the platform, to allow Mr Hudson and his small group to stand on that part of the red carpet that ran out onto the station concourse. The crowd stopped milling around and then silence descended on the gathering.

'What is going to happen?' whispered Den.

'I think Mr Hudson is going to make a speech,' said his father, quietly.

Sure enough Mr Hudson moved a few paces in front of his support group, and began to speak in a learned, measured tone—with a short break after each sentence. He explained that he was delighted to be back in his constituency and he conveyed greetings to them all from London, from the House of Commons where he worked, and from his fellow Members of Parliament who were doing their best to get the country back on its feet after such a long, hard-fought war.

Den was transfixed by what he was witnessing, and he listened very attentively to every single word that was delivered—without a note, without a microphone and in a confident manner, full of feeling and emotion. The crowd listened in silence and then applauded Mr Hudson at the end of his ten minute speech. He had explained what he had been doing on their behalf since he was last in Southport, he thanked them for their support and he finished by spending a few minutes briefing two or three newspaper reporters. Photographs were taken with flashes, and then Mr Hudson was driven away in a black saloon car which edged slowly through the crowd.

'What happens now?' asked Den. His mother said that they would be able to read all about Mr Hudson's visit to Southport in the local papers and even in the Liverpool Echo which would be out that evening.

Den could not wait to offer to go and buy the Liverpool Echo with money from his father, and he knew on a Saturday there was now the Sports Evening Echo that prided itself on being available for readers within an hour of all matches on that day having finished. Den wondered if Mr Hudson's photograph and speech would be featured in the Sports Echo.

At 5.25 pm that evening, he returned on foot to the main railway station where there were several newspaper sellers. He frequently ran the mile into town to buy the Sports Echo on a Saturday evening so that his Dad could read the match reports and see the first printed lists of all the Football League match results for the games played that day in the top four Divisions.

To his amazement Mr Hudson's photograph did indeed feature on the front page of the Sports Echo edition. It even had a short summary of his speech, listing some of the new projects and benefits that Mr Hudson had worked hard to achieve for the town over the last few years. Den could not wait to see the Tuesday Southport Visiter newspaper and the following Saturday's edition. He was going to see how important Mr Hudson's work really was. Indeed he resolved that very day to become a Member of Parliament for a town such as

Southport. He had never before realised what Members of Parliament did, but he was convinced that they worked very hard indeed for their towns, and were capable of achieving very impressive, and important, results. What a marvellous job to aim for! What a fine role model Mr Hudson was!

*****

Den had lived throughout the whole duration of the Second World War in the small semi-detached house in Stockton Heath. Whenever events in that war reached crucial stages Den's mother and her three sons strained their ears in trying to hear the often, almost inaudible, but strong and determined voice of their Prime Minister, Winston Churchill on the wireless in their back room. The boys would often creep down the stairs to be near enough to the door of the room, which was usually left slightly open—so that their mother could shout them if any emergency action was needed. They also suspected that she knew she would be able to hear any noises from upstairs with her well-trained ears, if the door was slightly open.

Those messages from Winston Churchill kept their spirits up, even in the darkest hours. He was a wonderful inspiration to the whole nation. Den had no idea that Winston Churchill was also a Member of Parliament and that he would know Mr Hudson because they both sat in the same Chamber of the House of Commons most weekdays during the period of the war. If he had realised that close link between the Prime Minister and Mr Hudson he would have been in even more awe of the Member of Parliament for Southport!

Chapter 20

Christianity and attending church was very important to the Dover family. The next day the whole family attended the morning service at St Philip's Church on the main road into Southport. Afterwards they decided to stroll onwards into the town centre. This time they ventured onto the pier that was one of the longest on the west coast of England. They even all climbed aboard the electric train at the pier head and were glad they did so, because it was nearly a mile long.

After a snack at the end of the pier they decided to walk slowly back and gaze at the sea, the boats, the yachts in Marine Lake and the hundreds of families who were playing on the sandy beach, and also spending time in Peter Pan's Pool—a well-attended recreation park with numerous fairground rides suitable for young children.

It was then that Den looked north towards the end of the impressive Southport promenade, heading off in the direction of Preston, the County Town of Lancashire. Den could hardly believe his eyes! He pointed, stared and pointed again in a state of shock towards the distinctive bright red row of hotels towards the northern end of the promenade.

'Alan, Keith, look along the promenade up to the north. What can you see?'

There was little or no reaction from the two of them, so he tried his mother.

'Mum, have we three boys ever been here before, with you?'

'No' his mother said. 'This is the first time we have all been out together to the pier and the seafront in Southport.'

'No' said Den. 'I mean have we, the three of us boys, been to where we are now—ever before?'

His mother thought most carefully and she was only too well aware of Den's photographic memory.

'Now you come to mention it, the four of us did come here once on a very important date. We travelled here one day from Warrington on VJ Day, when victory over Japan was celebrated on 15 August 1945.'

Den finally realised what had happened. All the three boys and their mother had spent a week on holiday in June that year. They had celebrated Victory in Europe Day in Douglas when hundreds of ships of all shapes and sizes covered the whole skyline, and most of Douglas Bay too. Later that year their mother had taken them off for a very long day indeed, to celebrate VJ Day. They had never, ever, before then in their lives been to the seaside except for their week on the Isle of Man. When the three boys and their mother had caught so many trains one day later that summer, they thought they had travelled to the Isle of Man again—without having to make a sea crossing. They had actually merely travelled to and along the west coast of Lancashire to the seaside resort of Southport!

Den was so delighted that his photographic memory had retained the picture he had committed to his brain all those years before. All the three boys had been so tired that day in August 1945 that it was a wonder they arrived safely back at their home in Stockton Heath, near Warrington. Den's elder brother Alan may have realised at the time where they had travelled to, but Den and his younger brother, Keith, were convinced that they had all had the unique experience of celebrating both VE and VJ Days in Douglas, on the Isle of Man.

Den realised his mistake, and thereafter he came to realise that Southport held a very special place in his heart and mind. It was the town where, together with his two brothers and his mother, they had celebrated Victory over Japan—after such a very lengthy, vicious war, conducted mainly in the jungles of Burma. That was the war in which their father had spent so much time and effort, and in which he had lost so many of his colleagues and friends.

Chapter 21

Albert returned to Newcastle by train very early the next day. He was keen to hear the results of any further discussions on the management and control of the Redevelopment.

He spoke to all his regular colleagues and caught up with them on the latest progress, and any problems they were encountering. He realised how very complicated the task of managing and controlling the creation of such a large and complicated factory and processing centre was. Nevertheless he so much wanted to devote his entire efforts over the next two years to the successful outcome of all the years of market research, planning, design, manufacture, assembly, processing, testing and operation.

Albert did not have long to wait. Bill Meyer called him into his office early on the Monday afternoon, and he had one of the Directors with him. Bill informed Albert that he had been chosen as the Project Manager for the overall Redevelopment. It would also be his task to be one of the three members of the trio controlling the project at all stages—including seeing it right through to the end of all the maintenance periods.

To say that Albert was pleased with this enormous distinction would be the understatement of the millennium. He was not just on cloud nine but at least cloud ninety nine. He did realise that he would be one of the busiest people in the manufacturing and processing world for the next two years, but that was exactly what he wanted. He had never shirked away from taking responsibility for any business opportunity and challenge. This would test him to the very limit. He likened his position to metal that had to be case-hardened to withstand the stresses and strains that it would have to resist during its working life. People were the same. They needed to be toughened up in their lives by rigorous, regular hard exposure to difficulties. This was what had often sorted out the men from the boys during his wartime experience. It was his firm opinion that industrial life could be just as tough and challenging as fighting wars. He was determined to make a huge success of his latest honour and appointment. In sporting terms he was resolute that 'He would not let the side down.'

Over the next two years Albert spent most of the weekdays in Newcastle since there was so much to be attended to, and so many decisions to be made. The trio concept worked very well indeed and there were only a few occasions when his casting vote was needed. This proved how very important it was to all concerned that the project progressed smoothly and efficiently.

The various Assistants he had appointed to key positions at the Old Trafford plant had all risen to the challenge. On the few days per month that he was in Manchester, plus several Saturday mornings, he was able to check on what issues were causing problems and helped to solve them. He was also able to inspect very closely all the bar charts and production achievement records. It was a joy for him to see how improved performance and productivity across all the departments had resulted in higher standards and lower costs. The additional product volumes had been achieved without any new capital outlays, good bonuses were being earned by all the floor operatives and financial targets were being beaten every quarter.

Albert realised that he would have to introduce the same disciplines at the Newcastle plant. He would be expected to achieve even higher output levels and lower costs because of the newer plant which had been designed to produce more 'product' at faster rates, and at lower levels of costs.

Albert had two regrets. First he was not able to spend as much time as he would like with his wife and family. Secondly he had had to give up not only playing football, but even cricket.

On the first of these he fully understood why Mr Shelby had decided to return to America while he was still fit enough to enjoy himself, and why he wanted to spend more time with his family as they matured over in America. On the second point Albert had always enjoyed being fit, keeping fit and being able to compete at a reasonably high level in league cricket. Lancashire was a real stronghold in league cricket and Albert felt he had several years of playing left in him—once he could achieve his aims and start to ease off. He also wanted to help his sons develop their own sporting talents to the highest levels they could achieve. He realised that tricky decisions awaited him once the

Newcastle Redevelopment was completed. Until then he would be stretched to the limit, but he would be 'as happy as a sandboy.'

Albert need not have worried about his three sons developing their sporting prowess to the highest possible levels. They had all been given an excellent start by their father, and had heard of his tremendous achievements in the world of sports. They wanted to prove to their father, and their mother, how good they each were at their chosen sports. They also wanted to show to their parents that they were both willing and proud to continue the Dover traditions—not only of education and training, but also of innate sporting abilities that were so often passed on within families. By his very high level of sporting and business skills Albert had done far more than most parents to instil in his sons the need to succeed in their chosen sports—and to practice, practice and then practice some more. He had also shown and proved to his sons that grit and determination were often more important than natural skills. These were lessons that all the three sons would never forget. They were deeply indebted to both their parents for the shining examples and high standards that they had been set.

Chapter 22

Alan Dover thoroughly enjoyed his six years at Manchester Grammar School among the other 1,400 pupils at what has been one of the best secondary schools for boys ever since it was founded in the year 1515. Its Latin motto was *Sapere aude* 'Dare to be wise.'

Alan had won a bursary grant to study at the school and he had graduated through the ranks of the school to the Mathematics Sixth Form where he spent his final three years. At the end of his second year in the Sixth Form he was awarded a State Scholarship based on the three specialist mathematics branches that he sat his Advanced and Scholarship examinations in. However, from the day he set foot in Manchester Grammar School, Alan's single ambition had been to win the highest level of Open Scholarship to Cambridge University.

Alan knew he had the innate intelligence to win such a highly prized Scholarship and he was willing to work extremely hard to achieve his aims. Somehow, at the same time he managed to become the highest scoring centre forward that the school had ever had, notching 37 goals in the final season. He also won the bowling prize at cricket for his medium fast seam/swing bowling. He had the very rare talent of being able to make the hard red cricket balls move away from the batsman (outswinger) or in towards the batsman (inswinger). This exceptional talent was clearly handed down by his father, who had claimed well over fifty wickets every season for several years in various Lancashire Leagues—bowling outswingers and inswingers for more than twenty overs a match, and being a very capable opening batsman with a few centuries and dozens of fifties to his name.

Alan was awarded a Major Open Scholarship to Cambridge University and took up his place in October 1951 in Clare College which boasted a magnificent white stone rectangular building four stories high next to the famous Kings College, both being on the east bank of the picturesque River

Cam. A new Memorial Court building had been built for the college next to the main University library, both to the west of the River Cam.

Alan was such a good centre forward at football and swing bowler at cricket that he played for the University Second XIs at both sports throughout all the three years he was at Cambridge University. Indeed in his final year he played nearly all the season for the football team. Despite suffering an ankle injury in late November he was awarded his Football Blue for playing at Wembley against Oxford University in the famous Varsity game held each December—although he spent much of the game on the bench.

Alan achieved his Mathematics degree in two years because so much of the syllabuses had been dealt with at his school. He then read for a degree in Economics and achieved this in his third and final year at Cambridge. He could have gained a First Class Honours degree but he considered that sport and girlfriends were just as important to his education as actually having to study for yet another three years!

During his years at Cambridge University Alan joined the University Air Squadron whose aim was to teach as many undergraduates to fly aeroplanes as possible. When he graduated in the summer of 1954, National Service of two years' service in the Army, Navy or Air Force was still mandatory, unless one of several reasons for exemption was satisfied. Alan wanted to get his National Service out of the way so that he could embark on an industrial career as soon as possible without having a two year interruption just when he had started to progress up the ladder. He enrolled for his National Service as soon as he could and, on the basis of his two years of intermittent flying with the University Air Squadron, he was included on what seemed to be an excellent fast track to becoming a fully qualified pilot for either the Royal Air Force or for one of the mushrooming, and highly successful, passenger airline companies.

Instead of spending around three months on 'square-bashing' as all the other National Service recruits had to, he only needed to spend three weeks on this seemingly outdated, and pointless discipline—particularly for someone joining the Royal Air Force. Nevertheless Alan devoted his complete mindset into coming out of the very repetitive marching, saluting and guarding duties with the highest grading levels possible. After that he was sent over to Canada to learn how to fly 'jets' as they were called. By then all the commercial airlines had begun to change from diesel fuelled engines and propellers to jet powered engines. These were much more reliable, cheaper to operate and had much longer ranges. The amount of military and civil air journeys throughout the world was increasing exponentially and Alan had found himself at the start of a whole new industry, thanks to the fast rate of improvement in living standards, the increase in air travel for holidays and the burgeoning international freight and passenger demands.

Alan loved Canada and managed to spend his weekends popping across the border into the United States of America—usually flying with a few of his colleagues and two trained pilot tutors who had to deliver various materials and goods to airstrips all over the most northern states. Alan's favourite destination was San Francisco and the Pacific coast cities of Seattle and Los Angeles. He managed to squeeze in overnight stopovers at Las Vegas, the Grand Canyon and Denver. He often felt more like a tourist than someone who was serving a compulsory period of military service on the orders of the British Government of the day. Nonetheless he was learning a great deal about air safety, navigation, radar, flight economics and a wide array of vital subjects relating to flying and national service duties. He felt completely at home in the armed services environment and was thoroughly enjoying the experience.

After six months in Canada all those on the base were summoned to a special one day briefing conference in the main training centre conference room, which was well equipped with all the latest audio-visual equipment. It was explained to them that there was an urgent need for a massive programme of nuclear bomb testing to be carried out, and their task would be to help over the next few years in the air transportation of the innumerable parts and components required for this activity. All of this testing would be carried out in a place none of them had ever heard of—namely on Christmas Island which was hardly more than a collection of tiny atolls in the South Pacific, about two thousand miles off the east coast of Australia.

This announcement came as a major shock to the newish recruits but many of the old hands took a wider perspective, realising that they might even become regular commuters to paradises such as Hawaii and the other South Pacific islands. It also seemed very likely that they would be able to visit Australia, and possibly New Zealand on their travels.

There was a buzz of very excited chatter at the dinner tables that night. Alan thought that some of the work might become boring, with what sounded like regular routines of very long air journeys of thousands of miles between the manufacturing bases and the testing facilities in the Pacific. However, he considered that it would all be marvellous experience, and would bring into his personal realm a whole new raft of trained personnel from many countries in the world with whom he never dreamed he would have relationships and experiences. He would soon come to appreciate the tremendous opportunity granted to him by the Air Force to visit many countries that he would otherwise never have been able to afford to travel to.

*****

At the end of his two years National Service, Alan realised that he needed to obtain an interesting job that would allow him, as far as possible, to use his academic talents and knowledge to the full. He was also keen to ensure that, whichever employer he began his career with, there was a strong likelihood of a good solid future career path and opportunities ahead of him. After so much globetrotting he had had very little opportunity to research the opportunities, but with his two degrees from Cambridge University, and his excellent academic and sporting achievements at Manchester Grammar School he assumed that there would be several potential employers eager to recruit him. Unfortunately, during his absence for so long a time out of the United Kingdom, the economy had started to decline and there was a real dearth of jobs two years after he had graduated.

Alan attended many interviews and was sending out job applications by the dozen. His father was extremely busy in both Newcastle-upon-Tyne and Manchester and had expected Alan to land a job with good prospects after no more than a few weeks. However, when Alan began to become dispirited about his employment prospects, his father had a long chat with him the very next weekend. It was clear that Alan had researched the potential opportunities very thoroughly indeed, and was not being at all unrealistic in his expectations.

Albert asked Alan if he would consider a position with Procter and Gamble. Alan said he would be delighted to consider anything that might be available. 'Beggars cannot be choosers.' he said to his father. 'I would be very grateful indeed if there was anything for me. However, I would not want to obtain a job with P&G only because I was your son. More important than that, I would not want in any way whatsoever to ask, expect or allow you to adversely affect your current positions in P&G by trying to help me to obtain employment with such a prestigious company—merely because you as my father worked for them.'

The next week Albert had a personal word with the Personnel Manager at Manchester who said that, although the market was very tight indeed, there were one or two openings with the Company—but these were not really suited to Alan's academic or personal achievements to date. Albert asked what kind of jobs were available and if he could be given a brief summary of these.

The Personnel Manager said that would be no problem but he pointed out that most of the openings were up in Newcastle. 'I am sure Alan would not mind working up in Newcastle at all. He is not yet courting strongly and he has often travelled to Newcastle to have a quiet look at our premises at the weekend, when I had to work a seven day week at the peak of all the Redevelopment work.'

Alan duly despatched to the Personnel Manager his various job applications, explaining in a covering letter that he was willing to put his whole effort into whichever of the vacancies they deemed he may be suitable for. Alan was then asked to travel up to Newcastle early the following week to meet one or two key people. He was so fired up—particularly after so many disappointments in his search for a job where he was really needed, and one into which he could devote his full energies and skills.

The only openings were in the design department which seemed a weird matching. However, market research had unearthed all the evidence to support and argue the need for a brand new luxury soap for high social group ladies. It needed to be pink to capture the market and to make the initial impact. Thereafter market research proposed other pale, but warm, colours such as peach, olive and lime or avocado. The unique reason why Alan was of interest to the Newcastle product experts was because they knew he would be able to carry out all the mathematical modelling and design calculations to ensure that the packaging was, literally, unique by being totally different to all previous luxury soap packaging. Market research had concluded that this 'totally new design concept' would sell their new product in millions across the world. Unbelievably the market research experts were spot on. After twelve months of feverish research and mathematical modelling, the unique wrapping for the Camay luxury toilet soap was launched. It became one of the biggest successes in manufacturing and marketing history—particularly because it was promoted and backed by one of the largest ever television marketing campaigns. Television marketing had truly arrived in Britain.

At the age of twenty five Alan married Pam Kershaw—a girl from Southport whose sister had been chosen as the English Rose Queen in the finals of the annual beauty contest held weekly at the Open Air Pool in Southport. They were married at the main parish church next to the Town Hall situated halfway along the Lord Street, famous for its high fashion and quality shopping. Den was the Best Man and made an appropriate speech at the wedding reception at the Belle Vue hotel, situated at the south end of Lord Street. It was the first occasion on which Alan and Den had ever worn morning suits, even though they carried their top hats rather than wore them.

After four years with Procter and Gamble in Newcastle-upon-Tyne, and the birth of their one child Carolyn, Alan was appointed as Transport Manager for Rothmans International—the worldwide tobacco firm owned by a South African. The new appointment was based at their European Headquarters in Basildon, Essex. Alan began a very successful career with Rothmans, later named Carreras Rothmans. He moved up the ladder and spent seven years based in Nicosia on the island of Cyprus. From Cyprus he was responsible for growing the tobacco leaves, transporting them to the appropriate factory, manufacturing the full range of cigarettes and cigars, and running the whole organisation—for the whole of the Mediterranean Area and North Africa.

For the final ten years he spent with Carreras Rothmans, Alan was based at their London Office and was the Overseas Personnel Director. His role was to recruit, train, allocate and promote all those employees and directors who were required to work anywhere overseas for the Carreras Rothmans International organisation.

Chapter 23

Den Dover had thoroughly enjoyed his life in Stockton Heath, Warrington in the house where he was born. While he remembered with fondness all the events that had taken place during the Second World War from 1939 to 1945 he realised that those had been very tough years for his family, with a dozen or more German bombers flying directly over their home several times a week both before and after targeting factories, docks and other important facilities in Manchester and Liverpool. There was nothing more frightening than knowing that during any of the raids a bomb could be dropped intentionally, or otherwise, on your home—destroying everyone and everything in it. Indeed round the first corner of the block of houses where they lived, one stray bomb had landed on a greenhouse and pieces of its shrapnel were traded on the boys' black market for years afterwards.

Den was so surprised and delighted to be disturbed one night when his father returned from the war, and fascinated by the myriad of tales he had related to his three sons in the months thereafter. All the family enjoyed their two years in Bootle where his father owned and ran the garage but since then his father had risen very rapidly through the ranks at Procter and Gamble, following the sale of their house and garage. The whole family was delighted to have moved their home to Southport in 1947, despite the fact that both their father and Alan had to commute on a daily basis by train to Manchester—one to his factory and the other to his school. Their father also had to work very regularly up in Newcastle-upon-Tyne where he was a very key figure in the Redevelopment project being carried out to provide a major new process plant and factory.

Den was not stretched at the St Philip's Church of England Junior School. The headmaster Mr Rimmer was very tall, distinguished and a strong disciplinarian. He was also a very good teacher whenever he stood in for any member of the staff who was away. The problem was that Den and Keith, his younger brother, arrived at the school halfway through an academic year. Keith was allocated into Class One and that suited his date of birth and his abilities. Den was initially allocated to Class Two and then upgraded to Class Three only a few weeks later. In Class Three Den experienced his first ever male class teacher, Mr Hill, who was also a strict disciplinarian. The personal warmth, understanding, kindness and interest shown by Den's female teachers to that date contrasted with Mr Hill's stern voice, firm orders and coldness. Nevertheless he knew his subject matter and instilled in Den a keen interest in all the numerous subjects that he taught the 48 children in his class.

Den realised that he would only be in Mr Hill's class for a few months and he was well aware that the Class Teacher for Class Four was a prim, bespectacled highly intelligent lady who had never married and had never had children. When he started the school year in Class Four he was one of the youngest of the 49 pupils. They had decided to put him in the top class ahead of his age, on the basis that—if he could not stand the pace—he would be allowed to have a further year in the same class, again under Miss Aldred. Miss Aldred was very aware that Den's elder brother, Alan, was attending Manchester Grammar School and that he had won a Bursary Grant to that very prestigious centre of learning on the basis of the excellent marks he had achieved in the most stringent examinations for any secondary school in Britain. The very high levels of performance that Manchester Grammar required for any new entrants were legendary.

Miss Aldred set herself the target of ensuring that Den Dover was the very first pupil from any school in Southport to gain entrance to the renowned and highly academic Manchester Grammar School. She had the firmness of resolve, the innate teaching ability and the patience to achieve her one ambition. She realised that the rest would be up to Den who was certainly a very well-behaved, intelligent boy—who was also very good at sports and keen to help out with any duties that needed undertaking by the pupils. In addition Den had a strong desire to work hard, and to try to match his brother Alan in his academic career.

Much of the teaching in Class Four concentrated on arithmetic and English, but there was also a reasonable amount of geography, history and music. Den loved the very frequent intelligence tests that were used at that time for most of the examinations at the end of junior schooling—ensuring that there was a proven measurable way of grading pupils by their Intelligence Quotient, that is their measurable level of intelligence. Den had never been keen on writing essays, nor on reading, until he discovered first Enid Blyton (with her "Five" books) and Arthur Ransome (with his tales of the adventures of a group of boys and girls)—including one where they chartered a yacht from 'Peter Duck' and sailed all the way to the Caribbean Sea and back! Den could never seem to switch off from everything going on around him—and he was incapable of devoting his total attention to reading a book, no matter how interesting or well known. He found the 'Five' books were easy to read and full of action. He also liked the way that girls were included in the famous five grouping because this meant the books were attractive to both boys and girls. He had no sisters and almost all his friends near his home were boys of his age, or somewhere between his older brother Alan (four and a half years older) and his younger brother Keith (nearly two years younger).

Considering that Den was almost a year younger than most of his classmates, he performed well in the class examinations held towards the end of each of the three terms. Miss Aldred knew it was a long shot but she recommended that Den should be put forward for the entrance examination for Manchester Grammar School. She accompanied this recommendation with the comment, 'Even if he doesn't make it first time round, he is young enough to try again next year. He will undoubtedly benefit from having sat the exams once, and might even win an award.'

Mr Rimmer was fully aware of Den's abilities but thought he was too immature to succeed first time—particularly at the age he was. He could not help wondering if Den would lose a fair bit of face, and perhaps a lot of confidence, if he did not gain entrance at his first attempt. Den wanted to press ahead as fast as possible but of course he was not consulted. He presumed afterwards that his parents, or at least his mother, had been asked for their views. After all, it was they who would have to pay all the high travelling costs to and from Manchester, plus any term fees that were charged (as they were for Alan, despite his Bursary Grant).

In the event Den did attend for the one day examination but he was not happy about his performance. It was mainly the very lengthy journey and having to focus his attention and efforts on two examination papers on the same day. He also looked aghast at some of the candidates who looked much older, and certainly more mature, than he was. They all seemed to know each other and they mixed in the way long term and close friends would. Den was unaware that he was the only candidate from Southport, and also from so far away (40 miles).

Den had no idea how long he would have to wait for the results. He was the only candidate from his school, and possibly from the whole of Southport (population 85,000). He realised that if it was the so called '11 Plus Exam' that he had just taken for the local grammar school in Southport (the girls would have sat the same examinations/tests as the boys—but they would be headed for the Girls High School, if successful) then all the pupils in his year would be informed of the results for the whole class at the same time that they learned how they had each fared.

After a period of several weeks, which seemed like an eternity, Den learned that he had not satisfied the standards required. However, the school had stated in writing that they would most definitely like him to enter for the entrance examination again because Den had shown that he was someone who would almost certainly reach the levels of performance they required, if he were to apply again the following year. Den was extremely disappointed, but he was encouraged by the school asking that he should reapply the next year. He realised that it would be a humiliating experience for him when word spread that he had failed. However, there was no dodging the issue, he had not reached the standard required this time round—but the door was clearly being left open for him to go for it the next time.

Little did Den realise that the disappointment he experienced at that time was something he would have to deal with on numerous occasions throughout his career and adult life.

*****

During the following academic year Den matured so much. He had covered the whole syllabus once before, he was no younger than the other pupils in Class Four that year, he still had Miss Aldred for his Class teacher—and he felt new confidence running through his veins. Miss Aldred was so keen to ensure that Den passed the entrance examination for MGS that she asked his parents if they would mind if she set additional homework for Den every evening. This caused her extra time and effort but it proved very effective. The additional work could be tailored to deal with any weaknesses that Den had shown, it would give him a deeper and broader experience of the subjects—and it would build up his confidence. Den was very appreciative and, in return, he offered to carry out any extra duties that Miss Aldred required. In this way Den built up his natural leaning towards working for and on behalf of others—and he improved his low level of experience in non-academic matters, such as keeping records, maintaining and storing equipment and stocks. It was all very new to Den but he enjoyed every minute that he spent serving and helping others.

During his final year at the Junior School Den began to show his sporting prowess. He had never been much of a footballer but he was very keen on cricket, indeed he even introduced the game to the Junior School he attended— and the school discovered that many of the girls were just as accomplished as the boys!

In his final year at St Philip's Junior School Den duly re-sat the unique Entrance Examination for Manchester Grammar School including two different styles of Arithmetic and English papers. Every year nearly two thousand boys living within a radius of around forty miles of Manchester entered this very rigorous testing process. The Part 1 papers were designed to be marked quickly, with multiple choice questions dominating the English paper and short answers characterising the Arithmetic paper. All the teaching staff members were involved in invigilating the candidates, and then marking the scripts so that on the same day the highest scoring 450 or so candidates could be ascertained and invited to take the second Part. The Part 2 examination was set and marked by members of the English and Mathematics departments. The English paper comprised an essay and a traditional comprehension test, with full written answers. The Arithmetic paper involved longer questions, with marks awarded for showing the working out as well as for the ultimate answer.

Within a few days Den was informed that he had met the high levels of achievement needed to enter the school of his dreams. However, for reasons which were never explained to him, a deal was struck between his parents and the brand new Headmaster at the local grammar school in Southport (Mr Dixon) that Den should attend the King George V Grammar School, only half a mile from their home, for his first four years of secondary schooling—and then transfer to Manchester Grammar School ('MGS') for his final three years of secondary education in their Sixth Form. Den had also passed the necessary examinations for KGV at the same time as he passed for MGS; indeed he knew he would have been able to gain entry to KGV a year earlier if that had been the original plan.

When recollecting in later life, about this decision made by his parents Den came to realise that the lack of finance was probably the main reason why they came to their decision.

Chapter 24

In September 1949, at the age of eleven, Den began his secondary schooling at King George V Grammar School in Southport. He was placed in the top stream at this all boys school and after a year or two he realised that the boys in his form were earmarked for sitting their Ordinary Level (later renamed General Certificate of Secondary Education) examinations after four years whereas the boys in the two lower forms would sit their first external examinations after five years.

There were 29 boys in Den's class and in their form room they were arranged in six rows of five desks, in alphabetical order of their surnames. This was very acceptable to Den because he was able to sit in the front desk of the second row, just to one side of the master's desk. Most of the subjects were held in the form room. Even when they went for lessons in special parts of the school—such as geography, history and science—the same layout of boys was adopted, so that the various masters were more easily able to remember the names of all the boys. A few of the boys from Den's Infant School were in his form but all the Junior Schools in Southport were represented in his form. He even recognised some of the faces from the other schools following several encounters on the football and rounders pitches over the previous few years.

Life at a secondary school was quite a major change. Whereas the boys in the first two years were only allowed to wear short trousers, all the boys in the higher years had to wear long trousers. Den soon realised that there were some quite tall and much older boys who wore special badges as 'school prefects.' Their job was to ensure that all the boys behaved sensibly, and they would often be left in charge of minding a class if the form or specialist teacher was called away at short notice.

In the two winter terms rugby union was played at the school and this was a totally new sport to Den. There was no football played at the school, and no hockey. Chess was a very popular activity and there was also badminton in the school gymnasium. There was a very strong Dramatic Society with Shakespearean and other plays performed throughout the school year. With his experience as a choir boy at the Walton and St Philip's Church of England churches Den was a natural candidate for the school choir. However, he had learned to play the piano and the violin from the date of the family's arrival in Southport. He soon realised that there were several very talented pianists amongst the pupils, far more able than he. Although his violin playing was only average he soon learned that in the school orchestra there were two grades of violinists—the First Violins and the Second Violins. The music teacher for all the forms in the school was also the Leader of the School Orchestra. He taught each class both musical theory and singing. Several of the boys already played various instruments and it was not long before notices were posted on the information boards asking for volunteers for both the choir and for the orchestra.

Den enjoyed the gym sessions and tried playing badminton several times after school. He also joined the chess club and the new recruits to the ranks of the second violins. There was certainly much to be done in his new school, and he was thoroughly enjoying himself. At all times he made sure that his academic subjects were given the highest priority. He knew he was at the school to pass examinations and to achieve qualifications, not merely to learn new sports and enjoy himself.

Den was intrigued by the House system operated in the school. All the boys were day pupils and travelled each day to and from the school. There were around 640 boys and these were equally divided up into being members of one of the eight Houses, each named after the surnames of the first masters who were the first eight House Masters. Each House would play the other Houses at all the sports and there were House league tables. In addition individual House pupils would be awarded points for good behaviour, for exceptional academic or sporting achievement and so on. The House system proved to Den that there were different loyalties that every pupil had to take into account. They needed to work hard, to do their homework, perform well in the classroom and behave well. They also needed to be loyal to their House in all that they did, and finally do well for the school. All these interacting priorities nurtured the correct spirit in the pupils and taught them to act well together in groups, to work and play as a team, and to achieve the best individual performances that they were capable of.

Den soon realised that every member of his form had different talents, aims and abilities. He made several long lasting friendships and he soon identified who were the boys who would be serious rivals when it came to examinations. There were very regular tests and marks were awarded and recorded for every single subject—even for Religious Studies! Den had been brought up in a fiercely competitive family with the three boys always challenging each other on a wide variety of tests of skill and knowledge.

Towards the end of the first term their form teacher announced that there would be an election held to choose the first Form Captain, followed by a further election for a new captain for the summer term. This was Den's first introduction to electioneering. None of the boys even thought that any canvassing of votes for themselves, or their favoured appointees was either a good idea, permitted, or of any help in the election of the Form Captain. Den thought it would be a high honour if he were elected, but he did not seek to obtain the votes or support of any of his form mates. A week before the end of their first term the form master announced that he would hold a ballot of all the members of the form to elect the Form Captain. This would be held from 1 pm to 1.30 pm in the Form Classroom on the following Monday, and everyone was encouraged to vote for the person they wanted to see as Form Captain for the Easter Term. At 1 pm the Form Master handed a piece of coloured paper to each of the boys and told them that they had to print the surname of the person they wished to vote for, fold the paper and put it into a wooden box with a slot on top, that he would keep on the top of his desk for the complete thirty minutes during which the ballot was open.

To his astonishment Den topped the numbers of votes by a large margin and he noted that Trevor Williams seemed to have obtained the next highest number of votes. The Form Master told Den that he would have a word with him at the end of school that day, to make sure he was aware of the duties he would need to take on, and why the appointment was important for the whole form and for the teachers who taught the pupils in it.

Den could not wait to arrive at home that evening and tell his family about his first ever election victory. None of them were surprised but they were all delighted for the honour he had brought on the family. Den resolved to make an excellent job of being Form Captain of what was the top stream in the first year at KGV and wondered if there might be any House points awarded for the position, but knew that there would not be.

Trevor Williams lived only a few roads away from the Dover family. Most evenings Trevor and he walked home along the main Scarisbrick Road towards Southport. They often discussed the various teachers, their fellow pupils and some of the details of the subjects they were studying. They took it in turns to test each other, particularly on history which was not one of Den's favourite subjects—although he was very adept at remembering all the names, places and dates with ease, due to his very efficient photographic memory. On the other hand Trevor seemed to have a much better grasp on the importance of the various political events, and their relevance to each other. In most of the subjects they studied one or other of these two friends came top and the other one second. However, there were some of the boys in their form who were brilliant at certain subjects but quite weak in many of the others.

It was no surprise to either Trevor or Den that Trevor Williams was voted into the post of Form Captain for the summer term when the election took place just before the Easter break. Any doubts about his likely success were probably very low indeed because Den acted as his unpaid and unofficial 'election agent' and recommended most of the form to vote for Trevor.

At the end of their first academic year Den came top of the form and Trevor was placed second. When they arrived back at school in the September there was a newcomer to their form. It was Neil Ziment who was a Jew and soon showed them both that they had a new rival for the position as top of the form. Neil and his older brother had just moved to Southport. Neil was not interested in athletics or sports at all but he was certainly highly intelligent. Trevor did not enjoy sports but he was very clever. Den was keen on both sports and learning so he resolved to keep up with his sports, as well as his studies. He was chosen for the Junior House team at both rugby and cricket. He was also included in the school chess team.

At the start of his third year at KGV Den chose the subjects he would be taking at the end of his fourth year. He was much more interested in science and mathematics rather than languages and the arts. However, he opted to sit the French and Latin exams, in addition to Music, Geography and a new course called English Oral. He passed all of these with high grades and he left his strong subjects of Mathematics, Physics and Chemistry to be sat at the Advanced and Scholarship Levels. This was the way that KGV decided to tackle the new forms of Ordinary, Advanced and Scholarship levels of the General Certificate of Education examinations.

During his third and fourth years at KGV Den grew by several inches in height and he was chosen as scrum half at rugby for not just the School Colts (Under 15s) but also for his House (Rogers) Junior and Senior teams. Indeed in the month he reached his fifteenth birthday (April 1953) he celebrated the winning of both the Junior Sevens Trophy and the Senior House Rugby Shield—triumphs that owed much to his distributive skills, tenacity and fitness in the kingpin position of scrum half.

Den also rose very rapidly through the cricket ranks at the KGV Grammar School in the 1952 and 1953 summer seasons. He had been a regular opening batsman for his Junior House cricket team for the first two seasons at the school (1950 and 1951) but during the 1951 school holidays he suddenly discovered that he had mastered the art of leg break bowling. He was promoted to the Senior House Team as a leg spinner in 1952 and in the following year he became the School First XI's leg break bowler at the tender age of fifteen, capturing more wickets than any of the other bowlers and at a better average. In that same year he also played for the Lancashire Schoolboys team, as their leg spinner.

Chapter 25

One very hot Saturday in June 1953 the Dover family spent the day at three different sporting events. The youngest brother Keith was, at the tender age of 13 years, competing in yet another high board diving event at the Southport Open Air Pool.

Alan had to travel by rail all the way to Manchester, and beyond, to play cricket for the Manchester Grammar School First XI. He was a brilliant medium fast seam bowler, and able to swing the ball into or away from the bat. Alan was no real batsman but was capable of swinging his bat and adding twenty or more quick runs to his side's total in a very short space of time.

Albert and Emma contented themselves by watching Den play cricket for the first time in their lives. The King George V Grammar School Senior House cricket final was to be played that afternoon in front of the whole school on their spacious playing fields next to the Southport Association Football Club's Third Division ground at Haig Avenue.

Den was proud to be playing cricket with his two parents watching him. It was to be his first spell of spin bowling in a Senior House Cricket final. The Rogers House team had been struggling to bowl out their opponents earlier in the season. However, the introduction of Den Dover as their demon leg spinner had transformed their bowling attack. After a few overs of fast bowling the captain, John Davidson, had learned it was best to bring Den on early. Most of the batsmen from the other Houses had never faced much spin bowling—and none of them even knew what a leg spinner was. Needless to say, the legend of such a demon bowler having to be faced, unnerved all the Senior House batsmen and they very quickly succumbed to the wiles of Den's spinning fingers. In the three knockout rounds before the House final Den had taken 6 wickets for 19 runs, 7 wickets for 24 runs, and 5 wickets for 12 runs. On the day of the Senior House Final he was able to excel himself with figures of 7 wickets for 13 runs against the Edwards House Team. This spell of bowling meant that Den's parents were able to witness his best ever bowling figures, have an early tea and then see the Rogers House Team knock off the runs needed to win very quickly indeed. This was the real launch pad of Den's bowling career because during that same season he played for not only the First XI of his school but also for Lancashire Schoolboys.

*****

Den had begun his cricket career as a capable batsman, albeit too orthodox, patient and slow, but he had been transformed into one of the rarest breed of cricketers—namely a leg break bowler. He owed this entirely to the KGV First XI wicket keeper, Mick Davidson, who was playing that day with Den, under the captaincy of his older brother, John, who was a brilliant batsman.

Mick Davidson had spotted Den's rare talent one year earlier when all the boys interested in playing cricket for the school teams were having an evening session in the outdoor nets at the start of the cricket season. No wicketkeeper ever stands behind the wickets in the nets, because there is not enough space behind the wickets for them. However, Mick was a reasonable batsman and he thought he could show some of the younger boys what a good batsman he really was. He walked down to the batting crease in one of the nets that evening and took guard. He kept his eyes carefully on the first two balls and drove them straight back past the bowler at great speed. However, he was completely bamboozled by the next ball that was delivered by Den. It was a slowish leg break that pitched on the line of his leg stump but then turned viciously away from him to hit the top of his off stump. He was so gobsmacked and shocked that he wandered down and had a word with Den.

'Who taught you to bowl leg breaks? That was an incredible ball' said Mick.

'My father used to play cricket in the Manchester Association, the top cricket league in the whole of the Manchester Area. He was a seam bowler and taught my older brother to become a very good bowler. He plays for Manchester Grammar School First XI and he is only sixteen years old.'

Mick put another question *to Den. 'What House are you in?'*

'*Actually I'm in the same House* as you and your brother John, that is Rogers,' replied Den.

'Well let's see whether you have any other tricks up your sleeve, and we'll have another word after I've finished my period of batting practice in the nets,' said Mick.

For the next ten minutes every ball that Den bowled to Mick was impossible to read, that is to assess whether it would be a straight ball or break away from the bat to the offside (a leg break) or break into the body from the offside (commonly known as an off break). By the end of his batting session Mick was completely at a loss for words.

He went up to Den and asked him how many variations he had in his repertoire. Den ran off the names 'leg break, googly and top spinner.' He added 'I'm sorry to say that I have never been able to make a ball swing, no matter how many times my Dad and my brother Alan have tried to show me how to.'

From that day Mick took Den under his wing and groomed him as a first class leg break spinner. He had a word with his brother John who was a first rate batsman and urged him to face Den's bowling in the nets as soon as he was able to, so that he could check back with Mick on his first assessment. John did this a few days later and was even more impressed than Mick had been. He praised Den on his bowling control and variations and told him that they must ensure he played for not just the Junior House XI, but also for the Senior House XI.

When Den returned home that evening his father and older brother Alan were absolutely over the moon. Up to then they had come to think of Den as a reasonable batsman but had completely failed to spot his amazing talent as a leg spinner!

*****

By the summer of 1953 Den's father, Albert Dover, was starting to play occasionally for the Southport and Birkdale Cricket Club in the Liverpool Competition—whenever his exhausting work schedule with Procter and Gamble in both Manchester and Newcastle-upon-Tyne allowed. Albert had been appointed to the Committee of the cricket club and was keen on developing the club into a leading contender for the Liverpool Competition League Championship, and also as a very suitable venue for Lancashire County Cricket fixtures. It would be able to draw large crowds to the ground, as a reputable seaside resort—particularly because the 'largest Flower Show in the

114

World' was held every year in Victoria Park, Southport in late August. This attracted more than 80,000 attendees over a period of three days and the Open Golf championships held at the Birkdale and Hillside courses in July drew even larger crowds to Southport every five or ten years.

Southport and Birkdale Cricket Club had three teams and several schoolboy teams including one for the Under 15s and one for the Under 18s. The schoolboy teams were breeding grounds for the three senior teams. Alan captained the Under 18s and Den captained the Under 15s. The two brothers would also regularly play together in the same team, often for the Under 18s, sometimes for the senior Second or Third XI, initially, and then later on even for the First XI—together with their father Albert.

*****

One very hot day during the 1953 school summer holidays Den was captaining the Under 15s XI against a team of the same age from Formby, ten miles along the coast, there was an end of season special tea. Den decided that the occasion should be marked by a short speech, thanking the devoted mothers of the home team who had throughout the whole of the summer holidays made and provided the teas at all the home games for the schoolboy teams. Den had never before made a speech but he knew instinctively what to do. He called the noisy teams to order and merely thanked the opposing side for several close games that season, the mothers for all the time and effort they had put into catering for all the home games and wished everyone success in their remaining games.

After the tea Den helped with the washing up, as usual, and a respected Senior Lady Member of the club complimented him on his speech—saying he was a natural speaker. Den mentioned that it was his first speech ever. Mrs Medrington was astounded and said to him 'I think you are cut out for a career in politics.' At that time Den had no idea that her son Stan Medrington was one of Mr Hudson's fellow Conservatives and key Party workers in the Southport Parliamentary constituency.

At about the same time Den's mother joined the local branch of the Southport Conservative Association. She would often pop into the constituency office in a small backstreet behind Lord Street. If Den's father was ever in Southport on a Wednesday evening—a rare occurrence—both his parents would spend the evening at the local Conservative Branch meeting. This was always held in a small hall adjacent to the very prominent Holy Trinity church, at the corner of Manchester Road and Houghton Street.

Chapter 26

Den was completely unaware that his parents had arranged to meet Mr Dixon, the headmaster of King George V Grammar School, where Den was nearing the completion of his first four years of secondary education. They were fully aware that Den had passed the Entrance Examination to Manchester Grammar School back in 1949, at his second attempt. They also knew that Den had set his heart on following in the footsteps of his older brother Alan—not just to Manchester Grammar School but also to Cambridge University. It was common knowledge that Manchester Grammar gained more than forty places per year at the two top Universities, namely Cambridge and Oxford. This contrasted markedly with the one, two or three maximum pupils per year that had gained places at Cambridge or Oxford University from King George V Grammar School, where Den was currently studying.

During the summer term of 1953 Den's parents had their first ever discussion with him. This was about which school he should attend from September that year. Den's heart was set on being admitted to Cambridge University. He had passed the Entrance Examination to Manchester Grammar School, albeit at the second time of trying, and he said it was a fact that if he stayed on at the local grammar school in Southport the likelihood would be that only one or two of their pupils in his year would go on to study at Cambridge or Oxford University. His father said that they had discussed that very point with Mr Dixon who had admitted that they were probably correct. However, he emphasised that he had only taken over as Headmaster in September of 1949, when their son had entered his school. He said that Den had been a model pupil, not just academically, but also on the sports field, and even in the school orchestra. Mr Dixon said he had been improving all the standards right across the school since his arrival and that he hoped to increase the annual numbers of admissions to Cambridge and Oxford year by year.

Mr Dixon had gone on to say that he thought Den should remain at KGV for the remainder of his secondary education. He said that Den would certainly be a very worthy applicant for the Cambridge and Oxford University Admission examinations. If Den stayed on Mr Dixon promised that he would become Vice-Captain of the school, at least. He explained that the choice of the Head Boy in Den's final year would be a close run race between their son and Trevor Williams.

After a lengthy discussion Den's parents left the meeting on amicable terms and shook hands with Mr Dixon. They said they would discuss the whole issue with Den and get back in touch.

Den was a little disappointed with the news that, if he stayed at the local grammar school, he might not become Head Boy. He was well aware that Trevor Williams would make an excellent Head Boy, although the choice was clearly being based solely on academic grounds—since Trevor played no sports at all, and had no ear at all for music. Den was a little surprised that Neil Ziment's name had not been mentioned at the meeting with the Headmaster. Neil had even ended up above both Trevor and Den at the end of one of the academic years; he had plenty of drive and a very high intellectual level.

Den's older brother, Alan, had left Manchester Grammar School two years before the discussion between Den and his parents. He had already flown the family nest and was busy at Cambridge University before globetrotting under the auspices of Her Majesty's Services. Alan was not available for advice and the decision was up to the three of them. His parents added that if Den decided to transfer to Manchester Grammar School he, Mr Dixon, had told them that he would send a very strongly supportive recommendation to Dr Eric James—the very distinguished High Master of MGS.

After a further half hour of detailed points Den's father asked him what he wanted to do. Den said he thought he should take up his offer of a place at Manchester Grammar School which had recently been confirmed in writing to his parents. He realised that he would have to travel every weekday to and from Manchester, and even at weekends for sports games if he was chosen to represent the school. Alan had successfully coped with all the train and bus journeys plus all the homework—and he had even been Deputy Head Boy at MGS.

Den's father duly sent a letter to Mr Dixon, thanking him for the meeting and advising him that Den would be leaving KGV at the end of the summer and taking up the place he had been offered at Manchester Grammar School—one which had recently been confirmed in writing by the High Master himself.

*****

In his last term at the local grammar school Den was not awarded his First XI cricket colours—despite taking more wickets than any of the other bowlers, and for a lower number of runs than any of the others. He wondered if there were any sour grapes involved in this decision, but he decided to put it down to other players deserving their colours more than he did. Several had played for more than one season and this would be their last year playing in any school team.

Den enjoyed playing several cricket games for Southport and Birkdale Cricket Club—often with his father, and even a few with his older brother Alan who returned from his two years of National Service—mainly served overseas.

Finally the big day arrived when Den walked down the road into the back entrance of Manchester Grammar School. All the morning buses from the city centre and elsewhere dropped the hundreds upon hundreds of boys off so that they could head for the Main Hall where the morning service began at 9.40 am prompt. The singing of the 1,400 boys rose above the sound of the organ played by one of the pupils. There were probably more than 250 new boys starting their education at Manchester Grammar School that day—but none more proud than Den. He was probably one of only a very small number of pupils who began their education at MGS in the Sixth Form.

Chapter 27

There were many Sixth Forms at Manchester Grammar School. These included Maths Sixth, History Sixth, Classics Sixth, Modern Languages Sixth and Den's own, namely Science Sixth Maths. Den was best at Physics followed closely by Mathematics, and then by Chemistry. By a weird coincidence one of his Physics masters from Southport began a period of several years of teaching that same day at MGS, where his own son John Caff had already been studying for five years.

There were three streams of boys starting their two or three years of studies in Science Sixth Maths on the same day as Den. There were 24 boys in each stream. Probably a quarter of those in the top stream would move on to Cambridge or Oxford University at the end of three years in their MGS Sixth Form. Perhaps a few of those in the second stream may do the same, but none of those in the third stream would be expected to attend Cambridge or Oxford as undergraduates. However, the expectation was that almost all the 72 boys who started in Science Sixth Maths would become undergraduates at one of the top ranking universities in Britain.

Den had to face up to a nasty surprise on that first day. He was not placed in the top stream but in the second stream, which by coincidence had Mr Caff as its Form Master. For the first few weeks it was not an easy settling in period for Den. He knew none of the boys, whereas all the others had spent four years at the school together—and studied the same subjects, often in the same forms. Nevertheless Den could sense the competitive spirit that seemed to flow through the veins of all the MGS boys. He was forming some strong personal friendships with some of his classmates and he soon realised that he could more than hold his own with them academically in the various science and mathematics subjects that they were studying. Indeed in some of the subjects an overall streaming system for all the boys in the same year was in operation.

This meant that the more able could be moved up and the less able moved down, for those particular subjects. All this was new to Den but it was a spur to him to try to impress and excel in his strongest areas—thus mitigating the effects of the initial positioning of him in the middle stream.

After six weeks had passed Mr Caff had a long chat with Den and apologised for the fact that he had almost certainly been placed incorrectly in the middle stream at the start of the academic year. He said that, without any further delay, he had been instructed to upgrade Den into the top stream of the Science Sixth Maths forms. Den was delighted with this news and resolved to keep working as hard and as well as he could. There were a few readjustment problems but after the break at Christmas he felt he had really settled into the top stream, thus vindicating the change to his ranking made half way through his first term at the school.

To ensure that he did not waste all his Saturdays travelling to and from Manchester for only a ninety minute football game, Den took up the game of grass hockey which was played by Southport Hockey Club, on the Southport and Birkdale Cricket Club grounds. He started in the Third XI but soon picked up the fundamentals of the game and improved on his basic skills. He was accordingly promoted into the Second XI and then he had a stroke of luck. He was not selected to play one Saturday, but took his kit along with him on his bicycle handlebars. The visiting team from Lytham St Annes were one short so Den was asked if he would be willing to play on the left wing for their Second XI against his own team. Playing on the left wing is one of the hardest tasks at grass hockey because a good, strong and accurate reverse shot with the curved hockey stick is not at all easy to produce. However, Den had practised this technique for many hours in his back garden and he had already become an effective inside left (or left inner) during his brief hockey career.

Southport Second XI took an early two goal lead against Lytham St Annes that day. However, the game was very well balanced and in the last fifteen minutes Den raced in to tap two opportunist goals into the Southport net. This evened up the scoring that day and it ended at two goals each. Den apologised to the Southport captain who said 'No, don't be silly. You spotted the chances and you made them both count. By the way, would you be willing to play on the left wing for us?'

Den replied by saying he would be delighted to play in any position for the Second XI. He said he was thoroughly enjoying playing hockey for the

Southport Club. It was not long before he became the first choice on the left wing for Southport's Second XI from which position he scored many opportunistic goals during the remainder of the season.

By the end of the Easter term Den had managed to achieve similar marks to the leading pupils in his form. This proved to the teachers that Den had enough intelligence, knowledge and ability to be up among the leaders in the top stream form. At the end of the summer term handwritten reports on all the key subjects were completed by all the teachers that they had. These were handed to each of the boys on their last day of term, and each of them also contained a handwritten sentence or two by the High Master at the foot of the report.

The High Master took Den's form for two subjects; one was the mainstream Organic Chemistry in which they used a textbook by the High Master. The other subject was a weekly personal discourse given by Dr Eric James as he strolled very slowly back and forth across the front of the form room. He spoke to them about the Forum and the Senate in Athens and the crucial places in history held by Aristotle and Socrates. For someone who was a latecomer to history, politics and philosophy most of what Dr James spoke about was way above Den's level of understanding. However, he could not help but be totally absorbed by the High Master's style of delivery. He stuck his two thumbs into the underside of his waistcoat and on top of the front of the black gown that he wore at all times. Dr James never referred to a single note and hardly ever posed questions to the boys, or asked for their involvement. The oft repeated phrase used by Dr James was to say to the boys 'It is yerr responsibility' in a curious local dialect which Den was unable to identify. However, these four words had a telling effect on the boys.

There was only one way of describing this monologue by one of the most brilliant brains in the education world. It was a fantastic personal account of why everything that the Greek philosophers spoke about, and debated, in their Forum and their Senate was of total relevance to the 20th century. It was still the case that everything present day mankind experienced, had to face up to and deal with was in many ways precisely the same situation as Aristotle and Socrates had to contend with. In days long gone, as in modern times, mankind had to solve any problems they experienced—using all the powers and means available to them.

The High Master's handwritten remark on Den in July 1954 was:-

'Dover finished 7th in his form of 24. He works hard and should not worry as much as he seems to.'

Den had never been a worrier in his life. However, he was willing to concede that Dr Eric James would probably never make an incorrect assessment or remark about any of the students under his care. Perhaps what had happened was that Den was so puzzled by his lack of understanding of the High Master's verbal addresses to his form that he had an unconscious quizzical expression on his face. To this day Den wishes that there were a written or sound recording of the words of wisdom spoken by the High Master to his fellow form mates because, even though Den understood so little of what the messages meant, he knew that they were of eternal importance, and just as valid in the twentieth century as they were thousands of years ago in Greece—the cradle of all civilisations.

*****

At the start of the summer term of 1954 Den examined the lists of cricket players for the practice sessions in the nets at MGS to no avail, because his name was not included. Having played for his previous school's First XI in Southport, for the Southport and Birkdale Cricket Club's three senior teams and Lancashire Schoolboys he was dismayed. However, he registered in his brain the distinct message conveyed by his absence from the lists. It was 'You need to show us what you can do here in Manchester. Your previous performances count for nothing. We will fit you into the team we judge to be right for you. Oh, and by the way, your older brother Alan did indeed win the bowling prize for his seam bowling, but you cannot gain any entry to our teams at MGS unless you earn it on your own performances.'

Den remembered two names from Alan's games of cricket for MGS. The first was the cricket master Fred Winterbottom and the second was the cricket professional, Arthur Booth. Den decided that he would have a word with these two key cricketing legends at MGS and ask for their guidance.

Fred Winterbottom had just finished a pep-talk that he had delivered in the school canteen. His aim was to spell out to all those interested enough to attend such a meeting the general rules that he expected all the boys playing cricket for any of the teams to abide by at all times. This was an annual affair that was held at the very start of the cricket season. Fred had already organised all the cricket activities at MGS for ten years and was expected to, and wanting to, carry on for many more years.

Fred started with a quick review of the results achieved the previous year, but emphasised that the previous season was literally history. He wanted to concentrate on what was going to happen in the season that lay ahead. He was delighted with the new cricket pavilion on the higher ground behind the bowler's arm at the north end of the First XI pitches. He announced that all changing into cricket gear could now take place in the spacious basement of the new pavilion, and he said he was very proud of the large balcony at the first floor level, again directly behind the bowlers' arm.

Fred Winterbottom continued by reminding everyone present of his requirement that they behave like gentlemen at all times, and also as sportsmen. He insisted that no incoming opposition batsmen should be applauded as they walked out to bat. He said they should feel free to applaud any opposition batsman who scored a fifty or a hundred against them, but only after they had deserved such applause by their skills and performance. He also said he did not mind if one or two of the opposition batsmen were applauded as they left the pitch at the end of their innings, if they had batted well enough to deserve praise. Fred's message was clear. We never applaud opposing batsmen on their way to the wicket—only when they are out, and therefore no further threat. No wonder MGS always achieved excellent performances, even against excellent opponents—especially when they played on the Annual Cricket Tour for four days during the Whitsuntide holidays.

When Den introduced himself to Fred at the end of his speech he mentioned that Alan Dover, who had won the Bowling Prize three years earlier, was his older brother. Fred recalled his brother very clearly and was delighted that Alan had played every season since for the Cambridge University Second XI. He was interested to hear that Den was a leg break bowler and encouraged him to meet the cricket professional as soon as possible.

When Den caught up with Arthur Booth he was surprised how old he was and how short in stature—being only five feet tall. Arthur had been a slow left arm bowler for the Yorkshire County Cricket team. He was at one end of the First XI pitch and asked Den to bowl a couple of balls down to the wickets at the far end of the pitch. Den did not deliver two particularly good balls but Arthur Booth seemed impressed. He encouraged Den to flight the ball as much as possible, and said he would show him the best level of trajectory. Arthur bowled two balls which he pitched exactly on the right spot, turning to the off (away from the batsman). He flighted these so high that Den was both surprised, and delighted, because he agreed with the cricket professional that deceptive flight was what earned most of the wickets claimed by spin bowlers.

Arthur closed the chat by saying he was always available for any help or guidance that Den ever needed. Den would never forget how high Arthur Booth had delivered the balls into the air, the very fast rotation rate of the balls and the audible whizzing sound as the missiles disappeared down the pitch.

In 1954 Den served his apprenticeship at cricket for Manchester Grammar School. One season earlier he had played for the KGV First XI team against the MGS First XI on their first team square. Admittedly KGV lost the game, Den did not bat very well, nor did he produce any of his bowling wizardry. However, he now had to face up to climbing through the ranks, starting in the MGS Third XI. It took him only three games to be promoted to the Second XI. The Third XI games were all played on very poor pitches and it was no wonder that Den was able to keep the batsmen guessing.

In his first game for the MGS Second XI he formed an excellent friendship and spin bowling partnership with Chris Druce who was a slow left arm spin bowler. For several games the Dover-Druce spinning partnership dominated the opposition batsmen and helped to set up a long run of victories. Just before the end of Den's first cricket season at MGS his partner Chris was promoted into the First XI and produced several magical performances. However, Den had to settle for a regular position in the Second XI. At least he had gained some very useful experience out in the middle, batting as well as bowling. In most of the Second XI games both sides had to bat nearly all the way down their batting orders since many wickets fell to some very poor shots at that level of cricket.

Chapter 28

When the school re-assembled after the summer holidays of 1954 all the boys beginning their second or third years in the Sixth form knew how very important the next nine months would be for their future careers. The only external examination that Den had sat in his first year at Manchester Grammar School was the General Paper which consisted of writing several essays in different subject areas. He was pleased with his performance in this recently introduced subject, and he was impressed and delighted that MGS were desirous of widening the knowledge of their pupils, not just restricting them to their chosen specialist areas.

Den was thankful that most of the Science and Mathematics teachers for his second year in the Sixth form were the same as those he had had in the first year. At an advanced level of education Den had realised that mutual confidence building between pupils and teachers was of paramount importance.

New subject areas were being covered at a very high speed in all his three subjects of Physics, Mathematics and Chemistry. Enormous amounts of homework were being set and these had to be handed in on a daily basis. Night after night the routine of a meal, homework and sleep was followed relentlessly and Den was so thankful that he had decided a year earlier not to play winter sports at the school. He could not have fitted anything else into his packed programme.

*****

Following a period of five years as Works Manager for both the Manchester and Newcastle factories of Procter and Gamble, Den's father had recently been appointed as the Works Manager at Cussons which was a British family owned firm based in the north west suburb of Manchester called Kersal Vale.

Den had mentioned his father's new appointment to his Chemistry master, Mr Clynes, who was extremely interested in hearing about all the new processes and manufacturing procedures at Cussons. He wondered if it might be possible to arrange an industrial visit to Cussons for Den's form—and perhaps for others too, if the first visit was a success.

Over the remaining two years of Den's time at MGS there was a steady stream of form visits to the Cussons premises. It was very revealing how few of the MGS boys had ever, in their lives, been inside a factory of any kind. The particular chemical processes employed in the Cussons complex were entirely based on organic chemical reactions and the visits provided an excellent opportunity for the pupils to see what large scale factory production looked like in real life, compared with the very small items of chemistry equipment that they had to use for their studies in the school's chemistry laboratories.

By this time Den was enjoying his hockey on the Second XI at Southport and even played the occasional game in the left inner position which meant a tremendous amount of running up and down the pitch—helping out the defence at one end and building an attack at the other. He discovered that the left inner position kept him heavily engaged throughout the whole game and he was able to keep in top fitness condition, especially with all the walking he had to do every weekday between the trains and buses.

He had settled into a very busy programme at school and with all the homework. He was so pleased he could relax on the hockey field, he enjoyed the fresh air and the change of scenery. The only two other outlets he had were attending the local Methodist church and teaching a young Sunday School class every Sunday afternoon. His parents had moved to a larger property in Leyland Road, Southport only 100 yards from the northern end of the promenade. This new home was large enough to allow his mother to run a small private hotel with eight bedrooms for holidaymakers. This had long been her ambition, and she proved to be a first class hotelier at the Kirkdale Private Hotel. Her one fault was that she worked far too hard and began with a full board option before moving down to evening meal, bed and breakfast before ending up with the most profitable, and least workload—namely bed and breakfast. In addition the three boys had to learn to respect the needs of their mother's clients.

Just after the Christmas holidays, Manchester Grammar School held a whole week of 'mock examinations' for all the boys who would be sitting external examinations in May or June later that year. These examinations gave an opportunity for all the teaching staff to gauge how their pupils were coping with the very detailed syllabuses for the various subjects. It also gave them a good guide to the percentage marks that each boy was likely to attain in the real examinations. Den only realised several years later that each subject master was required to predict the likely marks for each boy in each of the subjects. This enabled any rogue results to be examined at a later date, if needed.

Half way through the Easter Term Den played his one and only game of football on the MGS playing fields. There was a Sixth Form annual football championship where anyone in a particular Sixth Form at the school could play, irrespective of whether they were in the first, second or third year of that Sixth Form. Den ran out on the pitch and felt so proud that he was following in the footsteps of his older brother Alan, who had scored more goals than any other MGS player in his final football season in the school First XI.

The game was very evenly balanced and Den was playing in the half back line, where his father had played all his club and league football. He helped to break down several attacks by the opposing side, and he was quick to spot any openings in the defence that faced his own forwards. Den had the comfort of knowing that the First XV rugby full back, Nigel Starmer, was in goal behind him. Nigel latched onto any through balls using his excellent judgment and he booted the ball right down to the other end of the pitch, feeding his own forwards with several scoring opportunities. Halfway through the second half Den began to relax, and was confident that the opposition would not be scoring a goal past the solid Science Sixth Maths defensive system. That would enable his team to progress into the final of the Sixth Form Cup because of the scores they had registered against their earlier opponents.

Suddenly the opposing goalkeeper booted the ball all the way down the centre of the field and Den decided that the safest thing to do was to help the ball on its way towards Nigel Starmer who was standing halfway out of his goal towards the front edge of his penalty area. Den gave the ball the most gentle of taps, ensuring that the ball would bounce straight in front of Nigel—and be able to be caught comfortably by him in his very safe hands, developed during his years of playing full back at rugby. However, to everyone's astonishment Nigel approached the bouncing ball, let it bounce and then completely misjudged the height of its bounce—allowing the ball over his head and into his net. Den was shamefaced and so upset at what had happened. Despite a late continuous period of attack at the other end, no further goals were scored in the game. Science Sixth Maths would not be appearing in the Sixth Form football final whereas their opponents that day would be. Indeed they lifted the trophy the following week! Den was not asked to play for his Sixth form the following year.

Chapter 29

Den had opted to sit two of his Advanced Level subjects at the so-called Scholarship level as well. These two were Physics and Mathematics. While he got on famously with his Chemistry master, Mr Clynes, Den just could not master the enormous amount of parrot-fashion learning that was needed in the Inorganic part of the syllabus. However, he was very keen and knowledgeable about the Organic Chemistry part of the syllabus, perhaps inspired by the teaching on that subject matter by Dr Eric James, their High Master, in the previous academic year.

Each of the five examinations to be taken by Den were both graded and also marked by percentage. In the three Advanced examinations, plus the two Scholarship examinations, Den would be informed of both the grades he had achieved and the percentage marks he had been awarded. He would be told what total percentage he had achieved, out of a maximum of 500 percent. If he had exceeded an overall total of 325 percent, he would have been awarded a State Scholarship, meaning that he would have been among the highest overall percentage scorers throughout the land. Accordingly financial assistance towards his University education would flow from the Government coffers to his chosen university to cover the enrolment fees, the annual course fees, books and other materials.

Den's older brother Alan had scored well over the 325 percentage threshold for a State Scholarship when he sat his equivalent examinations in his penultimate year at Manchester Grammar. Alan had of course gone on to a third year in the Sixth Form and had sat the Cambridge Entrance Examinations in the month of December. In those examinations he had been awarded a Major Open Scholarship to Cambridge University which he took up for the three years of his studies at Clare College, Cambridge.

Den knew he was not as clever at his subjects as his brother Alan had been at his. However, he had always set his heart on sitting for Cambridge University in the December of his final year at Manchester Grammar School (his third at that school, and all in the Sixth form). He set himself the task of raising his game, if at all possible, in the three academic months of September, October and November of 1955. In December he was invited to spend three long nights in the picturesque white stone quadrilateral four storey Clare College with the River Cam on its west side and Trinity College Chapel and College on its south side.

The months of September, October and November 1955 were spent by all the MGS boys in their third year in the various Sixth Forms covering the few remaining parts of the Scholarship syllabus, and going through all the examination papers for the various subjects that had been set over the last twenty years. These would be completed in class, in discussions with the whole form, or as homework which would be marked and then gone through a few days later in class. No stones were left unturned and no preparation programme could have been more thorough than the Manchester Grammar School final assault on the Cambridge University examinations.

Despite the enormous effort that Den put into the final three months, he did not feel the confidence that he thought he would experience. Unfortunately he met several of his former colleagues from the King George V Grammar School in Southport where he had studied for the first four years of his secondary education. He also bumped into Trevor Williams who had indeed been appointed as the Head Boy at KGV in his final year at the school. Den asked Trevor how many KGV boys were sitting the Cambridge entrance examinations that week and the Oxford University entrance examinations in March of the following year. To Den's amazement Trevor informed him that fourteen were sitting the Cambridge examinations that week, and a further twelve would be sitting the Oxford examinations in the coming March. Years later he met one of these 26 former fellow pupils of his, and learned to his chagrin that all 26 of them passed the entrance examinations to Cambridge or Oxford Universities that year! How proud must Mr Dixon, Den's former Headmaster, have been with their performance? Indeed Den also discovered that of the 29 pupils who were in the first year of their secondary education with him at KGV, no less than five ended up by being listed in the renowned

Who's Who annual reference publication—proving what a talented class they were.

*****

Early in the Easter Term Den learned that he failed to gain admission to Cambridge University following his 'mediocre performance' (his own words). Nevertheless he vowed to strive to the utmost of his abilities to gain an admission to Oxford University when they held their entrance examinations two months later in March 1956.

Chapter 30

The preparation process for the March 1956 Oxford University Entrance Examination used by Manchester Grammar School was almost identical to what Den had undertaken over the three months prior to his attempt to gain entry into Cambridge University. These two world class universities were entirely in charge of their own selection procedures, although the syllabus for those sitting for Cambridge or Oxford places was precisely the same, for any given subject. Den detected a slight difference in the type of questions that Oxford had used, and it seemed to him that they were looking for different qualities in their applicants. Even in their quantitative examination papers such as statics and dynamics they seemed to be seeking to evaluate the thought processes of those sitting the papers. It was reasonably easy to spot the differences in the types of papers set by these two top universities, if you had spent three complete months on one type of papers followed immediately by the other type—as Den had.

Over the previous two years Den had befriended a boy called Steve Richardson who was wishing to study Zoology at Oxford University. He was the cousin of the best left handed batsman that Manchester Grammar School had ever been fortunate enough to have. Martin Richardson was the North of England javelin throwing record holder and he literally never needed to practise any javelin throwing from year to year, until the last few days before the event held annually in Manchester. Martin often explained to his schoolmates that he did not want to damage or disrupt the muscular movements of his shoulders, back and arms because he needed all of those for his batting and bowling for the whole of the summer season. He was often concerned that he might even jeopardise his cricket actions and abilities by the few days of javelin throwing that he undertook, with reluctance and strict instructions from the Athletics Master, immediately before the annual event.

When the Manchester Grammar School First XI went on their annual Whitsuntide cricket tour in 1955 Martin and Den shared a bedroom with a third player Peter Unsworth in Edinburgh. They played three matches against George Watson's College, Fettes and Loretto which were all within half an hour travel from the hotel in the city centre. Steve Richardson had also been included in the MGS touring squad of fifteen players although he was not normally a First XI cricket team player.

Den had played in the MGS Second XI for more than one season with Steve and had chatted to him on many occasions about the Cambridge and Oxford University entrance examinations. Steve had said he only wanted to read one subject, Zoology—and only at Oxford University. He said Oxford had 'a much better Zoology school than Cambridge.' Very few of the MGS boys expected Steve to gain entry into the Zoology course at Oxford University, but Steve proved them all wrong. That is why Den sought Steve's advice. He said that some scholars had been awarded places at Oxford when they had not even completed all the questions required for a particular subject! He had somehow fathomed out, or rationalised this situation, saying that they were looking for students with their own unique way of answering questions—rather than trying to obtain the one and only answer to a problem.

When Den set off for Oxford in March 1956 he recalled Steve's philosophy on what Oxford University were looking for in their undergraduates. He was also aware that he had occasionally spent far too long on some of the old Oxford University question papers. Exactly this phenomenon occurred during his sitting of two of the papers. He did not complete the required number of questions required, but he knew that he had greatly exceeded his normal abilities. He was confident his efforts would have won favour from the Oxford examiners.

However, by the last day of the Oxford examinations Den was not very confident about the outcome of his application. The final day included an oral interview with the Master of University College, the college he was hoping to be accepted by. He recalled his interview three months earlier with the Master of Clare College, Cambridge and how poorly he had coped with what was the first ever interview he had attended in his whole life! Den reasoned that he could definitely perform better at the University College interview—he could certainly do no worse.

The Master of University College and his companion began by noting that he had tried to gain entry to Cambridge University in the previous term. He explained that this was because his older brother had been an undergraduate at Clare College, Cambridge a few years earlier. The two men then told Den that they had been impressed by his wide and deep knowledge of the three subjects he had sat the examinations for over the previous three days. They went on to explain that they had a procedure whereby some of the applicants for admission were asked to undertake a single three hour practical examination on the Saturday morning. This was a procedure introduced several years earlier because every year there was quite a sizeable number of borderline students. They had found that such a practical examination was the most effective way for them to decide which of the borderline students should be accepted.

When the Saturday morning finally arrived Den entered the physics laboratory selected for this final trial, wondering what sort of experiment would be required to be carried out by each of the borderline cases, working entirely on their own. All the students were handed an instruction paper and they were asked to perform an experiment involving dropping metallic ball bearings down into a tube filled almost to the brim with a thick viscous transparent liquid. Stopwatches were provided, together with long measuring rulers and graph paper. This was an experiment that Den had performed many times in the laboratories of the two secondary schools he had attended. He was also fully aware of the theory behind the procedure—which he would be using to determine the value of the gravitational pull of the earth. He gathered his thoughts, decided the sequence of the actions he would need to take—and the times he needed to allocate for these various steps.

At last Den thought he could clearly see his way to obtaining an undergraduate place at Oxford University—and for a college that was among the most renowned at Oxford. He could hardly believe his luck! He was determined to perform the experiment, its recording, the graphing, the written descriptions of his methods, the tabling of his results and the drawing of his conclusions so well that there would be no doubt about his being accepted into University College, Oxford.

The three hours experiment started well but after half the time had elapsed Den suddenly panicked—something he had never done in his life before. He then lost half an hour getting nowhere and came to the sudden realisation that he would not be able to complete all the experiment within the time available.

He tried his best to recover the situation, but without success. To this very day he is still completely unable to explain what went wrong. Fortunately he has never experienced anything similar since that day. Perhaps he was just a victim of panic at the realisation of the importance of that moment to his whole career.

Den knew by the end of the three hour period allowed for the experiment that he had failed miserably in the task required. He knew he stood no chance of being accepted into Oxford University, and he had a thoroughly wretched journey by rail back up to Southport.

Chapter 31

Although Den was allowed to retake the Advanced and Scholarship examinations in Physics, Mathematics and Chemistry in the summer term of 1956 his heart was not really in it. He had failed to achieve his one over-riding scholastic ambition, namely to be able to study at Cambridge or Oxford University. With the experience of studying for both Cambridge and Oxford entrance plus an additional year of the Advanced and Scholarship examination syllabuses Den should have easily exceeded the target of 325 total percent in the three Advanced and two Scholarship examinations that would earn him the State Scholarship that he was now preparing for. Somehow he did not even achieve his total score of 310 percent of the year before.

When Den started the procedures for applying for a place at other universities he decided immediately that he would try for Manchester University. He had experienced some doubts when he resided in the Clare College, Cambridge and University College, Oxford halls of residence for the three or four days while he sat their entrance examinations. He began then to wonder whether or not he was really cut out to be a member of the top academic elite. Would he really enjoy mixing and mingling socially most evenings and weekends? Would he not feel safer and more at home if he were to treat his three years of university education as if it were a glorified technical college? After all, he thought, he had already managed to combine his studies with the very time-consuming commuting to and from Manchester and Southport.

For a while he thought about switching to entirely new pastures and carried out several days of researching the pros and cons of applying for a psychology undergraduate course. However, he decided that he would be throwing away all his years of study at the two grammar schools, all for a 'shot in the dark.' After a week of further consideration his mind was made up. He would apply to study Mechanical Engineering at Manchester University—particularly as his father had been a mechanical engineer all his career, after serving his apprenticeship in mechanical engineering with Metropolitan Vickers in Manchester. Furthermore he decided that he would commute, for the whole of the three years undergraduate course, on a daily basis between Southport and Manchester—if he was offered a place.

Den completed all the necessary application forms and was able to list the gradings and percentages he had achieved the previous summer, and to add that his local authority had awarded him a Grant on the basis of his 1955 results. He braced himself for the interview which was arranged at the Manchester University where he was to be interviewed by Professor Diamond who was a very well-known expert in the fields of thermal energy and university education. He had even been appointed as the Chairman of the Government's Working Party on the future energy needs of the United Kingdom.

Professor Diamond interviewed him for half an hour in his private office and asked why Den had not applied for admission to his school of Mechanical Engineering the previous year. Den explained that he had always wanted to study, for a degree, at either Cambridge or Oxford University—explaining about his older brother's three years at Clare College. The Professor said he would have accepted Den for his course the previous year, if he had applied. However, he said he would be delighted to welcome him onto the Mechanical Engineering three year undergraduate course at Manchester University, starting in October 1956. Professor Diamond explained that the first year was a very general course and explained that many students had to be brought up to certain minimum standards in all the subjects. This meant that he would be mixing with fresh undergraduates for other engineering courses, namely Civil Engineering, Electrical Engineering and Aeronautical Engineering. He also said that there would be a great deal of mathematics in the first year syllabus.

As Den left the building he realised that he had just found his home for the next three years. He was impressed by Professor Diamond. He looked quite a stern man, very determined but open minded. Den judged that the Professor thought he had made a mistake by not joining his course a year earlier. Den thought he might well have been right on that point. However, Den would now be able to get his head down and aim for the best possible class of degree he could achieve at Manchester University.

Chapter 32

Once Den had been accepted onto the degree course at Manchester University he was able to turn his attention to enjoying his last season of cricket at Manchester Grammar School in the summer of 1956. He had played in the First XI team for the last six games of the previous season as the leg spinner and a low order batsman. He was determined to be awarded his First XI colours in his final season and to really focus on all aspects of his game. The school had a potentially very strong First XI that year. David Green was one of the opening batsmen and went on to play County Cricket. The captain, Peter Hutson, was first wicket down and later gained a double Blue from Cambridge, in football and cricket. Martin Richardson was the brilliant, punchy left hand batsman with a wonderful eye—and he also usually opened the bowling with fast seamers. Barry Jones was a swing bowler and very capable middle order batsman. David Wrigley was a tall, dark haired, off spinner and useful batsman. Mike Crossley was only fourteen years of age but he was an excellent wicketkeeper. He was not often called on to bat because the side was very strong on batting. However, Mike rescued the team from suffering their only likely defeat that season by sharing a last wicket stand and helping to win the game. When he walked out as the last batsman there were still 18 runs needed to win and Mike saw them through, thereby securing his place in the First XI for the remainder of the season. Den was the leg spinner and also performed the unenviable role of going in to bat earlier than usual if there was a batting collapse. He was known as being able to prevent any more wickets falling at his end, while one of the better batsmen scored runs at the other end. The remaining team places were not taken up by regulars until half way through the list of fixtures.

In the same match that Mike Crossley saved the game, or rather won it, Den had captured six wickets against the local rivals, Macclesfield Grammar School. The opening bowlers for MGS usually made good inroads into the opposing batsmen. Den and David Wrigley would then be introduced into the bowling attack and would normally not take very long to trick one or two of the remaining batsmen into falling as victims to their accurate and economical spin bowling. By that time the MGS captain Peter Hutson would have worked out what was the best way of dismissing the rest of the opposing team for as few runs as possible.

Every year MGS played an MCC team. The MCC is the Marylebone Cricket Club with its headquarters at the Lords cricket ground, a mile or two north west of the centre of London. All the rules of the game are set, changed or agreed by top level meetings of the world governing body for the sport—generally meeting in London in the Lords cricket ground pavilion. The MCC also plays an enormous role in providing the opportunity for really talented up and coming players to show what they can achieve, often before they enter the County cricket arena. In 1956 the MCC cricket team played Manchester Grammar School in an all-day game starting at 11 am with breaks for lunch and tea.

All the boys attending school were allowed to watch the game by sitting on the grass surrounding the boundary line, and after school many planned to stay until the end of the game. There were two Lancashire County First team players in the MCC team that day plus one of Den's cricketing heroes who used to play for both the Lancashire County First team for years, and also for the England cricket team. It was Jack Ikin who was a very attacking left hand batsman and a slip fielder of world repute, standing in very close to the batsmen and never dropping any catches.

Den could hardly believe his luck. It was a 'dream come true' for him to be able to bowl against his lifetime hero. The MCC captain won the toss and decided to bat on the very firm wicket with a very fast outfield. The day was bright and sunny and play could last right through until 7 pm that evening. The MCC opening batsmen rattled up some early quick runs and looked very settled. The opening bowlers for MGS, Barry Jones and Martin Richardson, were not able to penetrate the solid defences of the opening batsmen and it soon became apparent that this was going to be a high scoring game. However, eventually there was a breakthrough and two quick wickets fell, bringing Jack Ikin out to bat with more than half an hour to go before lunch. After a few more overs David Wrigley was brought on at the end away from the new pavilion, and he was able to keep the scoring rate under control—but he was not confusing the batsmen or causing them to take any risks.

In every first class match it is common practice for the captain of the bowling side to bring his top spinner on to bowl around ten minutes before the lunch interval. Peter Hutson duly called Den and said he wanted him to bowl a couple of overs before the lunch break. The idea behind this move was that the two batsmen who were in at say twenty minutes before the lunch break would not 'chance their arm' and try to attack the bowling. They would always prefer to still be in at lunch and then start adding to their scores after lunch. At the same time, the fielding captain needs to tempt such batsmen into taking risks so he will bring on a spin bowler who could easily be hit for quite a few runs, if the batsmen took risks and lashed out. On the other hand a new, and slow, bowler just before the lunch break could often prove fatal for even the most experienced and 'well set' of batsmen.

Den bowled most of his first over to the other batsman—who was right handed—and only one of the six balls to Jack Ikin. However, when Den was thrown the ball to bowl the very last over before lunch, he knew his chance had come. His plan was to bowl two or three leg spinners that would spin into Jack Ikin's body and prevent him from scoring any runs, thus pinning him down at the batting end. Den had pitched the first two balls on exactly the right spot— namely just outside the line of the off stump, and quite well up towards Jack's feet. Den had performed the hardest part of getting his hero out. He knew that he now had to bowl his 'googly' out of the back of his hand, toss it slightly higher in its projection and pitch it one yard shorter than the first two balls. If he managed to achieve all these three things he was confident that his hero would fall into the trap (as so many of Den's victims had done, over the years).

Den took a long deep breath, went through the mental sequence of what he had to do, and then ran up to the bowling crease. He let the ball go and watched very intently to see what his hero would do. There was only one escape route. If Jack could 'read' Den's bowling action he would be able to tell it was Den's 'wrong un' '—but very few batsmen had ever been able to spot his googly, and distinguish it from his normal leg spinner. To Den's delight Jack Ikin took a step or two up the pitch, clearly thinking that he would hit this third leg break ball straight down the wicket for one or two safe runs. However, Den's googly was such an unusual ball that it dipped late in its flight and Jack Ikin was completely bamboozled. He was stranded up the pitch, he had played the wrong shot and he knew he would never be able to get back behind his crease line before the wicketkeeper would have gathered the ball and whipped off the bails. Jack Ikin even bowled occasional leg breaks and googlies himself and he should not have fallen into the trap. However, it was too late for him to stop himself being stumped.

Unbelievably the young wicketkeeper Mike Crossley made his one and only stumping misjudgement of the whole season. He was so excited by the chance of stumping this former Lancashire and England batsman that he 'snatched' at the ball. He did not take it cleanly. Indeed he fumbled with it—allowing Jack Ikin to shuffle his feet back behind his crease line, into the safety area. What a let off! Mike was disgusted with himself. Den was bitterly disappointed and Peter Hutson was very surprised, and also disappointed, that Jack Ikin had not ended up in the pavilion before the lunch break.

Over the lunch break Jack Ikin went up to Den and said 'If that was your googly, it was one of the best I have ever seen. I did not spot what it was, and I bet you get many wickets with that ball.' Den was deeply grateful for the compliment but nothing, no nothing, would be as good as having captured the wicket of his cricket hero, in full view of the whole school. Den thought the rest of the game would be an easy ride for the MCC team, particularly when they started to build up a sizeable score soon after the lunch break—but he had not bargained on the events of the afternoon and evening

*****

Jack Ikin was dismissed late in the first hour of play after lunch. The MCC then had four young professionals with County cricket experience who had been included in their team to push along the score at a fast rate. Den finished with just one wicket, that of a Lancashire County player, at the cost of 45 runs. This was a poor result for him but he had at least managed to keep the scoring rate down during his eleven overs. By mid-afternoon the MCC score was increasing too rapidly, and they were on target to pass the 200 run mark well before the tea break. This would allow them to bowl some fifteen overs before tea and take control of the game, if they captured a few wickets.

By the tea interval of half an hour, three MGS wickets had fallen for only 32 runs. In view of this collapse by the school team's batsmen Peter Hutson called for Den to come in just before the tea interval—by which time Peter himself had managed to master the best of the MCC's fast bowlers. As Den walked out to bat he knew exactly what function he was being required to fulfil. To reinforce the plan the captain met him on the edge of the square and said 'Den, you know exactly what I want you to do. You just HAVE to stay in for well over an hour of batting to take the edge off this very capable attack. I am not expecting you to score many runs, but you must NOT lose your wicket.'

Den applied the best rule for a new batsman facing a few balls before the tea interval, with his side in real trouble. He kept his eye on the ball, right up to his bat. In the many years he had spent honing his batting skills he had practised for many seasons against his older brother and his father, for hour after hour as they practised their phenomenal bowling skills. Both of them were extremely capable bowlers with years of top league cricket behind them, and had really tested Den to the limit.

After the tea interval Den also remembered that any batsman intent on staying at the crease had to watch the ball right out of the bowler's hand—so that he could pick up the trajectory of the ball from the very start of its journey up the pitch towards him. Den and his captain had a good rapport and a complete understanding of when it was safe to take a quick single. Slowly but surely the MGS score started to rise, but at what seemed a very slow rate to Den. The captain had several brief chats with him at the end of each over— telling him to just keep his eye on the ball, keep his end safe and be patient. Gradually the MGS captain asserted his authority over the various bowlers that the MCC captain employed to break the partnership. Half an hour later he was asserting his dominance and the team total was increasing at a very fast rate. By that time Peter Hutson, playing a real captain's innings, was approaching his half century—although Den had only scored 12 runs, all in singles. The MGS team score was by then 88 runs for three wickets, with Den and his captain having put together a half century partnership.

Even though the MGS team needed a further 120 runs to win, they had at least achieved the situation of being in the position of being able to play for a draw, if they needed to. However, it was abundantly clear to Den that the only result his captain wanted that day was a victory for the school. Both Den and his captain knew that their one demon batsman, Martin Richardson, was the next man in and what a batsman he was! They were only too well aware that Martin could score at an amazing rate if he managed to 'get his eye in.'

Just before the MGS score reached 100 runs Den was given out leg before wicket. He apologised to his captain as he left the pitch but Peter Hutson was full of praise 'Den, you have done exactly what I wanted. You have helped us to set up the possibility of the School's first win over the MCC for ten years. Martin and I can now push up the scoring rate, on the foundation we have built.'

Martin Richardson strode out to the wicket and had three words for Den 'Well done lad.'

As Den walked off the playing area he noticed that most of the large crowd of boys had left to catch their various buses and trains to enable them to arrive home on time and tackle their homework and revision work without a delay to their regular routine. Den, on the other hand, could afford the luxury of watching the rest of his team work like Trojans to achieve what would be a memorable victory over the MCC. He sat on a chair round the boundary line in front of the new pavilion with his other team mates. They were all feverishly calculating whether or not the required run rate could be achieved. After many projections they all agreed that Martin Richardson held the key to the possible win that they all craved. Once Martin settled in they knew he would be exerting his enormous body and arm strength to the full, and be able to rock the MCC players back on their heels.

Peter Hutson finally succumbed to a vicious fast ball from one of the younger MCC bowlers, who was anxious to prove his mettle. By then the captain had scored 68 runs compared with Den's relatively meagre score of 18 runs. Indeed Den had already noted that Martin had rattled up more than twenty runs in his first fifteen minutes at the crease. The springboard for the MGS team's success was in place, and Martin was even exceeding their huge expectations of him!

Before long, Martin's muscle power and body strength had built the team score to well over the 150 mark, without his new batting colleagues having to face many balls. When Martin drove three straight sixes into the new pavilion within the same over everyone on the ground—players and spectators alike—could only envisage one result to the game. Martin, unusually for him, curbed his over-enthusiasm and, with the help of one or two of the remaining MGS batsmen, he achieved the long awaited victory over the MCC. In a final gesture, typical of Martin, he drove the match winning six well over the long on boundary at a height of more than 50 feet off the ground. The ball hit the

MCC official flag atop the new flagpole, much to the merriment of all the MGS team players and their spectators who would most certainly remember this famous victory for many years to come.

Chapter 33

The Manchester Grammar School cricket tour of 1956 was to include three all day matches against Magdalen College School, Oxford followed by Radley College and ending with Eton. Den returned to Oxford only three months after his disastrous experience in the physics laboratory. This time he had a brief trip up the river in a punt that was so low in the water that another one or two passengers would have caused it to sink.

The match was keenly fought but MGS prevailed. Den took three wickets for 29 runs but did not need to bat. The next day, after a long journey by coach MGS arrived to see the Radley team were already out practising for the encounter. Radley won the toss and elected to bat on a rock hard pitch with a very fast outfield. It was clearly going to be a very high scoring game—and so it proved. The MGS boys were dehydrated before lunch but worse was to come. Radley stepped up their run rate in the afternoon session and Den was given his longest ever continuous spell of bowling. He somehow managed to vary his flight and pace sufficiently to prevent the Radley batsmen from 'having a go' at his bowling. One of Den's deliveries beat the batsman 'all ends up' and should have hit the top of the middle stump. However, the height of bounce was so great, because of the very hard pitch, that the ball sailed right over the stumps. Peter Hutson, the captain, kept on giving words of encouragement to Den who took four wickets for 68 runs from his tiring and frustrating long spell of 20 overs. He had never before been hit for more than 50 runs in a match, and he was a little embarrassed when the team walked off the ground, just before the tea interval, Radley having declared their innings at 210 runs for 7 wickets.

Fortunately the MGS batsmen enjoyed the perfect wicket just as much as the Radley players. All of them took the chance to improve their batting averages and there was never any possibility of the Radley bowlers dismissing the MGS team—the pitch was just too good and fast. At the end of the drawn match Den and the MGS players were enjoying the excellent showers and baths before catching the coach that evening for Eton. Fred Winterbottom, the master in charge of the MGS team, and who had been umpiring the whole game, came into the showers room and made a bee-line for Den. 'That was the best spell of bowling I have ever witnessed from any of the dozens of MGS teams that I have had the privilege of managing. You are to be congratulated, dear boy!'

Den was at a loss for words. His mouth was still so dry from his long, physically tiring spell and he was still disappointed that he had been hit for 68 runs in one game. Nevertheless he managed to mumble the words 'Thank you very much, sir, but it was just so good a pitch, and their boys knew exactly how to score runs on it.'

That same evening Den was treated to a brief trip on the River Thames at Maidenhead, by one of the Eton House Masters in his personal motorised boat. It was a splendid evening, with a deep red sunset at the end of a cool evening by the riverside. Needless to say Den slept very soundly in his tiny bedroom in the House Master's suite which formed part of the accommodation building housing all their boys in dormitories. One of the Eton cricket players treated Den to breakfast with all the boys from his House, and then all the MGS team and support group were privileged to join the entire school for their Service of Morning Prayers. Den, and no doubt all the other MGS team, felt a shiver down the back of his neck. It was a moment in his life that he would forever cherish.

The game against Eton was full of drama and proved that the MGS and Eton teams were both of a very high quality, and fiercely competitive. Before the start of the game Den noticed that all the studs on the underside of his cricket boots had been rubbed off, or reduced so much, by the rock hard Radley pitch that they were totally ineffective. He could not see how he could play that day in the same boots, until the Eton Groundsman of forty years spotted his dilemma and said 'Don't worry lad, I'll put fresh ones in for you in my boot room. All our players rely on me for the studs in their boots.'

Den only had to wait ten minutes and was delighted at the brilliant job that had been performed on his boots. He literally never had to change any of the studs inserted that day. Eventually, after many more years of cricket, the whole top structure of both boots disintegrated until they became an embarrassment to

Den. However, he had grown so sentimentally attached to that particular pair of boots that he decided he would keep playing in them for as long as possible.

*****

MGS won the toss that day and decided to bat. The pitch was a beauty and the MGS batsmen could not wait to get out in the middle on such a fine sunny day. However, disaster struck very early on and MGS lost both their opening batsmen before the score had reached 20.The MGS captain instructed Den to don his pads immediately. Even though Den was listed to bat at number 8 in the batting order, that is after six wickets had fallen, the captain needed him again to come in and steady the ship—just as in the match against the MCC. In the event what happened was that Den's best friend Martin Richardson went out to bat with the score at 17 for 2 wickets—knowing that Den would appear out on the pitch if another cheap wicket fell. However, Martin played the innings of his life, scoring 115 runs and destroying the Eton College's bowling attack. Den sat in the pavilion, with his pads on, for over three hours that day, and never batted at all!

The MGS ship had been rescued single-handedly by Martin Richardson and a declaration at 256 for 4 wickets was made by Peter Hutson. The whole of Eton College spent an enthralling afternoon, out of lessons, watching the Eton reply. This was spearheaded by Henry Blofeld—who decades later endeared himself to the BBC radio listeners to Test Match Special with his dulcet tones, gentlemanly manners and flowery language. That day Henry was a tall, strapping teenager eager to show the Manchester lads how well Eton could bat, and how very keen they were to win the match by overhauling the huge score amassed by Martin and his colleagues.

Henry literally blasted every ball straight back down the pitch on both sides of the wicket, relieving the monotony occasionally by cover driving or square cutting some of the shorter balls. Henry scored 50 runs inside half an hour, which was a phenomenal achievement for a schoolboy. MGS then had a tremendous stroke of good fortune which saw Henry leave the pitch with his head lifted high. Henry's opening batsman's partner straight drove yet another perfectly good ball from one of the MGS opening bowlers, just as hard as any Henry had hit. As the ball zoomed back towards the bowler he stuck out his arm to stop yet another four. The very fast return shot hit the arm of the bowler and then ricocheted onto the stumps at the bowler's end. The tragedy was that

Henry, quite correctly, was slowly walking up the pitch towards the other batsman—ready to run for a single. However, he had, not unnaturally, moved in front of the batting crease at his end. Consequently Henry was run out in that very moment and had no chance of regaining his crease because the incident was over 'in the twinkling of an eye'—to use a Henry Blofeld phrase.

The whole of the crowd of Eton boys realised what had happened and they gave Henry a tremendous standing ovation. The following batsmen tried to equal Henry's outstanding performance, but without success. Nevertheless the Eton score built up steadily, but at no time threatened to overcome the MGS total within the time available. Den was exhausted from his efforts the previous day and failed to take a single wicket in the four overs he bowled, conceding 20 runs. The MGS captain soon realised that Den was a spent force and he used David Wrigley, the off spinner to slow down the scoring rate, and ensure that the match ended in a draw with Eton on the very respectable score of 236 for 6 wickets.

During the rest of the season Den continued to take wickets at a very economical rate. This was a much easier task for him on the slow, grassy wickets of the MGS cricket square. Sometimes, if it rained on the match day, batting became nigh impossible. On days like that David Wrigley and Den would have a field day picking up wickets with ease and totally confusing the opposing batsmen, who were far more used to perfect batting wickets on their home grounds.

The MGS First XI did not lose a single game in the whole of the 1956 season.

It was a very proud day indeed for Den when he was awarded not only his First XI cricket colours, but the Manchester Grammar School Bowling Prize. He took 41 wickets in the season at an average of less than ten runs per wicket. This ensured a suitable entry in the Wisden Yearbook of Cricket for 1956. Furthermore Den was so proud to have followed his older brother Alan in being awarded the MGS Bowling Prize—exactly five years later.

Both the Dover boys were honoured to receive their Bowling Prizes from the hands of Lord James of Rusholme who had been ennobled and honoured with a peerage for teaching at the Manchester Grammar School, and for inspiring so many boys over the decades with the motto *Sapere aude* 'Dare to be Wise.'

Chapter 34

The first few days at Manchester University were spent finding out where various administrative offices were situated. Numerous forms had to be completed and the whole place was bustling. Den was one of the more than five thousand 'Freshers' welcomed each year into Manchester University, a figure that was growing annually because of its concentration on computing, engineering, mathematics and the sciences. All the other major faculties were provided but these were the mainstream subjects that had achieved regular headlines worldwide for Manchester University—with such significant breakthroughs as making the first ever computer, cracking the atom for the first time, developing a radio telescope to view deeper into the whole universe and inventing magnetic levitation for transportation.

Many of the usual general areas and lecture rooms were plastered with huge colourful and attractive displays designed to attract the first year undergraduates. Den was not drawn to the debating societies or the political parties, despite his ever-growing interest in such matters. He was intent on achieving the best possible class of final year engineering degree that he could. He knew he would need to devote all his time and effort to his degree course, rather than be distracted by other activities—no matter how important these were. He was also very conscious that he was intent on commuting every single day of the week between Southport and Manchester. He had heard that, unlike all the engineering subjects, most of the other faculties expected their undergraduates to spend much of their time in the libraries seeking and processing information away from the lecture theatre environment. The timetables for all the engineering and science schools were however totally taken up by either lectures in the numerous theatres or practicals in the very varied and extensive laboratories.

Although Den went for trials at hockey and cricket, he decided after two games for the First XI at hockey and only one game with the First XI at cricket, he would be far better off playing both these sports in Southport on a weekly basis—thus removing the need for him to add a sixth day of commuting each week. However, he really enjoyed his two sports at Southport because they ensured he kept fit and maintained his expertise and skills in case he decided after graduating that he should continue with these activities.

Professor Diamond had been absolutely correct in explaining that most of the first year engineering syllabuses were identical—with few lectures being unique to the particular disciplines associated with mechanical, civil, aeronautical and electrical matters. At the end of each term examinations were held in huge open halls such as the McDougall Sports Centre with literally thousands of students sitting numerous examinations, all of three hours duration. Den was so thankful that he had attended two excellent grammar schools at which all the subjects he was involved with at Manchester University had been taught extremely well and to the highest levels.

Den had chosen to study mechanical engineering because his strongest subjects at school had been mathematics and physics, and his father had been a mechanical engineer. However, he travelled every day by train from Southport with an undergraduate student studying Building at the University of Science and Technology (UMIST) based in the very centre of Manchester. They had regular chats about their various subjects and often discussed what possible future careers lay ahead of them. In early February 1957 Den learned that interviews were being held at UMIST for all kinds of students, and particularly building and construction—due to the huge housing and infrastructure programmes being undertaken by the public sector, and being carried out by private sector employers. He learned that the so called 'milk round' of interviews was being held over the next two weeks and anyone interested could apply. Den was very conscious indeed that his older brother Alan had found it extremely difficult to obtain a job, even as a Cambridge University graduate with degrees in both mathematics and economics. He took his travelling companion's advice and immediately submitted his name for interview for employment during the summer recess.

John Laing and Son Limited had been created in Carlisle by its original founder, John Laing. They had a first class reputation as one of the leading building and civil engineering contractors. This was the first employment interview that Den had ever attended. He was asked why he had applied for a vacation job with Laing if he was studying mechanical engineering. Den explained about his keen interest in building and construction, sparked off by his detailed conversations with his travelling companion. He was asked if he might consider changing his undergraduate course to civil engineering, because that was the type of undergraduate that they wished to recruit. He said he would, stressing that everything he had heard and read about building and construction was of the keenest interest to him.

Within two weeks Den received an offer of an eight week summer vacation appointment with John Laing and Son Limited, to be spent on a building site somewhere in the United Kingdom. The rate of pay was only at an annual rate of £350 but quite frankly Den was so pumped up about the prospect that he would have been pleased to offer his services free of charge! Den thought it sensible to advise Professor Diamond's office that he would be working for eight weeks during the summer vacation for a major construction company. He was very surprised and relieved by the response. Professor Diamond's secretary said that quite a few undergraduates switched their courses of study, particularly at the end of their first year. She said what Den should do was to write to Professor Diamond in early September, asking for an interview during that month, if he were minded to change to the civil engineering school.

Den was enthused by the prospect of a permanent and attractive career opening up before him. He concentrated on all his subjects and performed extremely well in all the examinations held at the end of the first year. A few weeks later he was notified by Laings that he would be working on the construction of a huge manufacturing plant on the other side of Southampton Water from the town itself. The client was the International Synthetic Rubber Company, an expanding American company.

Den had been asked to find his way from Southport to Southampton on the south coast. He would be met at the railway station, taken to the site and given instructions about the working and living arrangements. Unfortunately the person appointed to meet Den at Southampton station was diverted to an emergency and Den was asked to find his own way to the site which was only five miles from Southampton 'as the crow flies' but 25 miles by road around the northern tip of the Southampton estuary—with no direct bus route. Den discovered from Railway Enquiries at the station that his best bet would be to catch a ferry across the river to Hythe, a very small village on the southern coast of the estuary. That would take him to within five miles of the site, which sounded as though 'it must be in the New Forest.'

Den walked through Southampton to the ferry and was astounded to see that there was a seaplane in the harbour adjacent to the pier he would be leaving from. Den had been an avid reader of the 'Biggles' books and was delighted that he was able to watch the seaplane take off and land again before his ferry set off across Southampton Water for its twenty minute trip. On the other side Den asked about the local bus services and caught a bus to a tiny village which seemed as close to the site as he could manage by public transport. By then the time was 6 pm on the hot sunny day. He realised he would not reach the site during the normal working hours of 8 am to 5 pm. Den asked a few villagers where the site might be and they pointed down a gravel road that disappeared into a forest of trees. They told him the site was at least a mile down the gravel road so Den had an idea. He decided he would book in for bed and breakfast at a tiny house in the village and walk to the site early the next day.

The following morning he arrived at the building site on foot after a pleasant walk along the roadside through the New Forest. Every species of tree was to be found within a few yards of the gravel road which had clearly been carved out to form the route to the construction site for all the deliveries of materials and chemical plant, and for the construction and permanent workforce.

The construction site was truly enormous. Fifty individual chemical processing buildings were to be erected, some being similar to large aircraft hangars. There were to be massive pipe installations running between the numerous buildings along which the different chemicals were to be pumped. Massive boiler houses and other plant rooms were to be built, and the completed factory would almost rival the nearby Fawley oil refinery for size. Den was fascinated by the flaring off at this oil refinery which made it appear to be a lighted beacon marking the start of Southampton Water along which all the ocean going ships and boats entered and left the port of Southampton.

During his eight weeks working on the construction site Den witnessed at first hand all the innumerable building and construction processes involved in such a huge industrial construction project. He spent his whole time on the site setting out the positions, the heights and the depths of all the various buildings, drainage and sewers needed for the petrochemical installation. He worked under a graduate civil engineer and the two of them had a 'chainman' whose job it was to help them with their work. Charlie had been a chainman on several important construction projects and enjoyed the outdoor life. He was 'as fit as a fiddle' despite his age of nearly sixty.

The main tools of the trade for a site engineer were the level and the theodolite. The former was used to measure and mark the heights above Ordnance Survey datum levels, and the latter to measure and mark the exact location on the site of any item shown on a map or design drawing as needing to be constructed. These two instruments took several weeks of continuous practice before Den was totally confident that he had mastered them. The accuracy of the work was of the utmost importance. The whole of the new factory had to be constructed in exact accordance with the design plans. All the construction workers needed accurate 'lines and levels' for them to be able to build and install every piece of equipment and detail of the various buildings in the correct position.

Den thoroughly enjoyed being at the very 'work face' where the forward, or leading edge, of the construction was carried out. Part of his duties involved him frequently having to forage through the trees along the edge of the Southampton Water. He was required to mark out the routes of all the new process pipe-work and particularly the huge new sewers, up to twenty feet diameter, needed to discharge the waste into the various types of sewers and drains established over previous centuries and decades. While he was carrying out this work he would often be only 50 to 100 yards from the bows of the huge Queen Mary and Queen Elizabeth ocean going passenger liners as they arrived or departed on their Transatlantic voyages to New York and other exotic destinations, which Den could only dream of. Other ships that came close to Den labouring away in his workplace among the trees included the new Yacht Britannia, belonging to the Queen, and the United States of America passenger liner that had recently set the fastest time for crossing the Atlantic, thereby regaining the coveted Blue Riband for America.

Chapter 35

The eight weeks on the huge construction site for John Laing and Son Limited had been so fascinating and enjoyable that Den had no hesitation whatsoever in deciding that he should change his university course to Civil Engineering. He loved the outdoor life, the ever-changing workplace as the work progressed, the tasks he had been required to execute and the team spirit of the employees. He had a natural rapport with everyone on the site—whether they drove machinery, dug holes, laid pipes, erected steel, laid bricks or made the tea. It was one huge and impressive team effort by all concerned.

He had stayed in lodgings with a Southampton family and had commuted by coach to the site six days a week, picking up the coach at 7 am and being dropped off at 6 pm. He had attended a Methodist church just behind the landlady's house, played tennis on their two courts and joined their Youth Club. On his single half day free each week he had watched some very good cricket and travelled on a borrowed bicycle to various parts of the New Forest, and several local seaside villages.

In early September he applied to meet Professor Diamond to explain the reasons for wanting to change his course, and he had a brief interview with him a week later. Professor Diamond then introduced him to the head of the Civil Engineering Department, Professor Matheson, who quizzed him about his education to date, his reasons for wanting to change courses and why he was so convinced that he wanted to study for a degree in civil engineering. One of the reasons why Den wanted to change courses was that he did not want to spend all his working life in a factory; he preferred to be outside, pitched against the elements and trying to shape and build the future. In addition, Den had never been interested in how mechanisms or engines worked; he wanted to help improve the environment with more modern facilities such as homes, schools, bridges and shopping centres.

Within weeks Den was convinced he had made the right decision at the right time. Many of the undergraduate friends he had made at the university were still attending the same lectures as he was, and they compared notes on how the second year of their particular course was taking shape. After a very wide panorama of subjects in the first year, there was much more specialisation. There were more practical sessions in the wide variety of laboratories but at all times theory went hand in hand with experiment. The amount of research being undertaken by their various lecturers and professors was staggering. Much of it was at the forefront of science, technology and engineering. Fluid mechanics helped with tidal and river erosion problems, dams helped with energy conservation and water supplies, atomic energy was ensuring a new source of energy to meet the ever-increasing needs of growing populations, and soil mechanics was ensuring safe foundations and enabling sites with very poor ground conditions to be developed.

There was a massive workload of revision and examinations in the second half of the second year syllabus. Den hoped that the range of subjects in the final year would narrow down, and permit more specialisation. Nevertheless he emerged as the top student at the end of the second year examinations. On hearing this brilliant news he vowed on the train journey home to Southport that evening that he was going to stay in front and win the much coveted Taylor Woodrow Travel Fellowship awarded to the top civil engineering student in the Finals to be held in May of the following year, 1959.

At the commencement of the final year it was explained to all the civil engineering students that they would study certain important subjects up to Christmas, be examined on these in December and awarded degree classifications. These results would be taken into account in awarding their final degree grades. In the Easter Term other key subjects would be studied and the same process would be adopted. This meant that the final revision and examination results would take all the three terms results into account—preventing a huge upturn in workload in the final Summer Term which was short anyway because of the period during which the Finals would be held.

Although Den had enjoyed the first two years of his undergraduate studies immensely, he came into his own in the final year. One subject was Aerial and Geodetic Surveying. This involved three dimensional calculations, examining films taken from the air to calculate the heights of buildings and their distances apart—and even calculating what elevation, direction and speed a satellite would need to be launched at to ensure it would be able to orbit the moon and then be returned safely to Earth.

Another subject was soil mechanics in which earth dams and reservoirs would be designed for the retention of rainfall and the provision of water supplies to large areas of the country. Whole bridges in reinforced concrete and structural steelwork had to be designed, with detailed drawings and materials schedules produced. During a one week residential course the whole of an area of the River Ribble valley in Lancashire was surveyed and drawn up on a map using the theodolite and levelling techniques which Den had mastered during his vacation experience on the Southampton factory site. Den even spent two months of his second summer's vacation working, for Laing again, on the construction of the 53 mile long M1 Motorway in Bedfordshire and Northamptonshire. His job was to help to ensure that all the concrete used in the bridges, the road surfaces and the drainage was fit for purpose and meeting the very stringent strength and consistency requirements.

*****

Den had a really gruelling, testing time in one of the December 1958 examinations. It was his favourite subject of Soil Mechanics and the one he chose for his personal research project on sheet pile walls (executed in the first term of the third year). Professor Peter Rowe was literally one of the top world experts in soil mechanics and was hired around the world for his expertise in reservoir design, piled foundations and in extremely bad ground conditions. Den was keen to impress Professor Rowe with his performance in the last Soil Mechanics examination he would ever sit, to be held at the end of the Christmas Term in 1958.

There were nine questions on the examination paper and six of these were to be answered in the three hours allowed. Den read all the questions carefully and chose the questions he would score the highest marks in. After ten minutes he began to answer the questions. Soil Mechanics was not just a mixture of theory and calculation. There was much intuition and instinct required. Den seemed to have an innate feel for the subject and had been an ardent fan of all the work that Professor Rowe carried out for so many important clients around the world. He answered three of the questions efficiently and fully within the first hour and a half. However, Den then hit major problems in the next two questions he attempted. In the end he was reduced to explaining in words how both these questions should be attempted, and answered—even though he was unable to achieve this within the time available to him. Somehow theory and practice did not match on either of the questions. Den wondered if he was experiencing déjà vu as he recalled his disastrous experience in the Oxford University physics practical examination two years earlier.

Den kept his nerve and pulled through this unwanted, horrific period and eventually managed to present three excellent answers to questions, two others in which he had to explain how he should have answered the final parts—without being able to. This meant that he had only answered five instead of the six questions required. He realised that he had effectively reduced his potential percentage score in the Soil Mechanics paper to around 75% to 80% maximum. He was very disappointed, particularly because this was his favourite subject, and was to be marked by his favourite Professor. However, Den was at least satisfied that he had done his very best, even if that was far short of what he considered to be an acceptable level.

*****

The first day back at Manchester University in early January 1959 was taken up with looking at the results of the various examinations held the previous month, and with getting to grips with the new daily and weekly programme of subjects for the Easter Term. Den was delighted with his results in the Structures, Hydraulics, Aerial and Geodetic Surveying and Engineering Economics papers—in all of which he had obtained a First Class grading and was top of all the twenty Final Year Honours Civil Engineering students. He dared hardly look at the Soil Mechanics results. He took a deep breath and prepared himself for this one low grading. Instead of examining the list from the highest placed students at the top, he started looking at the list from the bottom up, covering the names further up the list with a large file of notes he was carrying. Slowly he moved the bottom edge of the file upwards, revealing one new name at a time. He had been expecting his name to be towards the bottom, even though this was his favourite subject, and the one he thought he was the best student in. Slowly but surely he raised the file up the notice board, one name at a time, until it was reaching the top. Den then wondered if he had done so badly that his name had been omitted from the final listing, perhaps on health grounds or because of an administrative error. Den could not wait any longer and he revealed the top three names in one final movement of the file. To his total astonishment he was right at the top of the list with a First Class grading—indeed he was the only one to be awarded a First.

Den had convinced himself that he had done so badly in the Soil Mechanics paper that there was no chance of him being anywhere near the top of the listings, so to obtain a First Class grading in that examination was more than he could ever have hoped for. Euphoria did not come close to how he felt. He now knew that all he needed to do was to keep his head down for the next five months, work hard, and a First Class Honours degree in Civil Engineering would be his—as well as the Taylor Woodrow Travel Fellowship to be awarded to the top Civil Engineering graduate of the year.

Away from university commitments Den officiated as Best Man at the wedding of his older brother Alan just before the end of the Easter Term examinations. This caused him great difficulty in squeezing an adequate amount of revision time for the various subjects into the wedding preparations. However, he was only too willing to carry out the appropriate duties at the request of his brother. It seemed to Den that whenever there were no distractions, he was easily able to concentrate on revising for all the subjects he was studying—but he found it difficult to combine any external priorities with his academic workload. Nevertheless he did manage to achieve acceptable grades for all the subjects for which he had to study and sit exams in that final Easter term at Manchester University.

Professor Matheson, head of the Civil Engineering Department, did however have a quiet word with Den about his Easter Term results, saying 'I think I know what you'll be doing for the next three months.' Den replied politely with the words 'Yes, so do I.'

This was just the impetus that Den needed to force him to get his head down, shut everything else out, and work on his revision for all the Finals examinations to be held in the Summer Term.

When the last but one examination had been held Den had to travel back to Southport in the afternoon and finalise his revision and swotting for the last paper which was Hydraulics. He started to study all the notes on the train to Southport, but his mind could not focus on the subject. He waited until he arrived home, had a quick tea and tried again. The result was the same. His mind just would not focus on the course notes, nor on all the other Hydraulics information that he needed to skim through, to commit to memory—or at least be able to call to mind when he was in the examination hall.

Try as he might, Den was making no progress as the hours passed. As a last resort he asked his younger brother Keith to have a short knockabout at cricket on the side garden—using a tennis ball—and he also asked Keith's girlfriend Deidre to join them. At last the blockage was cleared, although by then it was nearly 11 pm! Finally Den was eager to go right through all the Hydraulics notes, practicals and previous examination papers—brushing up his knowledge and making sure that no stone was left unturned. Den knew he had to rise at 6 am to catch the 7 am train to Manchester the following day but he did not turn off his bedroom light until 3.30 am, at which time he realised it was already daylight outside.

Den enjoyed his last journey to Manchester after three years of commuting to Manchester Grammar School followed by three years commuting to Manchester University. He started on the Hydraulics paper in fine shape. He was able to answer all the questions without any difficulties—except for the growing tiredness he experienced during the last hour. However, he gritted his teeth and ground out the last two answers, breathing a huge, but very tired, sigh of relief as he laid his pen down for the last time in a school or university examination.

*****

All the students who had been sitting their Finals that summer knew precisely the date and time at which their particular Degree Grades would be posted on the main University notice board beneath the beautiful arches forming the supports for the very fine central University buildings, a mile south of the city centre. Den travelled in by train that day with a strange mixture of feelings. One was elation that this was the end of his academic career, although perhaps the start of his learning process. Another was keen expectation about the possibility of good results. The third was a genuine concern lest he had not achieved the success he was sure he was capable of achieving.

Den planned to move his hand up the list from the bottom, as he had done with the Soil Mechanics results six months earlier. However, he had not reckoned on several other students on his course being by the notice board at the same time as he arrived to view it. Suddenly one of his colleagues was shaking him by the hand vigorously and shouting with joy 'Congratulations Den. You have topped the list and you've won the Taylor Woodrow Travel Fellowship as well.'

Den was overjoyed, and at long last—after many years of studying—he could take a well-earned rest—and try to fit in some relaxation. It was time to celebrate and also time to thank as many of the lecturers and professors that may be around on what was a very important day for him. He would remember and cherish this day for the rest of his life.

A few weeks later Den, his fiancée and his father and mother attended the Degree Day ceremonies in the beautiful surroundings of the Graduation Hall together with thousands of others who had successfully completed their university studies. On the way back to Southport they diverted to Stockton Heath where Den treated his parents to a celebration Afternoon Tea at the well-known Foxglove Hotel, only 100 yards from the Manchester Ship Canal. It was the first time Den had ever stepped inside this hotel because he had promised himself and his mother that he would never enter its doors until he achieved the first of his goals—namely to gain a proper and distinguished academic degree in a technical subject. This was his way of thanking his parents for the wonderful start they had given him in life—in spite of the humble beginnings they had all had to endure within a mile or two of the Canal and the hotel.

Chapter 36

Den had been asked in writing by the Personnel Manager of John Laing and Son Limited to inform him as soon as he received his degree results. Subject to Den obtaining an Upper Second or a First Class degree in Civil Engineering, the company had promised to offer him a Graduate Indenture which would commit them to employing him for four years during which he would be required to try to obtain the professional qualification of Member of the Institution of Civil Engineers. This organisation had its headquarters in Great George Street, London SW1 less than two hundred yards from the Houses of Parliament.

Den had thoroughly enjoyed both of the periods of vacation employment he had been granted by Laing. He soon learned from them that he would receive an additional annual salary of £500 for being awarded a First Class Honours Bachelor of Science degree in Civil Engineering by Manchester University. This was really the icing on the cake for Den because he was planning to marry his fiancée Marina Wright who lived in Southport and who had recently qualified as a teacher.

Den and Marina married on 8 August 1959 and on his return from their honeymoon he was informed that Laing wanted him to start full time employment with them in Swansea, on the south coast of Wales, before the end of the month. It seemed ironic that his older brother Alan was settling in with Procter and Gamble 200 miles north of Southport, just a few miles to the west of Newcastle-upon-Tyne whereas he was heading to Swansea, 200 miles to the south of Southport.

Den had to make several speedy decisions before heading off to Swansea. First he bought a car and found that he needed a guarantor to be able to obtain a hire purchase agreement. His father was only too happy to oblige and had probably helped Alan already on matters such as this. Secondly Den decided he would try to rent a flat in Swansea, but soon discovered that there were very few flats for rent in that area—only for sale. This was not what Den wanted so he decided to buy a smallish caravan that meant that he could easily move around the country to other locations with Laing—until he was able to settle somewhere on a permanent basis, and buy a suitable house at that time.

Den was surprised that, instead of being a site engineer, he was instructed to spend the first six months learning all about cost control and bonus calculations for the various tradesmen and labourers employed on the two contracts they had in Swansea. One of the contracts was for the construction of a large hotel and two rows of shops, located on a major roundabout in the town centre. The other contract was a major extension to Swansea Technical College.

The plan was that Den would take over the site engineering duties after six months, by which time he would be familiar with all the work on the two building sites. Den was delighted to hear that he had been hand-picked as one of several new graduate engineers with Laing to learn all they could about cost control and bonus calculations. The original founder of Laing was meticulous about controlling costs and the need to understand all aspects of the financial side of the building and civil engineering business he had created. Den thought this was a very forward looking attitude and he resolved to find out all he could—not just about costs and bonuses, but also about how long the numerous construction operations took to carry out, and the best methods to be employed. Den's industrial career had got off to a flying start and he was keen to progress as quickly as he could up the John Laing organisation. He was very impressed by all the people they employed, and particularly the bosses that came to visit the Swansea sites to see what was going on and to make sure that Laing achieved their motto which was 'Laing for completion on time.'

Two visitors to the Swansea sites took him by surprise. One was 'Sid Hodgson' who was a revered figure in the Company. He was 'Mr Cost Control' and he had built up this department over the last twenty years of his career with Laing. Den was called back into the office to meet Mr Hodgson and his travelling colleague, Ted Brian. The two of them were visiting all the sites in Wales and the South West Region, based in Bristol. Mr Hodgson opened by asking Den what he thought of the time he was spending on cost control and bonus calculations. Den replied by saying he was delighted to be able to start his post-graduate employment with the opportunity of helping to pioneer the new approach to graduates by asking some of them to spend their first six months on cost and bonus duties. He said he was learning a great deal very fast and was thoroughly enjoying his work. He asked if thought was being given to trying a similar period for graduates but on planning, programming and progress checking of the construction work. Mr Hodgson then explained that he would be retiring in the next year or so, and his companion Ted Brian was going to take over his role. At that point Ted Brian said to Den that he was extremely interested in his idea about adding planning, programming and progress checking into the graduate induction programme. He asked Den where he had learned about these essential operations. Den explained that his father had spent many years as Works Manager with Procter and Gamble in both Manchester and Newcastle-upon-Tyne. Den said he had been very interested and impressed to see how they programmed and controlled all their operations within their factories.

Den was not to know at that time how very important a role Ted Brian was to play in his life. Meanwhile Den took one of his mental photographs of Ted, for future reference. He particularly noted his wire-rimmed spectacles, his immaculate clothing and his rather incongruous heavy black leather boots. These were ideal for the building sites, but they reminded Den of the boots worn by the Lancashire miners at Clock Face Colliery, St Helens when he spent an afternoon down their pit on a school visit at the age of thirteen.

Den had an excellent tutor for his cost and bonus work on the Swansea building sites. David Prosser had spent many years with Laing and knew the cost and bonus system inside out. He was meticulous in his methods and data recording. He managed to balance the books to the penny every week, and there were never any complaints about the bonus calculations from the two hundred employees. One very important aspect of the work was to check all the materials on site—to ensure deliveries had been correctly made, that no materials were wasted and that the correct quantities of sand, cement and aggregate were used in producing the site-mixed concrete. A good liaison with the storekeeper was essential for smaller items of materials and equipment.

*****

Den was able to play hockey for the Swansea First XI team that contained three international players and two Olympic British Team players. This helped him to keep fit despite the lengthy, gruelling hours on the building sites. A major event also took place in Swansea while he was living and working there. The 1959 General Election was called by the Prime Minister Harold Macmillan with the very famous, and long lasting, catchphrase 'You've never had it so good.'

Undoubtedly after the long hard years of the 1940s this motto was very apt indeed. It caught the mood of the country and it delivered another victory for the Prime Minister, who even visited Swansea for a final campaign rally in the white stone-faced Town Hall near to the sea front. Den and his wife listened avidly to the election results on a small inefficient radio in their caravan. They stayed up very late indeed that night and Den knew he would be watching out far more carefully in future for what was happening in the field of politics. He was totally absorbed in the General Election night fever, for the first time in his life.

He was only too conscious that his parents had shown their keen interest in political affairs over the last few years without any of their three sons showing any interest whatsoever. That night Den resolved that he would start to take an active interest in politics as soon as his career allowed. He had been negligent in not being sufficiently interested or involved in what was the most important of all the vocations.

*****

Den was surprised how quickly the six months period on cost and bonus sped by. He was also impressed by the progress made on the two sites during that period. He spent a week with the site engineer, taking over his duties and making sure that he understood where all the Ordnance Survey reference levels were, and the grid line reference points that were required for setting out any new buildings and the adjacent roads, kerbs and sewage connections. Fortunately he had had an excellent grounding in all these matters at the Southampton site.

Over the next year Den had to help survey two additional building sites, one at Port Talbot and the other on the outskirts of Swansea. These tasks gave him the opportunity of carrying out all the initial setting out activities and transferring the Ordnance Survey levels onto the sites from the national reference points in the area. Den realised how immensely important the role of the site engineer was. Every gang of men was dependent on the engineer for making sure they had fully understood the intent of the Architect and the Structural Engineer. Moreover they needed to be fed with new information each day on the levels and lines for their particular work. Even when the finishing trades began to install plumbing, electrical and ventilation equipment—or tiling, doors, lifts and kitchen equipment—they needed constant attention to ensure there were no delays to the tight programmes for the contracts. Den ensured that he had a first class, cooperative relationship with all the Site Agents. These Agents were fully responsible for everything that happened on their sites but they often called on Den for a second opinion on any changes to the programme that should be made, any lack of progress by sub-contractors and any quality control matters. This was very educational for Den and helped him enormously in his later roles in Production Control and Site Management.

After a most interesting year as site engineer on the four sites Den was informed that he was required to transfer to a very large construction project in Bootle, Liverpool, on the well-known Dock Road that passes between the dozens of docks and the parallel road heading north out of Liverpool called Stanley Road that passed the end of the road where Den's father owned the garage back in the 1940s. This meant that Den would be working within 18 miles of Southport, and could probably easily find a suitable mobile home site for his caravan along the coastal strip.

Chapter 37

Just before 8 am on the last Monday morning in February 1961 Den arrived at the enormous construction site in Bootle where a brand new animal foods factory was being built for Silcock, the centuries old Liverpool headquartered company. The site measured 800 yards along the road and 400 yards in the direction at right angles to the River Mersey. The site had been chosen very carefully because literally across the Dock Road along its west side were the docks used for shipping goods around the world. On the east side of the site there was direct access by railway, thus allowing deliveries of raw materials to be brought into the site by rail in traditional rail wagons. Along the north side of the site there was a car park and all the offices, cloakrooms and canteens for the site staff and the total workforce.

Den entered the main office door to the administrative offices and asked the way to the Project Manager's Office. He had to look twice because there, staring him in the face was the name sign 'Project Manager—James Cryer.' Surely there was only one Project Manager in Laing called James Cryer. Yes, indeed Den was to be working on the site under the overall control of the same Project Manager who had been in charge at the International Synthetic Rubber Factory site on Southampton Water. He was still smoking the same slim, distinguished looking cigars with a reasonably pleasant smell. Den was very pleased because the Southampton project had been so well managed and controlled—all due to Mr Cryer's skills and abilities. He was convinced this project would run as smoothly but he had not reckoned with the enormous strength and intransigence of the trade union movement in Liverpool.

One of the Section Managers on the Silcock project was Bob Kliskey who had managed part of the Southampton site where Den had worked during his vacation four years earlier. On that site there had been a team of six site engineers. On the animal feeds factory there were four site engineers—of whom Den was one. These numbers reflected the relative sizes of the sites, the complications of the construction processes and the rate at which the work was planned to be carried out, in order to achieve the overall completion date set out in the contractual programme and documentation.

Just as at Southampton there were large excavators as well as queues of lorries delivering aggregates and sand, and removing excavated material. Large railway trucks were used for delivering huge precast building components to the site, and the various rail sidings within the site area were still being installed when Den arrived. All the concrete was to be mixed on site. This was transported around the large site using special dumper trucks and then either lifted up using building hoists or swung into position by one of the many cranes—two of which were able to travel along tracks and two of which were static and serving one major building each.

Den was initially engaged on completing all the railway lines within the site, and then he was allocated the huge and very complicated silo building as his single and challenging assignment. The first main operation on the silo building was to excavate an enormous rectangular hole in the ground 100 yards by 80 yards on plan and 30 feet deep. The east side of this enormous basement area had to be excavated even deeper into the red sandstone rock which underlies the whole of the city and which was used to build the Liverpool Anglican Cathedral—a project that took forty years.

In order to construct the complicated permanent reinforced concrete underground structure for the silo building, it would be necessary for a temporary coffer dam to be constructed over the whole of this deepened area which was 100 yards long and 30 yards across. This would be constructed by Laing as what would be called in contractual terms a 'temporary structure'—despite its huge capacity and the unknown ground conditions that would be encountered during the excavation and steel sheet piling operations that would be entailed.

Den might well have been very carefully selected to be responsible for the silo building, including its very dangerous and complicated substructure and the requirement for a 'temporary structure' design. However, to this day, he believes that it was purely by chance that this major challenge was to be tackled, and had to be overcome, by him with very little, if any, specific technical or design expertise being available within the Laing organisation. He knew that he would have to embark on a technical and research period—in his own time, and at weekends—to investigate the various types of coffer dam that could be designed, the soil and rock conditions and properties that were likely to be encountered and the dewatering techniques that needed to be employed.

First he checked whether any of the building operatives already employed on the site had in the past dealt with similar problems in the Liverpool area. To his delight his chainman, Billy Bowen—who had years before been the Welsh Rugby Union scrum half—had been a chainman on the original Mersey Tunnel project less than a mile away. Fortunately he had kept in touch with several of his former colleagues. When they heard from Billy about the need for a coffer dam to be built on the Silcock site they had immediately applied for a job with Laing, and had been successful.

Den spent many late nights and weekends going through all his Manchester University Soil Mechanics notes which he had taken down in long hand during the Professor Rowe lectures. He then paid a flying visit to his professional body, the Institution of Civil Engineers, in London to examine any relevant information they had in their famed technical reference library. He devised his plan of action. He decided that he would need to consult both Structural Analysis and Soil Mechanics textbooks—written respectively by Professor Matheson, his former Professor of Civil Engineering, and by Professor Rowe, his former Professor of Soil Mechanics—if he were to be able to calculate the earth pressures, the size of the huge timber members across the coffer dam, and the correct type and section of steel sheet piling to be driven into the bedrock by a steam or diesel hammer. He knew that Professor Matheson was by then Vice-Chancellor of the University of Melbourne in Australia and therefore not available for advice. However, he resolved to consult Professor Rowe once he had completed all his research, his calculations, his method statements and his written report on the whole of the coffer dam plan and its execution. He would also keep checking out what he was doing with the three experienced coffer dam 'specialists' that he was fortunate enough to have on site with him.

Den had a tight timetable to achieve and he knew that, although there were several boreholes that had been drilled in the area of the proposed coffer dam, there can often be major changes in the physical nature of underlying strata—particularly within a mile or so of river or sea beds. The Silcock site had both of these and the full scale of the problem would not be known until further samples of the clay and sandstone layers beneath the coffer dam area had been taken and tested at a reputable soil mechanics laboratory.

Den was surprised at the very large sizes of timber beams that he calculated would be needed for the coffer dam. He had decided that there needed to be at least two levels of timber beams, but he was reluctant to go for a third level because this would ramp up the costs and cause the working space for the operatives and their excavation equipment to be too confined. He explained his proposals to the three men with previous experience of the likely strata they would encounter. They were insistent that three levels of beams would be 'over the top.' This was solely based on their intuition, but in the field of soil mechanics Professor Rowe would be the first to agree that in many cases intuition was more important than theory. Professor Rowe was so keen to see his protégé succeed that he offered to carry out any tests on the clay and rock samples himself, and on an immediate turn round basis in view of the tight time schedules involved.

In the event, both the clay samples taken from the lowest levels of the coffer dam, and the sandstone rock samples too, showed that the original site investigation results were valid. This meant that the timber beam sizes and the two ring beams of timber would be adequate. However, it was an enormous relief when the steel sheet piling walls were able to be driven to the level required for the stability of the whole structure. The only possible problem was if there was a rogue storm brewing or if the coffer dam took longer to carry out than envisaged—thus causing the layers of clay and rock formations to weaken, soften and collapse.

*****

Den gave a huge sigh of relief when the permanent reinforced concrete basement slab in the area of the coffer dam was completed. The structural safety was thereby ensured, and the rest of the foundation works to the silo building could be completed in a safe environment. The whole of the perimeter of the building was then backfilled and progress on constructing the superstructure was commenced. The upper levels of the silo building were a combination of very large, standard, precast concrete units and complicated in situ concrete columns. Some of the first ever pre-stressing work on structures was carried out on the Silcock contract. However, the site was probably most famous for the major and lengthy strike of all the building operatives. This was a problem that was not confined to the Bootle project. At that time all the building operatives on the whole of Merseyside were flexing their industrial muscles. They had become too greedy and were demanding such ridiculous concessions that no building clients were willing to invest in a Merseyside project for several years. The differential cost of building on Merseyside compared with elsewhere had become prohibitive. This was a further lesson that became imprinted in Den's mind. In the field of industrial relations there needed to be intercourse, discussion, cooperation and compromise—but with common sense and consensus prevailing.

Chapter 38

A year after Den had arrived at the Silcock site in Liverpool he was advised that he was required to spend the next twelve months at the Laing civil and structural design office. The actual location was at Borehamwood, Hertfordshire only ten minutes by car from the Laing Head Office at Mill Hill—where Den decided to share lodgings with one of his Manchester University undergraduate friends, Ron Matthews.

The first week was an excellent introduction to the design services offered both internally and also to external clients. There were over three hundred design staff comprising architects, civil engineering, structural engineering, electrical, plumbing, ventilation and air conditioning. All the forty indentured civil engineers attending the course had been expanding their site experience since graduating a year and a half earlier. It was explained that they would all primarily be engaged on structural engineering designs that were carried out at Borehamwood, whereas the main design offices were at the Head Office complex ten minutes away at Mill Hill in north west London.

Towards the end of the week Den was asked to attend a brief interview with one of the Design Section Leaders, Peter Westwood, who had lectured to the incomers earlier in the week. Peter was a very well qualified civil and structural engineer and was clearly one of the best design experts in the Laing organisation. He told Den that they wanted him to spend his first eight weeks with a large bored piling subsidiary company of Laing called McKinney Foundations. They had bought this from an American firm and the McKinney office was only five minutes' walk away. Laing had noted Den's keen interest and expertise in soil mechanics and ground engineering. They wanted to give him the benefit of a period with McKinney Foundations which would be classed as very suitable design office training for his professional membership of the Institution of Civil Engineers. The aim of all the forty graduates attending the design office was to satisfy the professional body's requirements that they had been fully and properly trained in design office work in the civil engineering field.

Den was surprised by this development and wondered if it meant that he might fall behind the other 39 incomers in the informal rat-race that would develop over the next year or two while they were gathered together and gaining their design office experience. Peter Westwood explained that Den had been hand-picked for the McKinney assignment and he would do nothing but gain from the experience. Indeed the next two months turned out to be one of Den's most treasured periods of employment in his whole career.

There were less than twenty staff employed at the Borehamwood offices of McKinney Foundations Limited. Steve Nightingale was the Managing Director, Fred Bayliss was the Chief Engineer and Dr Ken Fleming was their ground engineering and soil mechanics guru. Brian Smith was an Assistant in the design office and was a permanent member of the McKinney team.

Fred and Brian explained to Den what their design services involved. They were responsible for ensuring that for every piling contract that the firm bid for, there were full and proper bidding documents, a detailed soil investigation report for the site and details of its location and boundaries. Using this information the design team would then prepare a fully detailed bidding document describing all the work that McKinney would carry out, the time they would require to complete the work and the overall price for the job. All the piling work was obtained on a competitive basis and each bid took several days to put together. This meant that Den was quickly immersed in the detailed procedures involved in the assessment of the soil conditions, the calculation or verification of the loads to be carried by the piling, and the preparation of the bidding document including the price, time and any contractual matters needing special consideration.

All the piling work was carried out in the Greater London area with the piles being drilled down from ground level to the well-known London Clay that had been formed millions of years ago beneath the River Thames valley and all the sedimentary soils beneath the river channel. The River Thames flowed from west to east across the middle of London and discharged out to the sea. The land surface to both the north and the south of the river rose gradually towards ranges of hills and higher ground.

In the yard at Borehamwood all the drilling rigs that were not in use were stored. Den was able to view these and tour the repair workshop to see what maintenance and repairs were being carried out. He was extremely impressed by the huge size of most of the drills which were up to fifteen feet in diameter, The lorries carrying the drilling shafts were large vehicles in themselves but the shafts were more than a hundred feet long, with the facility to double or treble this length of shaft for the longest piles which were often bored down into the stiff clay layers to a depth of several hundred feet. Den and Brian visited a few sites together so that Brian could explain to Den what were the important items to note such as overhead obstacles, poor access and sites that needed further clearance before drilling rigs could be employed.

Den was asked in his first week to carry out a complete site assessment, bearing capacity calculations, piling layouts and an estimate of the time needed for the contract plus his recommended bidding price. This was an exciting procedure for Den and he realised that the McKinney operation was a typical example of what the private sector did. It had to meet the needs of customers and clients in the most cost effective way. It had to give value for money, obtain work in competition and needed to ensure the work was carried out within the budget with an adequate allowance made for overheads and profit. This was why Den had become a Conservative Party supporter. They believed in competition and free enterprise. They were the ones who built up businesses and provided employment for both white and blue collar employees. It was the Conservatives who realised that the world was a fiercely competitive arena in which only the fittest, strongest and most able would survive.

Den completed all the work needed to submit the bid for his first contract within two days, of which half a day had to be spent reading a detailed soil and site investigation report containing borehole logs which had been carried out by one of the many soil and site investigation organisations who owed their very existence to the London Clay that had been deposited millions of years earlier. Fred and Ken Fleming joined Brian and Den to go through his recommendations. They were very happy with his work, after receiving satisfactory answers from Den on a few detailed points. They were particularly keen on ensuring that he had calculated the number of tons each bored pile would be able to support. All the load could be assumed to be carried on the circular base founded on solid London Clay. However, depending on the nature of the subsoil strata throughout the height of the pile, some of the load could be assumed to be borne by what was called 'skin friction' where the sides of the drilled shaft would take part of the load.

Some of the largest diameter bored piles were under-reamed, with a special extension piece fitted to the bottom of the drilling shaft—enabling for example a 12 feet diameter bored pile to be enlarged for its last three metres to become an 18 feet diameter bored pile. This simple device meant that more than twice the usual load could be carried by the under-reamed pile. Den had learned so much in his two months with McKinney Foundations that the routine reinforced concrete design of floor slabs, columns and beams throughout several industrial or commercial buildings that he carried out later seemed relatively dull. However, all the designs, drawings and calculations would be able to be used when he submitted actual working schemes as part of the documentation that had to accompany his face to face interviews with two or more very experienced Fellows of the Institution of Civil Engineers. Their job would be to ask Den about his site experience and design experience before recommending that he be approved as a fully-fledged professional member. The only other task he faced was to write three essays, inside a period of four hours, from a selection of subjects relating to civil engineering and its place in society.

*****

During the months that Den spent on his structural design work in the Borehamwood office any doubts about his career aim of being a Member of Parliament were completely removed. This was because of the battle of wits between President Kennedy of the United States of America and President Khrushchev of Russia. The whole world was at risk of becoming involved in a nuclear weapons war between these two world powers—without any opportunity of having any say in the matter. There was a head to head stand-off between these two world leaders who did not, and could not trust each other. Thankfully common sense prevailed after thirteen days of tension, but only after very detailed and lengthy exchanges had been played out with the whole world watching and wondering whether there might be a Third World War.

After his experience of the Second World War—and his father's six years in the Burma jungle—Den wanted to do all he possibly could to prevent any further fruitless conflicts between major world powers.

Meanwhile he had to qualify as a professional civil engineer, gain essential experience in managerial and executive positions—and start on what he imagined was a long, rocky road and a high, greasy pole for anyone wishing to become an elected representative of the people.

If Robert Hudson MP, the Honourable Member for Southport, had managed the political journey and the climb up the pole, so could he—given enough time.

Chapter 39

Den had no idea what lay in store for his future career with Laing until he was asked to meet Mr Frank Bryer, Head of the new Production Control Department, at his office in the Mill Hill headquarters of the Laing organisation. Frank Bryer was clearly earmarked for the top layers within the company. He had a distinguished Royal Air Force service record behind him, and he had recently been totally responsible for the overall management and direction of one of the largest Laing projects ever. This was a massive Head Office and production plant in Gillingham, Kent for Bowater, the world wide packaging firm. Laing had made an excellent film about the whole scheme, which Den had been highly impressed by.

After a few minutes of getting to know each other Mr Bryer explained how the Production Control Department had been formed over the last few months. It comprised cost and bonus, work study, planning and progress checking—including ensuring that all the design information and materials needed to execute the work on site were available in good time. Mr Bryer wanted Den to set up a new department, all on his own, based at Head Office. He explained that Den would be attached to the Mechanical and Electrical Engineering Department, under Mr John Stanley. He wanted Den to set up a Mechanical and Electrical Services Production Control Department and to spend half of each week up in Birmingham where Laing were building the Bull Ring Shopping Centre right in the heart of the city.

Den realised that he would be spending at least a further two years away from his wife and modest home up in Southport. However, he saw this new appointment as a tremendous opportunity to become more acquainted with all the Head Office top people, with the enormously important services installations that were becoming far more complex and important on all construction projects—and be a key player on the Bull Ring project. His lodgings were a five minute walk from the Head Office and he was issued with a modest saloon car for the days when he needed to be up in Birmingham, staying in bed and breakfast accommodation.

Den met John Stanley and there was an instant rapport between the two—both of them being civil engineers. John ran the mechanical, electrical, plumbing and air conditioning design services for Laing. Most of their work was for sites where Laing were the main contractor, but the 'M&E' department also provided services to property developers, housing firms, local authorities and even major airports. Den was introduced to all the section heads by John Stanley, and given direct access to any of them at all times. There were 120 staff in all.

Den immediately visited the Bull Ring site and realised what a very large site it was. It fitted into the existing shopping streets and was built over and around the main railway station in New Street. It was clear that construction and services installations would have to be very carefully planned if they were to be properly integrated into all the existing services and surrounding properties. After a discussion with the overall Project Manager for the Bull Ring contract Den met an invaluable member of the Laing team. Harold Williams was sixty years of age and had a very sharp mind plus an encyclopaedic knowledge of everything involved in the mechanical and electrical services field. Harold had worked, like Den's father, in the Royal Electrical and Mechanical Engineers (REME) in the British Army.

Den soon realised that he would be very dependent on Harold for detailed information about all the important parts of the various services installations—particularly boilers, air conditioning plant, ventilation ducting, testing routines and lift installations. In all these areas Harold knew all the important facts but his knowledge had not been put to its best use. He kept complaining, quite rightly, about the absence of knowledge about M&E services by all the Laing personnel. This was not surprising because Laing was a building and civil engineering firm that had only just realised that the services work was often more important than everything else, with huge contract values being provided by nominated specialist suppliers and subcontractors about whose work the main contractor on the site would have very limited knowledge or understanding. This was a major problem for the whole construction industry, and needed addressing and dealing with.

Harold had so much useful information in his head that Den decided he should attempt to capture it. This would help him focus his work on the Bull

Ring in the most effective way—and could probably be put to a much wider use throughout the Laing group. Den's first aim was to draw up detailed programmes for all the M&E installations, so that the large number of Laing personnel would understand how this work integrated into their own. He knew that all these programmes would need to have the progress actually achieved marked up on a fortnightly basis, so that any adverse trends could be identified immediately—and effective action taken. Den needed to visit some of the major suppliers and learn a great deal about the manufacturing processes involved. Den's work involved all parts of the Bull Ring construction site and some night shift working was introduced when key items of plant and equipment needed to catch up with all the other construction activities.

By the time the Bull Ring contract was reaching its completion Den was busy writing two important reference documents. One explained the important interdependencies between M&E work and that of the main contractors; it also showed the best ways of programming this work and integrating it into the main construction and finishings work. The other used readily available information within the Laing archives to enable the Laing estimators to price work for all the various types of M&E projects—even if they had very little knowledge of the work involved. The Deputy Chief Estimator in Laing was amazed that Den was able to use all the archived information to produce what became a main reference document for all the Laing estimating teams.

Towards the end of the Bull Ring project Den was surprised to hear that Ted Brian, whom he had met three years ago in Swansea, was now Head of the Production Control Department and Frank Bryer had moved to another part of the Laing empire as its Managing Director. Den had by then completed his two manuals,

Chapter 40

Den was not at all surprised to receive a telephone call asking him to meet the new Head of Production Control. He was however surprised by what Mr Brian wanted him to do. First he asked Den to call him 'Ted.' Secondly he brought Den up to date with developments in not only the Production Control Department but also in the ways that Laing were changing their whole approach to managing and controlling all their construction sites. Many of the senior management staff were reaching retirement age and there would be a lack of suitable managers coming up through the normal channels to fill all the gaps. Top level decisions had been taken to boost the role of Production Control on all the sites. This department had attracted many of the best graduates and qualified potential managers within the Laing organisation. All of these needed to be able to take over as Site Agents and Project Managers in the next few years, or they would become frustrated, impatient and wish to leave for other construction companies—particularly when higher levels of investment in construction were being made by both the public and private sectors.

Den agreed that Laing had correctly judged what the situation was, and he told Ted that he thought the approach being considered was a very wise and far-sighted one. It was then that Ted said 'Den, I want you to go immediately up to Chester where the city centre is being rebuilt by us, and where the present team needs beefing up—without delay.'

Ted explained that Den would be the right hand man to Bob Spencer who was nearing his retirement age, and had just built a fifteen mile new stretch of the M6 motorway through Staffordshire. There were several different contracts being built by Laing in Chester—the largest one by far being the Grosvenor Laing Development which embraced a new shopping centre and extensions to the famous Grosvenor Hotel. This stood alongside the East Gate part of the original Roman walls built around the city two thousand years ago.

*****

Den gave notice to his landlady in Mill Hill and travelled home to Southport on the Friday evening. He had just received confirmation that he had been accepted as a full professional civil engineer by the Institution at the earliest age permitted. He was now not just holding a First Class Honours Bachelor of Science degree in Civil Engineering, he was also a Member of the Institution of Civil Engineers. Den knew, of course, that qualifications were no good to any employer unless the person holding them was able to carry out the job allocated to them in an effective and efficient manner. He also knew that loyalty and service to a firm were essential attributes of any employee.

*****

Den allowed plenty of time for his car journey to Chester. The overall distance was 40 miles but he would have to negotiate his way to the best entrance in Liverpool for the Mersey Tunnel complex so that he emerged on the Birkenhead side where the main A41 road ran down the east side of the Wirral peninsula and headed straight towards Chester.

The journey took an hour and a half but he arrived well before his appointment with Bob Spencer in the Project Office just off Pepper Street. Bob was just a few inches under five foot in height. He had a full head of white, wavy hair, a grey moustache and a very craggy face, no doubt far more weather-beaten than most of the newer breed of project managers. Bob smoked one cigarette after another and was not at home in his office unless it was full of cigarette stubs. He greeted Den in a very friendly manner and started to explain the various contracts in Chester using the site drawings around his office walls. It was clear that Bob was enjoying carrying out the Chester Redevelopment contracts but he soon admitted to Den that he was not a 'buildings man.' He was really a Civil Engineering Project Manager and his last appointment had suited him down to the ground. He had indeed carried out an excellent job on the M6 Motorway contract, about which Laing were making a film which Bob was arranging to show one evening to all the Chester site staff, consultants and clients in one of the Grosvenor Hotel rooms.

Bob Spencer took Den round the various contracts that Laing were carrying out, all within the original Roman walls of the city. There was a Site Agent on each of these and they were all highly motivated, loyal Laing employees. Den then met Mungo Johnson who was supposedly in charge of the Production Control activities. He was very experienced on cost and bonus but had very little knowledge or experience of planning, progress checking and computerisation. However, he had spent all his working life with Laing and knew many people in the company.

Covering Production Control on two of the sites were two excellent staff members who had passed the intensive three year course in Construction Technology at the Liverpool College of Building. They had recently been accepted as Members of the Institute of Building and both of them were intelligent and hard working—but most important of all, they had good management and communication skills. Den soon weighed up that Eric Mitchell and David Booth would be his two henchmen. They had immediately responded positively to Den's introduction into the Laing team at Chester.

Unfortunately Den had to deal with some complaints from one of the Grosvenor Hotel's most loyal hotel guests—because of the noise of drilling holes through walls in the early hours. This was necessary so that dimensions could be taken by engineers and surveying staff when there was no disturbance from hotel guests or staff who would normally be milling around in the restaurant, dining rooms and bars used for conferences, meetings and other special occasions. The hotel guest involved was a permanent occupier of a suite in the hotel for many years. It was Sir Gerald Nabarro QC MP who was Member of Parliament for the town of Kidderminster. Despite his initial pompous and bombastic approach Sir Gerald was quick to understand why the work needed to be carried out at nights, and a rapid and firm agreement was reached whereby no such work would ever be carried out in future if the Honourable Member was 'in residence' in his suite.

*****

During the excavations to one of the important parts of the redevelopment area, Roman baths and an underground heating system were discovered. This meant that a six months delay to the original programme for the work in that area was inevitable, to allow the important archaeological investigations to be carried out. However, with careful re-programming Eric and David managed to maintain the original contractual completion dates. One of the major problems on the Chester contracts, before Den's arrival, was the slow production of the working drawings for the scheme by the very reputable architect's office in Shrewsbury. Den had to explain to all the design teams that there were lengthy delivery periods for many of the key materials and components; accordingly he negotiated and agreed precise release dates for the design information needed from both the architect and the structural engineer, an excellent firm based in London.

*****

One day there was a serious accident which could have turned out very nasty indeed. When the roof slab of the shopping centre was being poured, the dumper truck containing concrete in its large bucket, together with its driver, fell right through the floor to the level below. Den was standing only yards away and everything seemed to happen in slow motion. It was clear that the motion of the heavy load of concrete, being transported at only a few miles per hour, was sufficient to cause an overload on the temporary wooden formwork which was supported by metal strutting based firmly on the concrete floor slab one level down. The dumper driver was uninjured and the formwork was reinstated that same day, and the area concreted safely the following day— using wheelbarrows and a team of labourers to deliver the concrete safely across the roof area.

The date of this incident has always been imprinted in Den's mind because it was Thursday 15 October 1964. That was the date of the General Election which marked the end of thirteen years of Conservative government.

The General Foreman in charge of the concreting operation was stood next to Den on the roof slab when the collapse occurred. Bart Durkin was an Irishman who had been a General Foreman with Laing for more than thirty years. When the collapse happened he turned to Den and said 'Oh well, oi t'ink oid better go and vote.' Den pointed out to Bart that he could vote up to 9 pm that evening, so why the hurry? He had not realised that Bart's comment was just his Irish sense of humour coming to the surface, at a time of great relief that there had been no injuries.

That night the ten pin bowlers among the Laing Chester site staff had agreed to play challenge matches against each other right through the night. Nobody, apart from Den, was particularly interested in politics but this was a novel idea by the operators of the Bowling Alley minutes away from the site offices. Den had rented a bedsit room within the city walls and he could be on site within five minutes. The idea of staying up all night bowling with his best friends and business colleagues was very appealing. However, as the results of the voting in the hundreds of constituencies were broadcast on the television screens around the Bowling Alley, Den gradually realised that the overall result would be very close indeed. It was not looking at all good for the Conservative Party, under their new Leader Sir Alec Douglas Hume. It could well be that within a few hours Harold Wilson would be the new Prime Minister.

Labour won the election but had an overall majority of only four seats. Sir Gerald Nabarro did not stand in the election because of ill health.

*****

Bob Spencer had a tremendous temper and even at important meetings with the design professionals, with important Laing visiting managers, and at routine meetings with staff, Site Agents and subcontractors he would suddenly flare up and be unable to cool off for hours afterwards. Den was not surprised to hear one day from the head of the small secretarial team on site that Bob had been rushed to hospital with a suspected heart attack. This was a sad moment for everyone on site, but most particularly for his loyal wife and family members. Den visited him in hospital on several occasions but there was no real likelihood of Bob ever returning to his job.

Ted Brian visited the site within days, satisfied himself that Den was more than capable of assuming full responsibility for the Chester contracts—and also informed Den that he had a very interesting prospect for him, once the Chester work was into its final stages. Den had enjoyed the work at Chester enormously. There was an excellent spirit of co-operation between the manual workers and all the managerial staff. All the contracts were duly completed 'On Time' despite all the problems encountered. By then Den was totally immersed in his next appointment under the guiding hand of Ted Brian.

Chapter 41

After more than two years in charge of the Chester contracts, Den was asked by Ted Brian to set up the Production Control activities for all the industrialised building systems that Laing were involved in. The newly formed Industrialised Building Systems 'IBS' organisation was based in Edgware only ten minutes from Mill Hill where the Laing Head Office was, and only ten minutes from Borehamwood where Den had worked for McKinney Foundations and in the design offices.

Den was fortunate enough to buy the Borehamwood house owned by the Managing Director of Laing Housing who was being transferred to Canada to take over the extensive operations that Laing had over there. It was always going to be difficult for Den to be able to afford to buy a home around London because of the huge differential in house prices between the North West of England and London. With this transfer to London into a key posting the problem had been solved.

The Laing plan was that IBS would take over all the existing and future 'systems' or 'industrialised building' operations of the company. These were very extensive indeed. Laing had developed their own precast concrete systems for building schools, office blocks and housing up to four stories. Laing had also purchased the United Kingdom rights to employ a very fast and efficient French system using huge steel tunnels and ready mixed concrete for multi-storey housing 'SECTRA' and a Danish precast concrete system 'Jespersen.' The Danish system required three factories to be built and an entire fleet of special long trailers to be bought for transportation, and tower cranes to be used for hoisting all the units into position. All these operations showed that Laing were responding positively to the demands of both the Government and the people for far more homes to be built to house the ever-increasing population throughout the country.

Den headed up a team of specialist planners, work study, computer programmers and construction experts. They formed the central specialist team of experts who provided all the production controllers and training needed for all this workload. Den's team would go out into the various operating regions of Laing to carry out the services needed on the numerous sites and in the three Jespersen factories. All the local authorities and housing organisations up and down the country were eager customers for these services and Laing expanded its level of activity year by year. It was not long before Ted Brian asked Den to take over all the Production Control activities in the largest Region of all—the London Region stretching from Bournemouth up to Coventry and over to the Wash. Den had 130 Production Control staff under his control and there were 70 building sites including the enormous Barbican housing scheme in London, several major hospitals and the 40 storey new headquarters office complex for BP in Moorfields, London. When Ted Brian held his Production Control Quarterly Meetings, Den attended as the Regional Production Controller with by far the largest geographical area and number of staff. By then the importance of Production Control throughout the whole of the Laing organisation was both crucial and legendary.

Construction work was growing at such a pace that it was agreed that the London Region should be split into two, North London and South London. At the same time Laing obtained a large housing contract in north London where more than 500 homes had to be built in less than two years. Laing had no spare managers available to deal with this unexpected situation and Den was asked to set up from scratch the whole team to carry out this multi- site contract for the London Borough of Haringey. There were only six weeks to go before the contract starting date, however Den was thrilled to have his first management position—reporting to the former London Regional Manager, Les Holliday, who was now a Director of John Laing Construction. Den had built up a good relationship with Les Holliday, who had started with Laing decades before as a joiner in South Wales. When Les was London Regional Manager and Den his Regional Production Controller they had built up a first class construction operation covering all the South East corner of England.

By the time Den started his work on the Haringey project he had learned that Ted Brian had become the Chief Executive of Norwest Holst, with an annual turnover of nearly £80 million. Den kept in touch with Ted's progress via the technical journals, the broadsheets and the financial press—but they were both too busy to make contact with each other for several years. Ted quickly turned round the civil engineering firm Norwest Holst from big losses into huge profits—and increased their turnover at the same time. He was then appointed to the Main Board of Trafalgar House, the business empire of Nigel Broakes. This very newsworthy publicly quoted company was a highly profitable conglomerate with property development, shipping and construction as its main activities.

Chapter 42

Den began to make contact with several of his previous staff who had impressed him with their resourcefulness and determination. He needed three capable managers to take complete control of the three main building sites and he knew that all the existing and qualified Site Agents were totally engaged, working at maximum capacity in the various Regions. He needed people who lived within a half hour drive of Tottenham in north east London where his four sites were situated. He found that the former head of the Work Study Department was being refused a transfer into management. Gerry van Lottum had played cricket for the Laing XI under Den's captaincy and they had worked together on several tricky site problems. Gerry was trustworthy, hardworking and intelligent. He could manage the second site to start and help Den with all the main preparatory work for the others. One down, two to go.

One of the sites was on top of a very steep hill, called Uplands Road. Den considered that a civil engineer was needed for that site. Jerry Evans was not a top notch engineer but Den needed a manager. In the annual personal assessments of all the hundreds of staff under his control Den had pointed out several times that Jerry wanted to be a Site Agent—and that he was, in Den's opinion, a very suitable candidate. One of the Regional Managers had put the inappropriate comment 'He is as weak as water' directly under Den's contrary assessment of Jerry's ability. This incorrect assessment had been raised by Den with the Regional Manager concerned, who said 'Oh well. I hardly know him.' Den phoned Jerry without delay and found that he was about to leave John Laing for another firm. Den explained that he had a Site Agent vacancy on the Haringey project that needed filling immediately. His timing could not have been better, and Jerry moved into the small project office at Mill Hill with Gerry and Den.

The three colleagues knew exactly what steps had to be taken to ensure that the first three sites could start on time. All three were also determined that all the contracts at Haringey would be 'completed on time' to quote the Laing motto.

*****

The three colleagues carried out the most thorough pre-contract arrangements and procedures that had ever been undertaken. They each had every reason to want to succeed. This was a unique opportunity for them all to shine, and gain invaluable experience in their chosen route to the top. All the design information available from the architect, the structural engineer and the mechanical and electrical design team needed to be assimilated as soon as possible. Any long delivery periods for steel reinforcement and facing bricks needed checking. Temporary site office accommodation needed ordering and all the local suppliers checking out, to ensure they would be able to meet the Haringey site requirements. The arrangements for the large amounts of earth removal were checked, and the journey times and routes for the disposal lorries investigated. The various types of ready-mix concrete were designed, test cubes were made and tested to destruction at the Laing laboratories at Borehamwood.

Nothing was left to chance and all the key back up staff were chosen and briefed. Detailed planning of all the operations for the first three months was carried out and detailed works programmes produced so that weekly progress checks could be made. The pressure on the three key staff grew during the six weeks before site possession. However, as soon as the deliveries and erection of the temporary site offices and fencing began, it seemed that the pressure was starting to dissipate—because physical progress on the sites had begun, at last.

*****

Den was surprised when there was a knock on the door of his site office at the Tewkesbury Road site in Tottenham. Ken Williams had been told to report to Den at the site by his Area Agent in Hertfordshire where he had been a section manager on a sizeable housing contract. Den quizzed Ken about his work for Laing over his ten years with the firm, and told him what the Haringey arrangements would be. Den was happy to accept this new recruit

189

'out of the blue' but stressed that he would review his appointment as Site Agent at the end of his first month on the site. This arrangement worked well because Ken pulled out all the stops and showed what he was capable of.

Some of the most important positions on construction sites are held by blue collar workers who have never worked for the particular main contractor before in their lives. A large amount of good luck is involved in such appointments, with personal recommendations by previous work colleagues being the best way to ensure success and prevent unsuitable arrangements. Den had not realised what a focal point for building trade workers Tottenham had become. Cheap housing was available, large amounts of redevelopment had been carried out in the area—and Tottenham was a key and easy access point for tradesmen who travelled in from the north or east suburbs. Word of the new projects starting up in Tottenham spread rapidly and the Tewkesbury Road site office was an excellent recruiting centre for the experienced and reliable labourers, concrete gangs, joiners and bricklayers that were needed.

*****

After three months on site all the work was on programme and the three Site Agents were managing and controlling their sites very capably. A second site of traditional two storey housing had to be started at the Tewkesbury Road site, but Ken took this in his stride. Gerry van Lottum was enjoying every minute on his Kent Road site, only half a mile away. Up the hill at Uplands Road however a problem had emerged. Jerry Evans was dismayed at the huge amount of water that seeped into every excavation trench or drainage run—despite there being hardly any rainfall and the site being situated at the top of a hill.

Den and Jerry pored over the initial soils investigation report for the Uplands Road site. There was little or no reference to high water levels, and there was no instruction whatsoever for any piling work to be carried out around the eight residential blocks. Den demanded that there should be a special new soil investigation report carried out by drilling three boreholes close to the waterlogged areas. This work would only take three days and the results of any tests on the soil samples would only take a further three days. Meanwhile Den had a stroke of good luck. He read in his weekly professional civil engineer circular that Professor Rowe was speaking at the Institution of

Civil Engineers that very evening on the subject 'Difficult sites I have known.' This title was very apt and Den even put a question to his former Professor at the meeting. He also had a word with Professor Rowe after the meeting. Professor Rowe said that when the main railway line through Tottenham had been excavated decades before there had been tremendous problems with water seepage. From what Den described he said it was possible that a major earth slippage could take place. He volunteered to visit the site as soon as the laboratory test results of the soil samples were available. Meanwhile he said that it seemed to him that insufficient site investigation work had been carried out by the engineering consultants.

When Professor Rowe visited the site the following week he spotted clear evidence of underground water springs near the surface at the very top of the hill. He said that the whole site should have had a row of bored piling across the full length of the six and eight storey blocks of flats. He complimented Den on the swift action he had taken—and said he would keep in touch with Den on further developments. This involvement of the best world expert brought about a full acceptance by the civil and structural design engineers that they had grossly underestimated the underground problems associated with the site.

The final result was a complete re-design of the foundations for the Uplands Road site. The additional work was added to the contract documents and Laing, quite properly, lodged a major claim for all this extra work, for the extension of the contract period, and for the additional overheads and expenses. In retrospect it was fortunate that Den had been put in charge of all the Haringey work. It was inconceivable that anyone else would have spotted the danger signals, sorted out the problem so quickly and made the whole hillside stable and fit for residential accommodation to be built on it.

Den stayed on the Haringey project until the whole scheme was virtually complete. By then he had spent his first ten years of postgraduate experience with one of the best construction companies in the world. To his total surprise he was chosen to be the Deputy Chief Executive of the National Building Agency based close to the River Thames and Fleet Street. The 'NBA' was a quasi-government body charged with bringing the construction industry up to speed with the rest of industry. This was Den's first experience of working in the public sector, and he was set to enjoy the tough challenges that he would face.

Chapter 43

During the weekend before taking up his position as Deputy Chief Executive at the National Building Agency, Den mulled over the events of the last twelve months, and was amazed how rapidly his future family and career prospects had both changed and improved over this period. He had become the very proud father of a daughter, Amanda, who had made him think much more about his long term aims. He was carefully considering whether he should stay with Laing—the only firm he had ever worked for, both as a civil engineer and as a manager. He was still in his twenties and was only too well aware that the next step was to become a director, and there had never been a director in the Laing group under the age of forty. He was also pondering how he could pursue his long term vocational calling to become a Member of Parliament—a Servant of the People.

His mother had a favourite saying 'procrastination is the thief of time.' He decided to 'take a leaf out of her book,' and act without any further delay. He took his first steps to becoming an elected representative of the people. He had read in the press that Cecil Parkinson had been appointed to be the person in charge of the selection of all Conservative Members of Parliament. Accordingly he telephoned the Conservative Central Office in Smith Square, only a five minute walk from the Houses of Parliament. He spoke to Cecil's personal assistant and explained that he wanted to become a Member of Parliament, and asked what he needed to do to start the ball rolling. After a few questions to Den about his background and his business experience she told him that Cecil would want to meet him one evening in the Central Lobby of the Houses of Parliament so that they could have a brief chat. She offered three dates in the next few weeks and asked Den to make sure he would be available to meet Cecil on any of these dates. She would then ring him to confirm the date on which he would be seen.

Den recognised Cecil's face as soon as he breezed into the Central Lobby. He shook Den's hand and said he would be taking him into the Member's Bar on the same floor which overlooked the river. When they were sitting down for a chat, Cecil introduced Den to Sir Michael Havers QC MP about whom he said 'Michael was our Solicitor General, and he is a great friend of mine.'

After a drink and a chat Cecil summarised the situation by saying 'Den, your business experience to date is extremely impressive, but if you want to be a Member of Parliament you need to join the Party immediately, and become as active in the Party as you possibly can be, without delay.' At that time Cecil was a top accountant and director of a respectable house builder and developer, but not yet a Member of Parliament.

Den telephoned the nearest Conservative Party Constituency Office to his home address. It was in the Barnet constituency and the local Member of Parliament was Sir Reginald Maudling MP, who had been Chancellor of the Exchequer for the final two years of the Conservative Government. His constituency Agent was Arthur Fawcett and the office was only ten minutes by car from Den's home. Den agreed to go and meet Arthur the following afternoon. He was just over five feet tall, he had a large black beard and appeared rather forbidding, at first sight. Arthur could not have been more helpful. He explained to Den that one of the twenty two Conservative branches in the constituency was defunct due to the advanced age and ill health of its Chairman, Major Williams—a distinguished war veteran. There were only three months before the London Borough of Barnet Council Elections in May and they only had two candidates, out of the three required for the full complement in the Arkley Ward. One was the current Mayor of Barnet, Councillor Percy Woodruff, and the other was a local solicitor, Bob Stewart. Den learned from Arthur that the Arkley Ward even included eight roads that were in Borehamwood, where Den lived.

Den immediately offered his wholehearted efforts to helping out in the Ward. This offer was accepted with gratitude by Arthur Fawcett, subject to the formal agreement of Major Williams and his wife. Den started to deliver leaflets and knock on the doors of the local electorate in the Arkley Ward, after meeting the Mayor and Bob Stewart. They both said they would welcome Den becoming the third candidate for their ward, if he were interested. Den most definitely was interested, and within three months he and Bob had called on all the homes, delivered leaflets in every letterbox and, together with the re-elected

Mayor, they had won the three seats in the Arkley Ward election by a clear majority of over 900 votes for each of them.

Den attended a brief formal meeting of the Arkley Branch and was duly elected as the new Chairman. He soon surrounded himself with a bunch of young housewives and local business people on the branch committee. In retrospect, Den could not complain about the speedy progress he had been able to make in climbing the greasy pole of politics. Now, with his new job in the public sector, he would be much better able to understand the mechanics of government—at both the local level, and at the national level. Indeed the part time Chairman of the National Building Agency was a Member of the House of Lords, and he had been a General in the British Army.

At his interview for the National Building Agency, Den's positions as a Councillor for the London Borough of Barnet and a member of its Finance Committee, its Education Committee and its Public Works Committee proved no handicap whatsoever. The NBA carried out design and consultancy services for New Town corporations, health authorities and local authorities. The Chief Executive, Dr Bill Chan, and the Managing Director, Cleeve Barr, were most interested in his local government experience and considered that this would strengthen the role of the NBA. They would be able to work for both their public and private sector clients with a better informed understanding of them, helped by Den's intimate knowledge of their processes and procedures.

*****

Den spent his first few days at the National Building Agency meeting all the top people and his own staff of twenty who worked in the London office. He was also responsible for a proven team of six in Northern Ireland, four in Edinburgh, two in Newcastle-upon-Tyne and two in Manchester. In London there were three economics and market research experts, four construction engineers and thirteen others with a local authority, health authority or construction background. Much of the work carried out by his staff was obtained on a commercial basis following a bidding process against a limited number of rival organisations. However, more than half of the annual turnover was spent on what was called 'grant in aid.' This was money obtained directly from the government department responsible for the National Building Agency, namely the Ministry of Public Building and Works. Lengthy negotiations were carried out each year to explain and justify the various amounts of 'grant- in-aid' that the NBA should receive for non-project related research and development purposes.

Den attended his first Management Board meeting in his first week. This was held in the morning and on the same day as the Main Board Meeting, chaired by Lord Bourne and attended by the Board of Directors who represented the whole of the construction industry. On this Main Board were heads of major manufacturers, architects, civil and structural engineers, quantity surveyors, research organisations and the trade unions. These notable people met the Management Board over a buffet lunch and would sometimes hold a formal joint session in the afternoon. Den had heard and read a great deal about the various heads of industry on the Main Board and was very impressed indeed by all of them. These were the top people of one of the most important business sectors in the United Kingdom economy. It was indeed a privilege and a pleasure to meet and work with them.

The economics and market research section of his responsibilities was significant and impressive. They were charged with forecasting trends within the construction and allied industries, with statistics forming a large part of their workload. However, they had many experienced managers and former materials producers amongst their ranks. Their job was to help firms of all sizes to adapt their products to any changing demands before they experienced falls in their market shares. Continuous market research was carried out by the NBA and this helped to forge very strong bonds with the leading trade associations and major manufacturers.

At that time Northern Ireland was in turmoil and three staff cars were blown to pieces in the NBA underground car park during one of Den's visits to the province. Excellent work was being carried out in all the major hospitals, most of which were Teaching Hospitals, and of the highest standards. Major extensions were being built to four of the largest hospitals in Northern Ireland and the NBA were managing and controlling these huge investments in an efficient and effective way. Similar project management contracts were bid for and obtained to help with major extensions to the Southampton General Hospital, Hope and Withington Hospitals in Manchester, Arrowe Park in Birkenhead and the Ninewells Teaching Hospital in Dundee.

Questions in Parliament about the enormous and unacceptable over-runs on time and financial expenditure on hospital building work in the United

Kingdom were legendary in the 1960s. The construction time was often doubled and the financial expenditure was always grossly over budget. Den made sure that the team of planners, production controllers and progress chasers allocated to each scheme were of the highest calibre. Market fees were charged to the hospital authorities for this essential work which was extremely beneficial to the functioning of the National Health Service. Time and cost over-runs were dramatically reduced, and consequently no further questions were raised in the Houses of Parliament.

Den had realised for many years that the construction industry had inadequate training and education facilities in basic management and control procedures. He set up a very full programme of courses on these important matters. These were held around the country and in the NBA regional offices on a cost per course basis. They were all very well attended, much appreciated and profitable.

A new sector of work was provided for new town development corporations such as Milton Keynes, Runcorn and East Kilbride. This was pioneering work and very much needed by the small development corporation teams that were not experienced in large infrastructure work such as roads and sewers—nor the fundamental needs of large scale housing and industrial developments.

The reputation of the NBA in all these fields was growing, not just in the United Kingdom but overseas as well. Den was asked by the South African government to undertake a lecture tour round all their cities—paid for by them—including a speaking engagement at the Builders Conference in Durban, and advice on a large hospital they were aiming to build in Cape Town. The Managing Director of the NBA, Cleeve Barr, visited South Africa at the same time and put to Den his major fears that the new Conservative government under Edward Heath would want to close down the Agency which had been created by the previous Labour government.

Den explained that, in his view, the new government would—quite rightly—want even better value for money from the NBA. This meant there would probably be a severe reduction in the level of grant-in-aid. However, all departments of the NBA had proved over many years that they could match the private sector and carry out assignments, management or design, on a competitive basis—and cover their costs. Indeed Den, on his return to the United Kingdom, resolved that he would immediately reduce the level of grant bid for by all his staff to zero. Den created two strong new streams of activity—namely production control for construction firms and project management for very large property developers who had little, or no, idea how to manage and control the timetable and costs for their extremely complex schemes. Within months Den was fully operating all his NBA activities without the need for any grant from the government.

*****

During his time at the NBA the 1970 General Election was called by the Prime Minister, Harold Wilson. Den had made such an impact on Councillor Alan Fletcher, the Leader of the Conservative Group at the London Borough of Barnet that he insisted on Den putting his name forward to become the Member of Parliament for one of the four constituencies within the London Borough of Barnet, namely Hendon North, the northern border of which was only two hundred yards from Den's home in Borehamwood. Den reached the short list of eight but made the fatal mistake of saying that he would not be willing to vote for the death penalty, which was a key issue within the Party at that time. The Leader of the Conservative Group, who was an eminent barrister, then pleaded with Den to contest the vacancy that had arisen on the Greater London Council for the London Borough of Barnet as a whole. This covered four parliamentary seats and an electorate of around 300,000. Den came second in the voting for the GLC Conservative candidate vacancy, being beaten by a very sensible level-headed Jewish lady who had run the Citizens Advice Bureau in the Edgware and Mill Hill areas for several years.

The General Election campaign for the Barnet constituency in June 1970 was fought on the old constituency boundaries. At that time Reginald Maudling's constituency spilled over into the county of Hertfordshire, taking in the whole of Borehamwood and several towns and villages to the north of Barnet. At the same General Election, Cecil Parkinson was selected to fight the seat of Northampton, about 50 miles north of Barnet.

Den ran much of the Borehamwood part of the General Election campaign and was the 'warm up speaker' for the sitting Member, Reginald Maudling, who had a safe seat. Den's job as the 'warm up speaker' was to attend all the campaign rallies and meetings ahead of the sitting Member, speak to the audiences and get them 'warmed up.' He had to ensure that they were ready and willing to give 'Reggie' a loud cheering welcome and an attentive ear, while Den—having introduced the person they had all come to hear—moved on to the next venue. This public speaking experience was invaluable to Den, and much appreciated by the sitting Member—who was duly re-elected as the Honourable Member for the Parliamentary Constituency of Barnet.

The man appointed by the new Prime Minister, Edward Heath, to be Chancellor of the Exchequer in his new government was the very impressive, highly intelligent, Iain Macleod but he died after only a few months in office. By that time Cecil Parkinson had resigned himself, at the age of 40, to never being able to fulfil his desire to serve the people as a Member of Parliament, even though he had reduced the Labour majority in Northampton from 8.000 to only 1,000. However, the hand of fate enabled him to be chosen as the Conservative Parliamentary Candidate for the by-election caused by Iain Macleod's untimely death. This by-election was for the seat of Enfield West, only a few miles from where Cecil and his family lived. The by-election was held in late 1970 and Cecil romped home to victory. He had been chosen as the candidate out of 464 applicants!

Politics was even then becoming a profession for younger people who were replacing those who had served the people both diligently and well, after a distinguished career in industry, agriculture, the professions, academia, the unions and the armed services.

*****

After two years with the National Building Agency Den was promoted to the position of Chief Executive, taking over from Dr Bill Chan who headed off to set up his own consultancy.

Three other important events took place in Den's life at that time. His mother died suddenly from a brain haemorrhage at the age of 63, his son Timothy was born and his father died at the age of 65 while in hospital for a medical procedure. Den's main regret was that neither of his parents knew that he was intent on becoming a Member of Parliament. What is certain is that, if they had known about his calling, they would have given him all the possible support they could.

The year of 1971 was a trying time for Den but he was very fortunate to have loads of stamina and determination, qualities that were essential for someone heading for politics.

Chapter 44

One of the best known and well respected property developers in the United Kingdom was Capital and Counties Property Company Limited. It was quoted on the London Stock Exchange but it had strong links with development companies in Canada and North America. The value of the shares in all property development companies were climbing steadily following two years of sensible Conservative government. The property development market was very active and Capital and Counties realised that the large development programme they wanted to carry out was going to be very difficult to manage in terms of both cost and time, particular at what was already a busy period for the construction industry.

The Chairman of the Board of Directors of Capital and Counties was Sir Richard Thompson, a Conservative Member of Parliament for the safe seat of Croydon Central, only ten miles to the south of the Houses of Parliament. The company was keen to expand its activities overseas, including in Europe, and to develop their land holdings around the United Kingdom by building shopping centres and commercial offices. At that time the company owned two thirds of all the land and property in Knightsbridge, the very fashionable and high class shopping and residential area around Harrods and Harvey Nichols. They had identified several London sites ready to build on, subject to planning permission, to provide hotels and commercial offices.

Discussion at one of their board meetings had focused on their one major dilemma. The firm had many chartered surveyors who could value land and property, but no-one who understood the detailed design and construction operations involved in carrying out a major development programme. Nevertheless they would need to exercise very tight control over the numerous architects, consulting engineers, quantity surveyors and mechanical and electrical services consultants that they had appointed—if their ambitious programme was to be carried out speedily and cost-effectively.

Their United Kingdom property Managing Director, Ian Northen, and their Australian property expert, Ray Moorman, had both been highly impressed by what had been achieved by the National Building Agency on the first phase of their very large Eldon Square Shopping Centre up in Newcastle-upon-Tyne, 400 miles from London. This scheme had failed to make progress for more than ten years when it was handled totally by the Newcastle City Council. They had, in sheer exasperation, asked Capital and Counties to come in and help them out. This had allowed the first phase to begin but the second phase was much larger. One of their development team, Brian Hord, had been mainly responsible for achieving this progress—aided by the NBA—and he had recommended that they needed to expand their use of the NBA to cover the whole of Eldon Square, and perhaps even the whole of their development programme of design and construction. The Board directed Ian Northen to discuss this matter with the NBA to see what could be done. One or two directors even suggested at the board meeting that a specialist in-house Project Management team should be set up and led by a really top man in the field.

The Managing Director of the NBA, Cleeve Barr, had an early meeting with Den to see what could be done. Den immediately suggested that a specialist team would need to be recruited over the next few months if the Capital and Counties development programme was going to be controlled properly. This work could be carried out on the basis of an arm's length contract between C&C and the NBA, but this would be expensive for their client—who could, as an alternative, choose to appoint their own top man, who would then build up an internal Project Management team. Cleeve Barr asked Den to contact Ian Northen and put forward a proposal to satisfy their needs.

When Den met Ian Northen he heard how impressed the C&C Board were with the management and production control services that the NBA had carried out for them. They discussed the two options and Ian was convinced that the route his company would choose would be to set up their own in-house team—using Den's intimate knowledge of the type of staff needed and where they could be drawn from.

Den briefed Cleeve Barr on this decision by C&C and began to work on the people who would be qualified, willing and able to lead the team, and also the people who would be suitable to join the team. Ian Northen had a short meeting

201

with Den and went through the draft proposal, the timings, the costs, the job descriptions and the personnel specifications.

Den was keen to impress Capital and Counties because he knew that they would soon be one of the top three property developers in the United Kingdom, as they were intending to carry out three schemes in Europe, and they had plans to expand their American, Canadian and Australian interests. At his final meeting with Ian Northen he hinted at the kind of staff he would be able to attract to C&C if the NBA were awarded the contract to help them overcome their problem. Ian then posed two questions to Den.

'I am most impressed by everything you are telling me about what the NBA could do to help us set up a truly professional Project Management team. I would like you to start immediately on the recruitment process for the top person. How many candidates could you provide for us to interview for this position and is there a possibility that you might be interested in the position yourself?'

Den replied saying that he would recommend that they met a minimum of six people for the top position, and he would send their full CVs within the next ten days. He also said that he would be willing to be considered for the post himself, if that was his wish, but 'only if Cleeve Barr was happy for him to do so.'

Den immediately prepared the written proposal for this additional, new project for Capital and Counties, setting out the timetable and the fees associated—all in accordance with standard management consultancy practices. He had already given earnest thought to suitable people who would be ideal for the position—indeed he had rung the three strongest candidates for the post. All of them were thankful to Den for contacting them and were very interested indeed by the possibility, and promised to polish up their CVs in readiness. They were all on a one month notice period with their current employers—that being the standard period of notice in the industry at the time.

*****

The outcome of all this negotiation with Capital and Counties was that they interviewed all the six people recommended by Den for the Projects Director position, hired three of them for their largest new projects and appointed Den as their Projects Director—giving him overall control of all their design consultants and all their construction sites. Den quickly built up his team of three by appointing others from those he had recommended to Capital and Counties.

One new development was being started every two weeks. These ranged from the Eldon Square Shopping Centre at Newcastle, the Victoria Centre at Nottingham (in a former railway siding), the East Street shopping centre at Southampton, the Park Tower hotel by Hyde Park and the Howard hotel near the River Thames. Numerous new and refurbished commercial offices schemes were commenced in the centre of London at the Strand, Lloyds Avenue, Wine Office Court, Breams Buildings and Shaftesbury Avenue—among other locations.

The new team quickly stamped their mark on all the design and construction work being carried out for Capital and Counties in England. In Europe a new shopping centre was built in Hamburg on the Grosse Bleichen site just south of the Inner Lake, a six storey office block on the inner ring road in Munich, and a small commercial office in the 19th 'arrondissement' of Paris. All the European developments were designed using continental design professionals and Den took a few of their top staff around the appropriate UK developments so that they could question the C&C local employees and learn what was expected of them in Europe.

*****

Den and his team of project managers were extremely busy and did a wonderful job of ensuring that all the design information was available in good time for the construction work to be carried out to the programmes agreed with the various contractors. Den was very experienced in interpreting the very lengthy and complicated contracts and documentation for all the projects—and would deal with any problems that arose that could not be sorted out amicably by his chosen and appointed project managers. The placing of the main contract for the second phase of the Eldon Square shopping centre needed his detailed involvement because the contractor for the first phase had confidently expected to be awarded the second phase. They had been taken over by a national firm, Bovis, who had assured everyone concerned that they would boost the resources allocated to Newcastle-upon-Tyne and easily be able to run the two phases in parallel. However, it was essential that the overlap period of a year was adhered to. There was a crucial requirement that both phases must be open for trading by the major stores and hundreds of smaller units on the two phases by the end of October in two consecutive years—to catch the invaluable Christmas shopping peak, thus enabling all the retail units to trade with good profits from the outset.

Den dealt with the contractor already on site, and the bosses of their new owners, Bovis. He also spoke at great length to the very accomplished contractor Sir Robert McAlpine who had built many of Capital and Counties schemes in the past. Den decided that the second phase should be awarded on the basis of which of the two competing firms were best able to meet the very tight cost and time requirements, especially as the project had to be completed ready for Christmas trading. This would be ascertained by each of the two firms submitting their management structures, method statements, programmes and details of the key personnel who would run the second phase. This process would be followed by a detailed interview process lasting half a day for each of the two bidders.

Capital and Counties needed to be able to ascertain which of the two competing firms were best able to meet the very tight cost and time requirements. The interviews would allow the top C&C team to raise any points of uncertainty about the bids, and the opposing builders would be able to present their detailed proposals. At the end of that same day the contract would be awarded and the necessary documentation signed by the authorised representatives of the client and the successful main contractor.

The whole procedure was completely successful. Bovis allocated additional resources, at their own cost, to the first phase work which was being carried out by their subsidiary company. Sir Robert McAlpine came in and carried out the second phase within the tight time and cost constraints. Both phases were completed on programme before the end of October of the two consecutive years—allowing all the hundreds of stores and shops in the Eldon Square development to maximise the benefits of opening for business just before their best trading period of the year.

*****

Den ended his three years of service as a London Borough of Barnet Councillor at the end of his second year with the NBA. During his first two years with Capital and Counties he was so busy travelling around the United Kingdom and Europe and raising his family that he had very little time to spend on his plans for a political career. However, despite his very heavily committed work programme, he did make three attempts to have his name included on the Approved List of Conservative Parliamentary Candidates—all within the five year period starting in May 1968 when he became a Councillor.

On each occasion he was required to attend an interview lasting only half an hour with one or two sitting Members of Parliament. Following each of these, Den was not surprised, but nevertheless extremely disappointed, to receive an absolutely standard impersonal brief note from Conservative Central Office each time. The wording on each occasion was identical and informed him that his name would not be added to the list, but expressed the hope that he would continue working for the Party.

By the time that the February 1974 General Election was called by the Prime Minister, Edward Heath, the whole country was suffering from the 'three day week' caused by the shortage of energy supplies arising from political problems and the price rises demanded by the Middle East oil and gas suppliers to Europe and the United Kingdom. It was clear that the General Election was called at the wrong time, and for the wrong reason. The cry was 'Who runs the Country?' The answer should have been 'a Government that completely deals with a major problem and only 'goes to the electorate' when they have done all they can to sort out problems on behalf of the people of the Country.'

*****

By the start of the three weeks leading to the General Election of February 1974 Den was Chairman of the Conservative Party organisation for two thirds of the recently formed South Hertfordshire Parliamentary Constituency. The Parliamentary Candidate for the new seat, brought in following the recent Boundary Commission Report (held every fifteen years or so) was Cecil Parkinson who was already the Member of Parliament for those parts that were in his existing constituency of Enfield West.

Den threw himself into the battle to win Cecil's new seat in the cold dark days of February 1974 knowing that every vote counted, not just in South Hertfordshire but throughout the whole of the United Kingdom. At the age of 35 he was at peak fitness and he was determined to ensure that Cecil could build a new base for his on-going political career—and move on to high office. The result in South Hertfordshire was very difficult indeed to predict, with half the area historically a Labour stronghold and the other half being a Conservative stronghold. The outcome was a victory for Cecil Parkinson and the Conservative Party of just two thousand votes.

In the Spring of 1974 there was a weekend Conservative gathering in Newcastle-upon-Tyne and Den spoke during the Saturday morning session shortly after Dame Irene Ward, who had been for many years one of the local Members of Parliament. After his speech she came over to compliment him and said how important it was for more Conservative Members of Parliament to come from the ranks of industry. After this compliment a young dark haired girl, Roberta Baron, and her mother came over to chat. They asked if Den had stood in the recent General Election and he said 'No, but I was extremely active in Cecil Parkinson's constituency in Hertfordshire, where I live. We managed to win it by two thousand votes.'

'Well we both think you should stand for Parliament, and as soon as you can' said Roberta, and her mother concurred.

'Why don't you have a word with Farmer Giles from Wales, who is looking for good candidates to fill the last few vacancies he has?' said her mother. 'He only told me on the phone last night that he was desperate for any new candidates that we might meet here at the conference.'

'Hang on' said Den. 'I am not even on the Approved List of Parliamentary Candidates. Indeed I was rejected for the third time a year ago.'

'Don't worry about that' said Roberta's mother. 'You just have a word with Farmer Giles who I'm sure will do all he can for you. He told me that they were interviewing for the last few seats in Wales within the next two weeks. Please promise us you will give him a ring this weekend, and make sure you have your CV ready to send off to him right away.' Roberta had the telephone number for Farmer Giles and Den wrote it down, thinking to himself 'nothing ventured, nothing gained.'

*****

The next day Den rang Farmer Giles and they had a very friendly conversation lasting about ten minutes. Den explained about meeting Roberta Baron and her mother. He also added that he knew Wales very well, having lived and worked in South Wales for eighteen months—and having played hockey for Swansea 'all over the valleys'—putting on his best Welsh accent.

He openly admitted that he had tried three times, unsuccessfully, to be accepted onto the Approved List of Candidates.

'Never mind that, young lad, you send your CV to me immediately and leave the rest to me' said Farmer Giles. Either he was a force to be reckoned with, or he had an unrealistic view of his power to influence people, thought Den. He posted off his CV immediately and was delighted to receive a telephone call from Farmer Giles a few days later.

Farmer Giles explained that they were inviting eleven prospective candidates to attend two sets of interviews. The first pair would be for Bedwellty and Caerphilly. The second pair would be Abertillery and Merthyr Tydfil. All the eleven prospective candidates would be interviewed for the first two on the first day, with the nine unsuccessful ones attending the second pair of interviews the following day.

The Bedwellty nomination was won by Peter Brook who later became a Cabinet Minister, and Den came second. Later that day Den won the nomination for Caerphilly against stiff opposition from his opponents who included two other future Cabinet Ministers. On the long drive back to Hertfordshire, Den felt flabbergasted and honoured to have been chosen to fight at the next General Election to become the Honourable Member of Parliament for the Welsh constituency of Caerphilly.

The General Election was held only three months later because the Labour government needed a larger overall majority if they were to be able to get their legislative programme through, and stay in office for four or five years. Den spent all his annual holiday period in Caerphilly and travelled down to Caerphilly every Friday evening, returning to Hertfordshire very late on the Saturdays. During those three months he built an effective campaign team who worked very hard indeed. However, in those days too many Welsh people voted the way their parents had, year after year. Socialism was almost part of their birth right. Den obtained five thousand votes for the Conservative Party but the seat was won by the well-respected Fred Evans who had been a local headmaster. Fred had also been born and educated in the heart of the Caerphilly constituency.

*****

During the last of the three years that Den was their Projects Director, the Chairman of Capital and Counties retired from the House of Commons. Brian Hord had stood in both the February and October 1974 General Elections as the Conservative candidate in Darlington (40 miles south of the Eldon Square development)—losing by three thousand votes both times. Den fought his first of several General Election campaigns, as the Conservative candidate for the Caerphilly constituency in South Wales (a very safe Labour seat). In newspaper reports he was described as 'a very energetic civil engineer.'

Unfortunately in the second half of 1974 there was a severe 'crash' in the share prices of all the property developers quoted on the London Stock Exchange.

Den saw the shares that he had purchased in the open market at an average price of 144 pence fall in a single day to the unbelievably low figure of 7 pence. Capital and Counties sold off their European company, of which Den was a Director, and they made a 'public statement' that they would not be starting any further property developments for several years.

In these dire circumstances Den offered to take over all the key staff he had moved into the company, charge a market rate for their services for C&C and then build up a production control and project management consultancy. This proposal was rejected by the Main Board of Capital and Counties and inevitably Den and many other high quality employees were declared redundant.

Chapter 45

The output of the construction industry has for many decades been seen as the most reliable measure of the state of the United Kingdom economy. This was certainly the case in the spring of 1975. For the first time in his life Den saw clear evidence that the only construction opportunities for professional staff were in the overseas markets of places like Nigeria and Iran where multi-discipline contractors were required. Before he left Capital and Counties he accepted a major construction appointment in Nigeria with the famous Taylor Woodrow group but the project was cancelled at the last minute. He then agreed to join George Wimpey to head up their Joint Venture with John Laing for some very large contracts in Iran. He would be based in the Head Office of Wimpey in Hammersmith, reporting to Andrew MacDowell who was a Main Board Director.

Andrew was a very dynamic and direct personality who was responsible for both Wimpey's largest region in the country, London, and also their joint venture with Laing in Iran. He had known Den for the previous two years because Wimpey had built a sizeable office complex for Capital and Counties at Witham in Essex, which had been awarded to them on a competitive basis by Den in his role of Projects Director.

Den shared an office, and a secretary, with Ned Sparkes who had been based in Aden with the British Army for many years, and spoke fluent Arabic as a result. Ned was the Wimpey representative responsible for their joint venture with John Laing in Saudi Arabia which was led by a local firm, as required by Arabic law. The joint venture was called Laing Wimpey Alireeza. Wimpey had a long history of working in the Middle East so Ned was given the notional responsibility for any work obtained in Iraq, and also for trying to obtain the final payment of almost a million pounds from the Iraqi government for a major contract completed several years earlier.

A large dry dockyard was being built by Wimpey Laing at Bandar Abbas on the south coast of Iran. Wimpey had had to recruit well over a thousand South Korean workers to meet their commitments. The South Koreans were very skilled and conscientious workers who relished the opportunity to work away from their home country, and send back money to their wives and families. The Iranian Navy had been delighted by the efforts of the Wimpey Laing joint venture on the dry dock. The Shah of Iran was on the throne and the country was intent on putting its enormous oil reserves to good use by planning to set up major industrial manufacturing facilities—including plastics and a very large battery manufacturing plant, for both civil and military production. Monthly payments were made by the times specified in the various contracts and relationships between Wimpey Laing and the various Ministers and members of the Royal Family were excellent.

Den was swiftly able to finalise the contract documentation for a new navy training centre, again at Bandar Abbas, only half a mile from the dry dock project. His job was to ensure that all the design information was produced in sufficient time, the materials ordered from suitable suppliers and transported out by road or sea, and professional staff recruited and posted out to Iran. He had to ensure that client relations were good, that all the design team effort was coordinated, that the management teams on site were suitable and able to cope with the extremes of climate and the problems of working overseas. It was essential to have a happy team of staff on site because the working environment was all that they would experience.

At Bandar Abbas the joint venture had built a small township of temporary housing units, including a school, because there were so many Wimpey Laing staff who would only accept an overseas posting to Iran if their wives, and children up to age seven or so, were able to accompany them. Additionally teenagers were able to be educated, free of charge, in boarding schools—and even allowed to travel out to Bandar Abbas twice a year. All these costs were essential to ensure that suitable professional management and technical staff were able to be attracted to working in the very hot and humid working environment.

Den did not enjoy doing business in Iran because of the differences in culture and the difficult circumstances. However, he did do a very good job. Tehran, the capital city, was where the Shah was based in an enormous palace complex on the edge of the city. All the government officials and ministers were based in Tehran, which was a bustling city with only a few western hotels. It had a gridded road pattern—with each block being one hundred and fifty yards by one hundred yards. Each taxi only ran up and down one grid line, and had to be shared with up to four other passengers who would jump on or off whenever or wherever they wanted to. A passenger would have to stand on a corner and travel in one direction, until reaching the correct road to switch taxis to another one heading in the correct direction towards their final destination. Every evening there were solid traffic jams covering most of the central blocks—all caused by the rigid gridded road system. The standard of driving was appalling and there were some horrific traffic accidents. A red light at a junction would mean that the driver could turn left, but not, theoretically, go straight ahead or turn right—however they often did.

Tehran was not the place to be out at night time. Den would occasionally pop out of his hotel for a short walk in the relatively cool evenings. However, he found a very unfriendly environment. First there were packs of completely wild dogs running wild and secondly there were always footsteps coming up behind him, particularly down the darkest back streets. After his first few visits he never ventured out at night, and he was always relieved when the aircraft took off for London from Tehran airport, usually at 6 am, so that he could be in his London office by 10 am that same day, due to the differences in the time zones.

Andrew MacDowell would spend three or four days in Iran every three months. Den and he would visit the various contracts and deal with any of the government officials regarding any possible new contracts. The turnover of the joint venture was more than a hundred million pounds a year and good profits were made. Den would attend the monthly Wimpey International board meetings every month to report on all aspects of the work in Iran. All the managers responsible for the numerous overseas territories dined in the same dining room, whenever they were in the United Kingdom. There were some very interesting discussions about the similar problems encountered by them all in trying to obtain new work, keep to the programmes agreed for all their contracts, hire and retain good staff, and ensure that all their United Kingdom designers and suppliers were giving a reliable and timely service.

*****

Den was still Chairman of two thirds of Cecil Parkinson's organisation in the South Hertfordshire constituency. He had recognised the need to appoint chairmen for each of the main branches and he was gradually able to rely on a slick efficient organisation for raising funds, building up membership, and finding candidates for election to both the local borough of Hertsmere and the county council of Hertfordshire. He realised that by the time of the next General Election, say in 1979, he would be over forty years of age himself. He just had to find a marginal seat to fight at the next General Election because none of the sitting Conservative Members of Parliament would be likely to stand down, with the strong possibility of the return of a Conservative government—following their two election defeats in the February and October 1974 General Elections.

Den loved to check on all the statistical information for the 635 Parliamentary constituencies. In February 1974 Labour had won 301 seats, increasing this figure to 319 seats in October. The Conservatives had won 296 seats in the February 1974 election but only 276 in October. In the October 1974 election 30 Labour MPs had been elected with majorities of less than 2,000 votes and 37 Conservatives with majorities that small. Den reckoned that he needed to be chosen as the Conservative Party candidate for the next election for a constituency where the Labour majority was less than 2,000 and one that was situated in Lancashire, his 'home county.'

Once the political season began in 1975 (by Den's definition this was September 1st) he was checking on all his information sources to ensure that he was aware of which parliamentary seats were starting to choose their candidates. He only had to wait a few weeks before hearing that Bury North and Preston North were starting their selection processes, and hoped to choose their candidates by the end of the year. Den wrote into Conservative Central Office in Smith Square, London saying that he would be interested in being considered for these two seats, and pointing out of course, that he had been the Party's candidate in Caerphilly in October of the previous year.

Den reached the 'long list' of around 15 for both of these seats and was interviewed on consecutive weekends. He reached the 'short list' of six for Preston North but not for Bury North. Two weeks later he attended the final interviews for Preston North but failed to reach the final three. Nevertheless Den was pleased with his performances, and he knew by now what the Lancashire selection committees were looking for. Before he could catch his breath he received notification that the seat of Chorley, also in Lancashire, was opening up their selection process. Ironically the Chorley constituency was situated a few miles north of Bury and a few miles south of Preston. It was also only fifteen miles from Southport, where his political idol Mr Hudson had been the Conservative Member of Parliament all those years ago when Den was just a boy. This was the town from which the football team had travelled to Southport more than twenty years earlier, together with their broad Lancashire supporters shouting 'Cum on Charrley.' Oddly enough Den and his family spent one of their 1975 summer weeks of holidays staying at the M6 motorway service station hotel at Charnock Richard, in the Chorley constituency. This was an easy point from which to spend time in Southport with their relatives and in the Lake District where they loved to go fell walking.

Den was chosen for the long list of interviews at Chorley and these were spread over several evenings in view of the unbelievable number of 129 applicants. Den was informed of this number by his Wimpey colleague, Ned Sparkes, who was a personal friend of a former Conservative MP who had applied for the seat but was not even listed for an interview. It later transpired that a further three former MPs had applied for Chorley and also one serving Member of the European Parliament. Den knew that the Labour majority in Chorley at the October 1974 General Election was 2,713 which meant he would have a tough fight on his hands to win the seat, even if he managed to be chosen as the Chorley candidate.

Den spent several days up in Chorley over the Christmas break and visited the library to read all the local papers and the Lancashire Evening Post for the last few weeks. He soon picked up what the key local issues were and he was able to verify the constituency boundaries, as well as reading much of the local history of the coal mines, textile mills and the farming community. He learned that Hoghton Towers was just inside the constituency and he remembered how his history teacher at the Southport KGV Grammar School had pointed out from their first floor classroom the impressive structure of this historic building. This was the former castle where William Shakespeare wrote and produced many of his plays. It was also where the ruling King of England was so pleased with his meat joint that he christened it with the title 'sirloin.'

Den chose to highlight in his five minute speech to the Selection Committee two former residents of Chorley centuries before who epitomised the two most important characteristics of mankind. One was Mr Tate, founder of Tate and Lyle, the world wide sugar manufacturer. The other was one of the 'founding fathers' who sailed across the Atlantic and settled near Boston. Both of these had shown the pioneering spirit and enterprise that all Lancastrians possessed. Questions from the audience were confidently responded to because Den was so well briefed about the huge local demand for Chorley to have its own District General Hospital, the problems of the Central Lancashire New Town ruining the local landscapes and the closure of so many textile mills. When he was asked if he would buy a house in the constituency Den said he most definitely would do so, within weeks.

Den was chosen to be one of the short list of only three candidates to face an open meeting of all the Conservative Party members who wished to attend, and vote for, their new Prospective Parliamentary Candidate. This was held in the largest hotel in the centre of the town, directly across the road from the Chorley Conservative constituency office and club for members—where the first selection meeting had been held in a large second floor room. The Chorley Conservative Agent was a six foot tall, silver haired, former marine who was born in Scotland and known to be one of the best Agents the Party had. He had arranged for the other two finalists, both ladies, to bat first on the basis of 'Ladies first.' One was the former Conservative Member of Parliament for Preston North and the other was a sitting Member of the European Parliament. There were nearly two hundred members of the Party present for this final selection process. The Chairman was Peter Birtwistle who stood no nonsense. He had been a net cord umpire at Wimbledon for several years and had even stood up to John McEnroe in front of all the television cameras. The first vote was counted and no candidate had the 51% of the votes needed to be declared the winner. After a short break in the proceedings a second ballot was taken, with only the top two being voted for. Den emerged as the winner and the Chairman broke the news to him and the other two candidates by coming to the small waiting room where they had been waiting nervously.

There were extended celebrations that evening across the road in the Party's offices. Den was introduced to all the key personnel in the Chorley Conservative Association and was on an enormous high. When he and his wife left the building they had to drive to Warrington where they had left their two children with Den's favourite Aunt. From there it was a three hour drive back to their Borehamwood, Hertfordshire home where they all had a good night of sleep, except for Den. He had agreed with the Leader of the Conservative

Group that he would be back in Chorley by 10 o'clock the very next morning. Ian Sellers was a former Main Board Director of Pye of Cambridge and had been a high ranking intelligence officer in the British Army throughout the Second World War. Ian said that he wanted to talk through several important policy matters and introduce him to key members of the local Party. First of all however he said he had one very important question that he had to put to Den.

'Have you any skeletons in your cupboard?'

Den had never been asked that question before, and it had never had the importance then that it has had over recent years. He firmly and deliberately replied with the words:-

'I can give you a categoric assurance that I have never had, and do not have, any skeletons in my cupboard.'

The rest of the morning was spent with Ian Sellers with whom Den built one of the closest relationships in his life. At all times they were able to share problems, deal with issues and focus on the most important policy matters—at both local and national levels.

Before leaving Chorley that day Den visited the Wimpey new housing development in the village of Euxton, a mere mile and a half west of the Chorley town centre. He was impressed by the show home and decided to buy it without hesitation, without any employee discount. This took five weeks and enabled Den to honour his promise to buy a home in his Parliamentary constituency 'within weeks.'

*****

There was still much work for Den to complete with Wimpey. Early preparations were being made for an enormous tank manufacturing facility in the desert in the middle of Iran, near to the well-known city of Esfahan. Thousands of workers would be needed and hundreds of professional staff. Temporary offices and a large village of timber temporary buildings were planned to be built, including a school for the children of the British staff based on that site.

The talks on the provision of an enormous battery factory—with Wimpey Laing linked with Lucas Batteries—were proceeding in a spirit of full cooperation. The huge dockyard contract at Bandar Abbas was being built exactly to the agreed programme and the internal electrical and computer installations were being installed in the nearby navy training centre.

Everything was going to plan when suddenly the World News bulletins were running the huge headlines that the Shah of Iran had been deposed. The Ayatollah Homeini, a religious fanatic, had taken over the whole of the country's affairs.

Did this count as a coup d'état? What would the effect on Wimpey Laing and all their employees be?

All these questions and thousands more would need to be answered quickly, but the future for all involved was looking very uncertain indeed.

All payments to Wimpey Laing from Iran stopped immediately. The Ayatollah's representatives insisted that all the contracts should be continued, even though they refused to make any payments. After a short period of stalemate, Wimpey sent a formal written communication to the new Head of State making it abundantly clear that unless further monies were received within the next fourteen days all work on the various contracts would cease. Thereafter measures would be put into immediate effect to repatriate all the workers and return any materials that could be usefully recovered, with appropriate adjustments to the Final Account.

*****

Ned and Den spoke to each other back in the London office and concluded that it was extremely unlikely that any further work would ever be carried out in Iran by Wimpey Laing. With his long term intimate relationships with various countries in the Middle East, Ned was one of the best people to consult on such a tricky and unpredictable issue.

A week later Ned showed Den an advertisement in a national paper, repeated in several of the technical journals, advertising the position of Director of Housing Construction at the Greater London Council. Ned checked on a few points in Den's previous career with him and concluded by saying that this was just the sort of job that Den should apply for.

Den duly prepared his job application and checked it out with Ned over a drink one evening. At that stage the Greater London Council was run by a very left wing Labour administration, and Den doubted that they would seriously consider him. The post advertised was for a five year fixed term of office.

Would the Labour controlled Greater London Council even consider employing him, particularly when they read in his application that he had been selected as the Conservative Prospective Parliamentary Candidate for the marginal constituency of Chorley in Lancashire? However, on the basis of 'nothing ventured, nothing gained' Den submitted his application and awaited developments.

*****

Within the next month all work by Wimpey Laing Iran had been stopped and the necessary steps taken to repatriate the workforce, including all the South Koreans. By that time Den had attended his first and only interview for the post of Director of Housing Construction with the Greater London Council at County Hall. Around the very large square of tables were several well-known Labour politicians who held important Chairmanships within the Greater London Council 'empire.' Den presumed that the twenty or more gathered round the tables were all members of the Housing Committee and the meeting was chaired by Sir Reginald Goodwin, who had been a major Labour figure in London politics for years. He also assumed that the six or so men sitting on chairs around the perimeter of the room were Officers of the Council, presumably all the top housing staff in the Council.

To Den's great surprise there were no questions at all about political affiliations. The Selection Committee members wanted assurances that Den would be willing to serve the best interests of the people of London at all times, that he would be available to start work with the Council after giving his 28 days' notice to Wimpey, that he had no outside remunerated employment that could constitute a 'conflict of interests,' and that he would at all times work in the best interests of the Greater London Council. Den gave firm assurances on all these points and answered an array of questions about labour relations, safety matters, construction contracts, project management and financial controls.

Within a further week Den learned in writing that he had been chosen by the GLC to head up their entire Housing Construction operation which employed 3,500 men on 63 building sites within a 20 mile radius of County Hall, the GLC headquarters situated on the south bank of the River Thames diagonally across the river from Big Ben and the Houses of Parliament. His appointment as a Chief Officer meant that Den would be reporting to the Controller of Housing, Harry Simpson, who had formerly been in charge of the Londonderry City Council in Northern Ireland.

Chapter 46

The offices of the Housing Construction directorate were in refurbished buildings a five minute walk from Lambeth Bridge, the next one to Westminster Bridge. The Director of Personnel for the Housing Department of the GLC, Geoff Manning, met Den on his first day. This allowed him to introduce Den to a Deputy Director, Tim Liddell, and his two Assistant Directors. There were four Contracts Managers, a Commercial Manager, a Chief Estimator and an Administration Manager. This hierarchy seemed far too top heavy to Den but he would have to assess the merits of all of them and take any necessary action. Geoff Manning explained that many of the Councillors on the Housing Committee were being contacted by the so-called shop stewards, one of whom was on each of the 63 sites. Den soon discovered that each of these shop stewards spent all their working day dealing with trade union matters, instead of just an hour or two which was the maximum allowed on equivalent building sites in the private sector. It was abundantly clear to Den that the Project Managers on the large sites and the Site Agents on the smaller sites were being subverted by the direct links between the shop stewards and the elected Councillors—who had no authority whatsoever to interfere in the running or organisation of the sites.

A chauffeur driven white Vauxhall saloon car was available for Den to visit any of the sites, at any time. There was a full-time efficient elderly lady who was Secretary to whoever headed up the Department. She had been in post for fifteen years and knew everybody in the head office building where there were around 80 staff. Far too many of these held various grades of clerical positions within the Department, directly mirroring the civil service system that backs up Ministers in the various Government Departments in Whitehall. Den had learned—through his experience at the National Building Agency—that throughout the Government Service the same grades of civil servants received the same pay and conditions, irrespective of the nature of the particular

219

government department they were employed in. Everyone in the Housing Construction Directorate was a union member and very proud of it. The same conditions of pay, salary increases, promotion arrangements, periods of notice and overtime working were in force throughout the British Civil Service and local government at that time.

One of the questions asked of Den at his interview for the job he now occupied, was about what steps he would take to make sure that the Direct Labour department became more like the private sector, and better able to compete with the private sector. In his first few days Den realised the enormity of his task. It would be a matter of how quickly, or perhaps how slowly, he would be able to make the far reaching changes that were undeniably necessary to ensure that his department was as efficient and effective as the private sector house builders and contractors.

Den made sure that he visited all the 63 sites in his first week. At that time his chauffeur John's excellent knowledge of all the shortcuts in London, plus the best times to travel was invaluable. None of the sites was more than thirty minutes' drive from the office in Lambeth. There was always room for the Director's car near the site offices, so parking was never a problem.

On each site there were many private sector subcontracting firms. The directly employed trades were mainly bricklayers, scaffolders, joiners, painters and decorators, plumbers and general labourers. Some of the sites were building more than a thousand dwellings, most were building several hundred dwellings and some were only building a few dozen homes. On all the sites there was a small management team of section managers and general foremen who coordinated the various operations of all the specialist operations on the sites. There were hardly any programmes for the construction work, and none clearly on display on the site office walls. However, this would soon be remedied by Den with the introduction of graphical programming for all the sites. At the National Building Agency the graphical programming (or line of balance) training courses were the most popular of all, particularly for house building, and the easiest programming method to use.

On all housing contracts there has to be a well-defined order of activities in every block, on every floor and in every room. This sequence of trades is most easily shown in graphical form, with the number of dwellings on the site marked up the vertical axis and the timescale along the horizontal axis. The graphical programme for even the largest contract can be drawn up within a few hours, with one large programme showing the sequence of the trades and the number of dwellings to be constructed. The actual progress achieved is shown on a weekly or fortnightly basis and compared with the programmed rate required. Any visiting manager can calculate how many weeks the site is ahead or behind the programme literally within minutes of looking at the graphical programme.

*****

No sooner had Den taken up his position than Tim Liddell went off on sick leave. He was an enormous man, well over six feet in height, and he had developed a problem with sciatica—with a trapped nerve affecting his hip, his back and the outside of one of his massive legs. He had great difficulty in sitting down comfortably—and could hardly walk at times. During Tim's absence Den took the opportunity of finding out more about what his two Assistants were doing. He was not surprised to find that they had far too little to do and they were each heading quickly for their sixtieth birthdays. The presence of these top three in the management organisation was not essential so Den had a discussion with Geoff Manning to see what could be done, within the over-prescriptive rules relating to the terms and conditions of senior management personnel.

Geoff was a man of long experience and he said to Den 'I'm not at all surprised by what you say. I wondered how there could be room for so many top managers in the organisation.' Den said he thought Tim would probably welcome an early retirement package on health grounds and that the other two seemed obsessed by the level of pension they would lose if they took early retirement. Den left it with Geoff to do his homework and report back to him regarding all these three managers. He pointed out to Geoff that a case could be made on redundancy grounds for the two Assistant Directors. This was because, while there were currently 63 contracts, Den had calculated that within six months this number would be down to 45 sites, and down to around 30 within twelve months. If the Labour control of the Greater London Council changed to Conservative control at the forthcoming May elections, to be held throughout the whole Greater London area, there may not be many more, if any, new building contracts awarded to, and begun by, the Housing Construction directorate. Den knew this because he had, completely by

221

accident, found himself sitting next to the Leader of the Conservative Group on the GLC, Sir Horace Cutler, at the recent Conservative Party Conference held in Blackpool. Sir Horace chatted to Den and was interested in his construction background, and the work he had done at Capital and Counties. Sir Horace said the Labour Group on the GLC was intent on expanding the Direct Labour department whereas, if he had his way, he would want to close it down. Sir Horace was a builder by background, with his own family business. He was a fervent supporter of the private sector throughout the whole economy.

Den had formed an immediate strong bond with Jack O'Brien, an academic looking and studious man, who—as Commercial Manager—was in charge of the Quantity Surveying, Estimating and Cost Control departments. He had been in the private sector for many years and with the GLC for the last fifteen. However, he was fundamentally someone who believed in competition and the need to run a very tight ship. He was insistent that the Housing Construction Directorate needed to be able to offer the Housing Development Directorate— the client for all its work—new build or refurbishment contracts in direct competition with the private sector construction companies. Jack lived in North London and was, like Den, an early starter and a late finisher. Den often picked Jack up from his home and ran him back home in the evenings. Jack and Den had so many detailed issues to discuss that these two half an hour, one to one sessions in the car avoided the need for them to have meetings with each other in their offices.

The Finance and Administration Manager for the Housing Construction directorate was in charge of all the Clerical Officers and Administration staff. He was meticulous with the huge number of orders, payments, timesheets, invoices, statements and control procedures that he was required to be responsible for. He was efficient, helpful and a real asset to the whole operation.

In a construction operation what really counts is the quality of each site manager and the person one level higher (usually a Contracts Manager in charge of several sites). Detailed matters below these two levels will be in total disorder if these two levels of management are ineffective and incompetent. Den knew that his number one priority was to set in place a first class team of Contracts Managers whom he would have to select, appoint, encourage, motivate and guide. With their help he would then be able to ensure that each of the site managers in charge of one particular site were fit to fulfil their role, be able to control their men, their subcontractors and their suppliers. They would then be able to complete their contracts on time and within budget.

*****

The complete re-jigging of the structure, the reporting procedures and the controls took two months of hard effort. However, this paid off because there was a new esprit de corps within the Housing Construction directorate by then.

During these reorganisations Den had been able to identify where the strengths and weaknesses were. It was abundantly clear that there were two remaining problems. One was the trade union representation throughout the organisation, the other was the whole area of specialist subcontractors. Both of these would now be able to be dealt with effectively and efficiently because he had his full and best team of Contracts Managers and Site Managers in place.

*****

Geoff Manning did not take long to sort out the problems relating to the three top managers in the directorate. He was able to confirm that Tim Liddell would be able to be offered, and had already accepted, an early retirement package on health grounds. He was still virtually unable to move around and had promised to come in and say 'cheerio' to Den and others in the Head Office when he was fit enough. The full details of the two Assistant Directors had been examined in detail, and any earlier, similar cases studied. In view of what increasingly looked likely to be a decrease in the number of sites under construction, linked with the advanced age of both individuals, it had been accepted that they would both be taking early retirement on a package approved by the Council itself. Accordingly they would both be written to, but they had already confirmed that they would agree to the packages offered to them, provided no further changes were made. These three 'barriers to progress' had been removed, very smoothly and effectively, by Geoff Manning who had more than proved his credentials with Den in the process. He had shown himself to be a person who could be trusted with confidential matters, relied on to achieve a task, and discreet in his dealings—all qualities that Den would need to depend upon in future.

Two levels of management had been removed within the first few months. Furthermore three very high salary packages had been removed from the overheads of the organisation. However, the most significant benefit of these changes had been that the number and responsibilities of the Contacts Managers could now be re-jigged as appropriate to ensure that the new arrangements offered scope, incentives, career development and better reporting procedures throughout the whole organisation.

The largest sites were now headed up by proven Project Managers who would report direct to Den, thus enhancing their importance, independence and status. The remainder of the sites were divided into groups of between six and eight contracts with each group headed by a Contracts Manager. Some of these were promoted into that position under the new arrangements, having proved themselves to Den in his first few months. The others had already carried out their duties to Den's satisfaction and had been rewarded by taking on additional sites.

The Project Managers and Contracts Managers agreed with Den that the trade unions had, for far too long, exercised too powerful an influence on their sites—and within the whole organisation. This had been partly brought about by elected Councillors on the Greater London Council, and even from the scores of individual Borough Councils within the GLC area, encouraging some of their political supporters to link with the trade union representatives on the sites in their area—and often to report back to the elected Councillor, or even arrange for them to visit the site and start issuing instructions!

However, the main problem was one of much more significance. The worldwide trade union movements had earmarked the Greater London Council as a key target for causing major disruptions. Labour unrest about working conditions, rates of pay and unsafe working conditions were the chief causes of complaints that were espoused by the top union activists. Nevertheless they were merely bargaining chips in a very subversive and dangerous campaign to undermine management on the construction sites and arouse passions among the site workforces. On each of the major sites the full time union representative was from one of the major countries around the world, and famous for causing disruption on construction sites. These immigrants had been deliberately planted into the United Kingdom to destabilise the industrial system. The concentration had been focused on construction sites and the Direct Labour Organisations of the major local authorities around the country. These DLOs were easy to infiltrate because they were all in major conurbations with left wing controlled Councils and large labour forces of directly employed operatives ranging from general labourers up to tradesmen. Building workers from around the globe had been encouraged to emigrate to the United Kingdom, obtain employment in the Direct Labour Organisations, aim to be elected as the top Shop Stewards (Convenors) on the sites, and be ready to cause maximum disturbance and disruption when called upon to do so.

Den had learned from years of front line industrial experience that the best way of handling trade unions was to keep them involved in what was going on, to ensure that there were no unsafe conditions anywhere around the sites, to be firm but fair in any dealings with them, to always make sure that there was ready access to the management team, and always listen to what they had to say—even if you were not able to agree with what they were saying.

By ensuring that all the Project Managers and Site Agents adhered to these guiding principles, and by underlining the importance of them, Den was able to have three dispute free years as Director of Housing Construction at the Greater London Council. The trade union representatives and Site Convenors (the top Shop Steward on a site) were only allowed 'essential time for union duties.' If any safety matters needed to be discussed with site or higher management, Den was insistent that this should be done immediately.

There was one occasion when Den suspected that the trade unions were intent on causing problems, on a very large, new site in Hammersmith. He asked his Project Manager to start the first ever joint meeting of management and the unions on that site within the hour of his telephone call to Den. Den explained that he wanted to attend—to explain to both management and the trade union representatives what the system of constructive relationships on the site would be. He asked the Project Manager to prepare an agreed list of any points of uncertainty for when he arrived—to save time for all concerned. Den spoke for five minutes to those assembled as soon as he arrived on site. He dealt with all the listed points, thanking the person who had raised each one, and giving an immediate response—or instructing the Project Manager to deal with the issue within the next 24 hours.

After the first six months of Den's arrival as the Housing Construction Director it was noted by several members of the management team that the leading troublemakers in the union movement were leaving the Directorate and returning, in many cases, to their own shores. Throughout the first three years of Den's term in office there were no serious accidents at all and there were genuine meetings of minds on all trade union and safety matters. There was a spirit of cooperation that helped achieve excellent progress on all the sites. Very few new contracts were awarded to the Directorate because the new Conservative political masters at the Greater London Council had decided that there was now very little need for any new homes to be built for rental to its own tenants. Housing Associations had mushroomed in London, with the arrival of a Conservative controlled GLC, and the likelihood of a new Conservative Government in Westminster.

*****

Every main contractor in the construction industry carries out some of the main operations themselves, depending on what they have traditionally decided to do over many years. All the remainder of the activities and specialist trades are subcontracted out by the main contractor on, most usually, a competitive bidding process. The Housing Construction directorate had, like most main contractors over recent years, decided to use subcontractors for all the excavation and foundations work—because of its special nature and the very large cost of the necessary plant and equipment. In addition most of the superstructure (above ground) construction was subcontracted for similar reasons—especially because every housing scheme was a one-off design by the architect and the structural engineer. The directorate had chosen to carry out almost all the brickwork on its sites, and employed many very skilled craftsmen in this field. The other trades for which the GLC used their own men were scaffolding (for historic reasons), plumbing and joinery (which helped to train apprentices), plastering, painting and decorating (very important activities for their refurbishment contracts on scores of five storey blocks of flats built in the 1920s and 1930s) and general labourers (for cleaning and temporary office duties).

When the new build construction activities of the Housing Construction branch increased rapidly in the 1970s they had great difficulty in finding sufficient specialist subcontractors to carry out certain key activities—particularly the excavation, foundations and reinforced concrete superstructures (which had replaced structural steelwork for fire protection reasons). The firms that they did employ at that time relied heavily on the Construction Branch for most of their workload. Three private sector specialist reinforced concrete firms were, within a few years, carrying out more than half the superstructure erection work needed by the GLC direct labour organisation. By the time Den arrived, this monopoly situation within the directorate was clearly visible. However, nothing could be done about it, even if no further contracts were placed with the three firms involved. Indeed as the construction branch completed, and handed over two contracts each week, to the Housing Development Division, the situation was visibly seen to worsen. The three firms in question were becoming even more dominant within the Construction Branch—especially because no new contracts were forthcoming.

Den ensured that all the construction contract clauses in the copious documents and agreements with these three firms were being fully and properly applied, at all times. Jack O'Brien, the Commercial Manager, was well aware of the position and was a tremendous ally in spelling out to the firms concerned that proper accountability was absolutely essential. The three firms were performing extremely well on all their contracts with the GLC. Indeed they were forging ahead on the contracts to recover any delays incurred before Den's arrival.

John Stringer was the key link man with the main Finance Department of the Greater London Council, at County Hall. John was a sensible and intelligent man who had worked for the GLC for many years. He was fully aware of all the financial rules and regulations applying to Local Government and he reported to the Finance Comptroller for the Greater London Council who operated at the same level as Harry Simpson, Controller of Housing, who was Den's one and only superior.

John Stringer had several meetings with Jack O'Brien about the amounts being paid to the three firms involved—and received very full and detailed responses to all his queries which were fully supported by the appropriate documentation. In the end Den and Jack produced a twenty page written official 'Report to the Housing Committee of the Greater London Council' which explained all the payments made, the progress of each of the three firms on their various contracts, and the important clauses and particulars for all the contracts for the Greater London Council which they had entered into with the Housing Construction Direct Labour Organisation.

Not one of the contracts in contention was entered into during Den's period as Director of Housing Construction. All of them had been agreed, signed and commenced months or even years before Den arrived at the GLC in September 1977. Den was asked to wait outside the Housing Committee Meeting Room while his item was discussed. This was usual practice, in case the Officer or Director of the Council needed to be consulted by the Members of the Committee, in which event they would be requested to enter the Committee Room to answer any queries that needed to be answered.

*****

When the minutes of the Housing Committee meeting were issued there was no follow up action required to be taken. John Stringer had been closely involved in the preparation of the Report and he was satisfied with all the information provided. He was clearly content with the outcome of the Committee meeting.

Den continued his tight control over all the contracts and was able to reduce the number of current contracts from the figure of 63 when he became the Director of Housing Construction down to 30 by the end of 1978. Meanwhile he had held several discussions with Geoff Manning about the need to be able to reduce the workforce in the Housing Construction section at a faster rate than natural wastage was allowing. Den stressed that there were no new contracts that would be able to absorb any excess labour.

'Would it not be possible to introduce a voluntary early retirement scheme for the Housing Construction employees?' was the crucial question put to Geoff by Den.

'There has never been an early retirement or voluntary redundancy scheme in local government in the United Kingdom. I cannot see any early possibility of such a scheme being introduced' was Geoff's response, but it set him thinking. 'I will discuss your suggestion with experts in the field and come back to you in the next few weeks' added Geoff.

Den thought that would be the last he would hear about his suggestion for many months before being told it was an impossibility. To Den's delight Geoff rang him two weeks later and asked if he could pop over for a chat and an update on the question that Den had posed about a voluntary redundancy scheme being made available in local government.

When Geoff arrived his mood was entirely different from what it had been two weeks earlier. He said he had discussed Den's suggestion with top officials in the relevant Government departments. They had admitted that the Greater London Council was not alone in this field. Other local authorities had been pressing for a voluntary early redundancy scheme to be made available for local government staff, but their requests had related to office staff ('white collar workers') whereas Den's inquiry was solely related to construction workers or staff who were clearly 'blue collar workers.'

Den saw Geoff's response as a sign of light at the end of the tunnel. He encouraged Geoff to keep up the pressure, and said he was sure that if there was a new Conservative Government the following year, they would be only too willing to bring in such a scheme. Den was not trying to be at all political but he needed to be able to reduce his workforce at an even faster rate over the coming year because the completion rates on the various construction sites had increased due to the better management and tighter controls being exercised on all the sites.

After a further month Geoff finally came up with the exact answer that Den had been wanting. He said that he had been granted permission to undertake a questionnaire of all the Greater London Council workers who might be interested in partaking in an early voluntary redundancy scheme. Would Den agree to his entire workforce being approached on this matter? Den was delighted and said that he thought the take up rate would be very high. He confirmed that any such early retirement would need to be subject to the Greater London Council having the right to refuse or delay an application, if they needed to retain the employee concerned, to complete duties that they were currently engaged on.

This effective action by Geoff Manning was a major breakthrough, and would help the timely reduction of the number of employees within the Housing Construction directorate in line with the rate of completions of the remaining contracts. It would also incentivise the thousand or more directly employed operatives under his control to look for employment elsewhere. They might then be able to set up their own small businesses or become self-employed. In these ways their early voluntary redundancy money would be re-circulated in the economy and create new jobs and wealth for those who took up the Council's offer.

Chapter 47

In early October 1978 the Prime Minister, James Callaghan, ducked the possibility of calling an immediate General Election. Had he done so the nicknamed 'winter of discontent' could have been avoided, a Labour Government might have gained a further mandate from the electorate, and Den might have completed his five year fixed term of office as the Director of Housing Construction with the Greater London Council.

The long dark cold winter of 1978/1979 was not a good time for the Labour Government. Both television and newspapers concentrated time and time again on the enormous piles of black waste disposal bags strewn everywhere on the streets of Britain. Against this background the electorate gradually lost confidence in the Labour Government and examined more closely what policies the new Leader of the Conservative Party, Mrs Margaret Thatcher, was offering to the British voters.

*****

In September of 1978 the Housing Construction directorate was asked to bid, in competition with five private sector contractors who were on the Greater London Council's approved list, for a 'large' contract for six hundred low rise housing units (up to three floors). By then the Direct Labour Organisation needed more work if large enforced redundancies were to be avoided. The price submitted by Den's team was a sensible, but keen, one that would have been sufficient for them to carry out all the works with a small 'profit.' The overheads of the operation had by then been drastically reduced, the output rates achieved by the various trades were very satisfactory and this would be the first test of how much progress had been made in sharpening up the operation, by proving that it was now competitive.

The tenders for the work were opened in secret without anyone present from any of the bidders, in accordance with strictly laid down procedures. It transpired that the Construction Branch had submitted the lowest price for the work—and their bid contained no conditional clauses. When the news spread the reaction was one of pleasant surprise by the white and blue collar workers within the Branch. A contract such as this would normally be started within a few weeks of being awarded. The older and wiser heads wondered if the Housing Committee would press ahead with the contract, and allow their internal Direct Labour Organisation to begin the works.

After a few weeks the new Conservative controlled Greater London Council decided that they would award the contract to the lowest of the private sector bidders, without making an official announcement about the matter. This decision meant that the need for an early voluntary redundancy scheme for the DLO workers was now of paramount importance. Hundreds of the workforce would have been ready, willing and able to make a concerted start on the new contract which was situated just to the east of the main road from Lambeth to Brixton. Indeed the site was less than one mile from the Head Office of the Housing Construction operation. Fortunately the early redundancy scheme had been introduced and had attracted very large numbers of volunteers, thereby assisting the rundown of the Construction Branch.

The decision to award the contract to the private sector had been met with bitter disappointment from the internal staff, who blamed it on the new administration. Perhaps the two decisions were taken simultaneously. The outcome was that Geoff Manning's office in the Personnel Department of the Council was very busy indeed for the next six months. During this period the total labour force of the Branch was reduced from 1,350 to a mere 800. At the same time one contract per week was being completed, and handed over to the Housing Development Branch—so that it could be occupied by the ever-increasing numbers of local residents who would rather be housed by the Council than a private sector landlord who charged them a very high level of rent, and often refused to offer any maintenance services whatsoever.

*****

At that stage Den was travelling up to his constituency of Chorley, in Lancashire, every Thursday or Friday evening to ensure that a very large number of electors could be canvassed by his voluntary team of Conservative Party workers. Every Sunday Den totalled up the cumulative pledges in each of the 30 electoral wards—to see if there were any trends emerging and to see if the results were better or worse than the last few sets of annual local authority election results for the Chorley Borough Council and the Lancashire County Council.

He was constantly preparing new leaflets for delivery through the thirty thousand letterboxes within his constituency. He was also writing plenty of letters to the local press, and making sure that he was active in and around all the 24 villages surrounding the market town of Chorley. All these villages were part of his constituency and contained many of his strongest supporters, and Party workers. The local Conservative Association operated from an office one minute from the Town Hall and only three minutes from the offices of the two local weekly papers. One of these had to be paid for by the reader, the Chorley Guardian, and the other was a 'free issue' journal, the Chorley Citizen. In addition the Lancashire Evening Post was printed daily. They had an office right in the centre of Chorley and a circulation area which covered Chorley and the surrounding fifteen miles.

The local secretary of the Conservative Party, Elsie Whittington, took excellent shorthand and was brilliant on punctuation and grammar. She typed out all the letters and press statements for Den. His Agent, Howard Stirling, liaised with the local printers, raised money for the Party, arranged local events and dealt with any matters relating to election procedures, voting and the electoral registers. Two local authorities made up the Parliamentary constituency. The Town Clerk for the Chorley Borough Council was based in Chorley Town Hall. The Chief Executive of the South Ribble Borough Council that covered a quarter of the Chorley Parliamentary Constituency—was based in the adjacent town of Leyland.

Den had been 'nursing' his constituency for more than three years since his selection as the Conservative Prospective Parliamentary Candidate in January 1976. For the first half of this period he had been in charge of the Wimpey and Laing work in Iran, for the second half he had been Director of Housing Construction at the Greater London Council. In those three years he calculated that he had driven his own car up and down the M1 and M6 Motorways the incredible distance of 150,000 miles. He and his family had not had a relaxing holiday for four years because all his spare time, and much of theirs, had been spent at their home in Chorley which was so conveniently situated one mile from the Chorley Town Hall and only three miles from the South Ribble Council Offices.

Den was frequently asked why he bothered with politics at all.

'Surely it is a dog eat dog trade where everyone ends up as a loser? Why don't you sit back and relax at the weekends instead of going all that way without any guarantee that you will ever become a Member of Parliament? You must be crazy for wanting to give up a secure and well paid job in your chosen profession. Why bother?'

Den was constantly asked these questions by people whom he knew very well and whose opinions he respected. However, as every political candidate knows, once you get the bug you cannot back away and retreat from the battlefield. You have to go on, and on, and on—until you have no other option, and all doors are firmly shut. At one stage in his career Den had even been offered the job of Director of Development for the largest food retail operation in the United Kingdom where there was a massive forward programme of retail design and construction to be carried out. Five hundred applicants had applied and Den was selected for the post. However, the Chairman and Managing Director of the whole Group had insisted that Den would have to end his political career for good if he agreed to take up the appointment. Den made it abundantly clear that, with the deepest regret, he could not accept the position on that basis. It was several years later that Den realised that the man in charge of the whole operation, and the single shareholder, had been very keen indeed to become a Member of Parliament himself but had seen his potential political career terminated prematurely—without good reason.

*****

Den was thrilled one day when the North West Region Chairman of the Conservative Party telephoned him and offered to arrange for the Leader of the Conservative Party, the Right Honourable Mrs Margaret Thatcher MP for Finchley, to spend two hours on a factory visit in Chorley. This was arranged very efficiently and the visit would be to a high technology mechanical engineering and automation firm based half a mile from the centre of Chorley.

Brian Taylor and his brother Ron had built up their private firm over many years. It was expanding and thriving, even after a long tricky period for the

British economy. Brian knew Den very well and was delighted that the Chorley Conservative Association had chosen Den to fight the seat at the next General Election. He was fully aware that Den was a civil engineer and that his father had been a mechanical engineer and a top man in industry in the North West and also in Newcastle-upon-Tyne.

The visit went like clockwork and Mrs Thatcher received a huge ovation. As an industrial chemist she was fascinated by all the technology, the robotics, the automation, and the mechanical handling equipment that had been developed in the Chorley enterprise. She made a wonderful speech at the end of the visit and helped boost support for Den by taking the time and trouble to visit his highly marginal seat during what could well be the final year or so of her period as Leader of Her Majesty's Opposition.

The following day Den had been asked to bring his personal car to the main reception door of the Manchester Piccadilly hotel right in the centre of Manchester. Conservative Central Office had made all the arrangements for Den to drive Mrs Thatcher and two others all the way down to her home in Chelsea. Detailed checks were made well in advance about the personal ownership of Den's Ford Granada vehicle and its registration and other details. It had to be an acceptable make, for political and security reasons. Political vetting and checking had clearly been developing for many decades—and had become so important. Indeed the next top level Conservative politician to visit the Chorley marginal constituency was the Right Honourable Airey Neave MP for Abingdon—who had escaped from Colditz in 1942, and who was tragically murdered by terrorists planting a bomb under his car which detonated when he was driving out of the House of Commons car park.

Den arrived in good time and parked his car as near to the main entrance door to the Piccadilly Hotel as he could. Two Security policemen descended immediately and they checked all his personal and car details. They told him that he would be accompanied by a motorcycle escort out to the M6 Motorway and then they would leave him to head south unescorted, after he had left their designated area. This was a tricky and unusual task for Den. The police procession sounded their sirens at each set of traffic lights and went through several red lights. It was a weird feeling for Den to drive through so many red lights, especially when he was escorted and surrounded by the forces of law and order.

Mrs Thatcher spent the first ten minutes chatting with her two fellow passengers about detailed matters of that day, arising from a few more constituency visits to marginal seats—and an important speech she had just made to leading members of the North West business community. She then turned her attention to Den and said how much she had enjoyed her visit to Chorley the previous day:-

'What a splendid man Mr Taylor is. We have some very good business people in our Party and they deserve a better Government. What about you Den? Tell me a little about yourself.'

'I was born in Warrington which we will drive past in the next twenty minutes. I went to Manchester Grammar School and Manchester University—both of which are only a few minutes away from where we are now. I was a Councillor on your local authority of Barnet for three years. I fought Caerphilly in the October 1974 Election and I have been nursing Chorley for the last three years.'

'Splendid, Den. We have to make sure we get you in up here. It is a very important part of the Country for us' were the last words Mrs Thatcher spoke until she woke from her sleep two and a half hours later.

The other two passengers in the car on the journey south were Mrs Thatcher's Parliamentary Private Secretary, John Stanley MP for Tonbridge and Malling, and her personal security guard who was an armed detective. Fortunately the non-stop journey was a smooth and hassle-free one. Mrs Thatcher was so tired that she slept all the way from the edge of Manchester to, rather aptly, the Finchley Road in north London only a few miles from her home in Chelsea.

Den had been given very strict instructions that he must not, under any circumstances, accept any invitation by Mrs Thatcher to enter her home. John Stanley MP asked to be dropped off just before St John's Wood, at the John Barnes store by Finchley Road underground station saying his London residence was just round the corner. The private detective asked to be dropped off a few hundred yards west of Hyde Park Corner, oddly enough outside the Iranian Embassy, which was to be the scene of the three day armed occupation by terrorists a few years later.

By then Mrs Thatcher was straightening herself up, knowing that her home in Flood Street was only three minutes away. When Den parked the car right outside the front gate there were no security guards or police in evidence, which Den was most surprised about. He opened the rear door of his car for Mrs Thatcher and escorted her to the front door before returning to pick up her small case and belongings from the boot. She opened the front door with her keys and then popped her head inside the doorway.

'DENISSS, DENISSSS!' she shouted in her most powerful voice aiming it up the staircase. This was exactly the same powerful voice that Den heard Mrs Thatcher use eleven years later to shout 'NO, NO, NO' towards the end of her last speech as Prime Minister in the House of Commons.

'Oh, where is he?' she said in a muted voice. Then 'Oh, there you are. I'm coming up and Den is with me' she said standing on the bottom two steps.

Mrs Thatcher motioned to Den to sit down and Denis appeared in the front first floor lounge, without any further delay. 'Well old boy, how about a drink?' he asked, being polite and hospitable.

'No, no—I don't drink and I must be off,' said Den.

'A soft drink then?' said Denis.

'No, really, I must be off,' repeated Den, conscious that he had already broken his promise not to enter the home, which was in immaculate condition.

Mrs Thatcher came sweeping into the room 'Have you got rid of that car yet?' was the question Mrs Thatcher posed to her husband.

'Yes dear, I think it will have gone by the end of the week.'

'I know I keep going on about it, but it IS a real security risk with DEN123 on its number plates. Do please try this time to get rid of it.'

Den thought it was time he left the two of them alone, but before he did so he noticed that Mrs Thatcher's observant eyes kept glancing at his leather shoes, with a quizzical expression. He had visited one of his local farmers that day and had not had time to pop home to clean his shoes. It was a lesson that Den learned for the future. He had never been a Boy Scout but he knew their motto was 'Be Prepared.' Ever since then Den has kept at least one spare pair of shoes in the boot of his car. Ironically Den only discovered many years later that Mrs Thatcher had a fetish about men's shoes. What must she have thought?

Chapter 48

Back in London the number of applications for early voluntary retirement was growing daily. Those employees who had the least period of time before they would be entitled to retire at their normal retirement age were given priority and after that it was a matter of 'first come, first served.' The Housing Construction Directorate would not be charged with any of the additional costs of the early retirement scheme. These would be borne by the Greater London Council itself. However, there was a strong possibility that the Government would accept part of these costs, particularly because they were on the point of accepting that all local authorities would be eligible for help in such circumstances—subject to a fully argued case being submitted to the relevant Government Department.

The Construction branch was continuing to work efficiently and effectively on all its remaining sites and one contract every week was being handed over, as complete. There was now a requirement to see if any of the Project Managers or Site Managers should be considered for some kind of transfer to suitable employment elsewhere in the Council, or offered a similar deal to the 'blue collar' workforce.

*****

On the evening of Thursday, 29 March 1979, after several further very busy weekends of intensive campaigning up in Chorley, the one major uncertainty in Den's life was removed.

It was that evening that the Prime Minister, the Right Honourable James Callaghan MP was winding up at the end of a very heated and noisy debate on the Motion that 'This House has full confidence in Her Majesty's Government.'

Den listened to the last two hours of the debate on an old-fashioned radio situated in the kitchen of his home in Borehamwood, fifteen miles to the north west of the Houses of Parliament. He had often queued up to attend important late night debates on matters of policy affecting his constituency of Chorley, in Lancashire. These Adjournment Debates were very informative but never aroused any strong emotions in the Members of Parliament, or the members of the public viewing and listening up in the Public Gallery. There would usually only be a few dozen members of the public at such a late hour, always after 10 pm, who were sampling 'the best theatre in London'—and completely free of charge.

That evening the House had been full to overflowing for the whole six hour debate, with some of the best political speakers from all sides taking part. The requests for speaking time were so numerous that a time limit of five minutes had been laid down for all speakers, apart from the Party Leaders of the main Parties.

Den would have given his right arm to be in the Public Gallery that evening but he had been busy in the Head Office of the Housing Construction Directorate across the River Thames until 7.30 pm. He had a quick snack at home before waking his daughter, who had insisted that he must do so, in time for the voting at 10 pm. He listened intently to the radio commentary which was not very clear. At one stage it seemed that the Labour Government had survived the vote, but when the final voting figures were announced it was clear that the Government had been defeated by a single vote.

The commentator had made it abundantly clear that a defeat by even one vote would mean that the Prime Minister would be forced to call an immediate General Election. The kitchen ceiling nearly collapsed with the noise of shouting and screaming by Den, his wife and his eleven year old daughter Amanda. Meanwhile his eight year old son slept peacefully through the whole night, oblivious to the drama that had unfolded, and which might well mean even more boring and tiring three hour journeys for him up and down to Lancashire.

Chapter 49

Den completed as much of his workload at the Construction branch as he could the next day and then headed north for discussions with his Election Agent, Howard Stirling, and his main campaign team. They had decided to fight the General Election on a ward by ward basis, with several smaller wards being grouped under a Coordinator. One of Den's biggest jobs was to write his General Election leaflet that would be hand delivered to every household in the Constituency. These 30,000 leaflets would contain several photographs of Den around the whole area, and concentrate on both the key national political issues and the ones of a local interest. These included the need for the new hospital—which Den had pledged he would deliver—retention of the Green Belt and the future of British Leyland which was based in both Leyland and Chorley, his two main towns.

Howard Stirling had fought many local and General Elections and he was a proven professional Party Agent. Only five years earlier he had headed up the Conservative Party organisation in both the February and October 1974 General Elections in Chorley. He knew the geography of the whole area, as any ex-Marine would. Den and Howard had several meetings during the first weekend of the election campaign and set out their overall programme for all the wards. It was essential that Den met as many of the people of Chorley as possible so the programme for the four final weeks was divided up into three sessions each day. The first was 10 am to 1 pm, the second was 2 pm to 5 pm and the evening session was 6 pm to 9 pm. Den was thankful that he was as fit as a fiddle, and he looked forward to walking, and often running, about twenty miles per day on each of the Mondays to Saturdays inclusive right up to Polling Day on Thursday 3 May 1979.

*****

In the first three days of the week commencing Monday April 2nd Den met with all his top managers either in his Director's office in Lambeth or out on the twenty three current sites. Three of the remaining contracts would be entirely completed before the date of the impending Election, leaving him with the task of overseeing only twenty contracts after that date. Den knew he was in for a really tough fight up in Chorley but this was what he had always craved since the seed had been planted as a young boy—the opportunity to win a General Election and become a Conservative Member of Parliament, working for the people.

Some of the management team asked Den what would happen if he won the election up in Chorley. They knew he was on a five year contract and, now that no further building contracts would be awarded to the Construction Branch, they were clearly fearful that they may become redundant as the number of current contracts dropped below the twenty level. All these managers were aware that the early voluntary redundancy scheme for the 'blue collar workers' employed by the Construction Branch had been introduced at the instigation of Den, and they were pleased that it was being effective. Den wondered if they were asking surreptitiously if it might be possible for there to be a similar scheme for the 'white collar workers' in the Branch.

Den pointed out that the number of contracts would drop to twenty within a month. It was almost certain that no more work would be taken on by their organisation, so there would be a gradual reduction in the need for managers, agents, general foremen and office staff such as financial, cost control, materials scheduling and clerical work. He promised that he would make an early request for a similar early voluntary redundancy scheme to be made available to them all, whichever way the election in Chorley went. His relationships with his staff were excellent and he pointed out that he had been employed on a five year contract—which he would be seeing through to the end. He added that he was most unlikely to become a junior Minister or an aide to a Cabinet Minister, if there was a Conservative government in a few weeks' time. He pointed out that there were hundreds of Conservative Members of Parliament who were much more experienced than he was, and many of these would—quite rightly—be expecting to step onto the first rung of the promotion ladder in a few weeks' time. In any case there might well be no change of Government.

Chapter 50

Den had saved annual leave time especially for the General Election and it was vital that he spent as much of his time in Chorley as possible. He had to be the figurehead of the whole election campaign and lead by example. He needed to be available to everybody at all times.

Ever since he had been selected as the Prospective Parliamentary Candidate for Chorley in January 1976 he had been writing letters to the Editors of all the local and regional newspapers. This had ensured that his name had become very well known in the general area—and particularly in Chorley, Leyland and the surrounding villages forming the Chorley Parliamentary constituency. There were 81,016 electors who would decide his whole future career on Thursday 3 May 1979 by casting their votes between 8 am and 9 pm that day. The only exceptions would be those who, for health, business or family reasons needed to vote by post instead. The majority of these people would have registered their wish to vote by post with the appropriate local Council Electoral Officer.

A whole procedure was followed by all the political Parties to make sure that, particularly in marginal seats like Chorley, none of the potential postal voters were ignored. It was well known that these very people were more likely to cast their votes than those who would be voting in person on the actual Polling Day. Squads of Party volunteers would focus on making sure that all the Postal Voters received a copy of Den's Election Address or leaflet through their letter boxes several days before the deadline for Postal Voting. The name of the Member of Parliament elected for a constituency had so often been decided by which Party these postal voters had chosen to support, so Howard Stirling and Den had to ensure that enough resources were directed to these voters within their organisational planning.

For six days each week Den adhered rigidly to the carefully prepared programme of the three sessions for 'walking the streets.' Fortunately the weather was reasonably dry on most days and the Conservative Party workers were very keen indeed to play their part, and work hard right through the election campaign period. These were the same volunteers who, for the last three and a half years had been out working alongside Den whenever he came to their village or part of the town. They knew many of the local people and some of them were Councillors for Chorley Borough Council or South Ribble Borough Council, and devoted much of their spare time to political and local Council matters. During the daily sessions of three hours each, 10 am to 1 pm, 2 pm to 5 pm and 6 pm to 9 pm Den and his team covered the whole of specific electoral wards by knocking on all the doors. They ensured that Den had a word with everyone who was in, and left a leaflet with each household— sometimes mentioning particular issues in each locality they visited—and answering any questions they may have.

The ideal team for one of these two hour sessions would be eight to ten fit, sure-footed men and women who knew their areas well and could keep up with the fast pace that Den set for them all. The group would be accompanied by a loudspeaker van plastered with election posters with a few key words such as VOTE CONSERVATIVE. VOTE DOVER. All these posters would be in the special distinctive Conservative 'true blue' printing, large enough to be seen and read from a distance of fifty to a hundred yards.

The purpose of the nine hours per day on the streets was to show that Den and his Party were anxious to make themselves available to all the people in the constituency. Den had already personally called on almost all the houses in the constituency by foot slogging on Fridays, Saturdays and all his holiday time— thereby becoming known in all the areas, building up his local knowledge and meeting people throughout the whole constituency. Den's contention was that you needed to meet and know your constituents, and your constituency, if you were going to be able to represent them properly, and be an effective and efficient Servant of the People.

In the one hour periods between the three daily sessions of door to door campaigning it was possible for Den and two or three of his supporters to pop into the nearest village or town shopping area and hand out leaflets to all the people they could see—especially on market days. This was very important and allowed Den to pop quickly into all the shops and local businesses to shake hands, have a quick word and then press on. By the second week of such intensive campaigning Den had several blisters on his feet but a good hot bath every night worked wonders for him. He did not have any difficulty at all in sleeping at nights. He was happy to go to bed totally exhausted provided he had achieved his declared aim for each day, namely to meet as many of his constituents as possible.

Chapter 51

On the first Sunday of the campaign Peter Birtwistle, Chairman of the Chorley Conservative Association, had requested the presence of Den, as the Parliamentary Candidate, at a meeting to be held in his home in Upper Brinscall—a village five miles north east of Chorley. Den was flabbergasted to walk into his large lounge to find a crowd of local Conservative Branch workers. They were already highly organised on various clerical jobs but they stopped when Den entered the room and the Chairman announced that they would be starting the meeting forthwith.

Peter's wife Sheila was a formidable lady who had been the official driver for several top Army staff in the Second World War. She organised all that she did along military lines, and clearly the hundred or more present at the meeting were waiting for their next instructions. She went through the detailed arrangements that they had all agreed to for the next four weeks operations. As she addressed the group of people from each village, one after another, they gave her a detailed progress report on what they had been doing, and what they intended to achieve over the coming weeks. This very same meeting had been held in Peter's lounge for both the General Elections in Chorley in 1974. There was a real buzz in the air and everyone was so enthusiastic. This was the only occasion when they would all meet before the election because they would be so busy, out on the ground, carrying out their instructions as outlined by the Birtwistles.

During a short tea break Den spoke to the meeting about the arrangements that were being followed around the rest of the constituency. He emphasised the scale of their task in having to overcome the Labour majority of 2,713 votes in October 1974 and pointed out that the Labour MP for Chorley had now had more than five years' experience and had been very active and quite popular in the area. It was vital that Labour should be defeated and he would be doing everything possible to make sure that they secured a good majority—pointing out that Chorley was one of the most crucial of the marginal seats that would decide the outcome of the General Election.

Howard Stirling, Den's Election Agent, then addressed the meeting on a few important points of electoral procedure and promised that he would always be available for advice and assistance in his office in Chorley. There followed a buffet lunch during which Den circulated and made sure that he shook the hand of every person in the room. He needed their time and assistance and he thanked them in advance for all they would be doing. When Howard and Den drove back into Chorley they chatted about the prospects for a Conservative victory. They both agreed that Mrs Thatcher was being very punchy and had, quite rightly, gone onto the attack from the outset of the campaign. She had been emphasising the need for private enterprise and condemning Socialism for preventing Britain from achieving its full potential.

Howard and Den went through the photographs and the wording of several leaflets and the main Election Address that would be delivered to every household. Den enjoyed the creative work of preparing and finalising these important items, but he could not wait to get out and about on the streets where he could make a physical impression on the voters, whilst the leaflets and paperwork were mainly aimed at the minds and hearts of the voters.

There was a series of public meetings that had been arranged by pressure groups concerned about matters such as overseas aid, abortion, farming, the health service and unemployment. These were all held in the evenings which meant that Den had to start his three hour period of electioneering on those evenings almost an hour early and down a quick cup of tea and a biscuit in one of the homes of his team of helpers that afternoon. These pressure group meetings were sometimes just with Den alone, but more usually candidates from the other parties were present to put their points of view. Each candidate would give a short introductory speech and a shorter wind up at the end. All these meetings were informative and helpful, both to the members of the public who attended and to the candidates. Usually there were several dozen people present but any meetings regarding the lack of adequate health provision, and the need for a new District General Hospital, were standing room only. Undoubtedly this was the issue of the moment, and Den was conscious that there had been public marches in both Chorley and Leyland a few years earlier with 30,000 people walking right through the centre of the towns.

On the hospital issue there was one large public meeting during the election period. It was held in the Chorley Town Hall and it was packed. The sitting Labour Member of Parliament, George Rodgers, was standing for re-election and he tried to explain that the health service was doing all they could to meet the health needs of the people of the area. However, he seemed to give the impression that the current arrangements were satisfactory, and gave no promises of any improvements.

Den gave a very strong and positive speech. He was able to say that he had helped to build several excellent new District General Hospitals around the country, and that is what was most certainly required in Chorley. He pledged his full support for the campaign and promised that, if elected, it would be at the top of his agenda at all times. He pointed out that the Royal Preston Hospital had been built in the wrong place for the wrong reasons. The over-ambitious plans for a Central Lancashire New Town meant that it had been built five miles north of the River Ribble instead of seven miles south. This meant that anyone in the two large and growing towns of Chorley and Leyland had to travel all the way through Preston to reach the hospital or go twelve miles up the M6 Motorway—instead of being able to attend a hospital on their doorstep.

In many ways this was the key turning point in Den's campaign because everyone was so impressed and excited by the fact that the Conservative candidate, Den Dover, had made a rock solid, firm pledge to deliver a new District General Hospital. One which would be able to serve the people of Chorley and the surrounding areas—who deserved better, and would literally 'get better' if a Conservative Government was elected on May 3rd.

Chapter 52

April was passing by so quickly as the election campaign progressed and the date of the General Election approached. Den needed every day of that month to make sure that he had done all he possibly could to convince the electorate in Chorley and to maximise the Conservative vote. Howard Stirling and Den's complete team of voluntary workers were highly motivated and eagerly awaiting the big day. They knew exactly what they had to do in the last few days and on the day of the election.

Knocking up is the terminology to include all the various ways of harnessing a larger vote than just letting things happen. Committee Rooms were set up in every polling district and lists of all the voters' names and addresses (also telephone numbers if available) were pasted onto large sheets of cardboard. A small team of helpers would rotate shifts through the whole thirteen hours during which voting could take place. One or two other volunteers would sit outside each polling station and collect the electoral register numbers of those who had cast their votes, irrespective of which Party they had voted for. Lists of these numbers would then be taken to the local Committee Room every hour or two, so that the numbers, names and addresses of those who had voted could be crossed out—with no further action needed.

All this activity was vital to check on how the voting was progressing. In each polling ward the Conservative Party had many experienced election specialists who would quickly be able to produce lists of the constituents who had not voted, and who needed to be called on by a volunteer and encouraged to vote. This could be done by walking around the polling ward, or driving round with one or two helpers to get out the vote. All these activities were designed to maximise the Conservative vote and to ensure that all known supporters had voted before the close of polls that day.

It was very clear that most of the listed Conservative supporters were very keen to vote. However, nothing was left to chance and all the Committee

Rooms throughout the Chorley constituency played their part in maximising the number of Conservative votes cast that day.

Den had decided that he should pop into all the Polling Stations and thank the officials for their efforts, have an encouraging word with the tellers outside the Polling Stations and visit all the Committee Rooms. This was a full time commitment throughout the thirteen hour voting period, with only time for a quick hot drink at a few of the houses being used as Committee Rooms.

Den was able to be accompanied during part of the day by his wife Marina, his daughter Amanda and his son Timothy—because all their schools were being used as Polling Stations and were therefore not open to pupils or teachers. Den and his family, travelling together, portrayed the happy family image that was part and parcel of the Conservative message. Both children enjoyed the hours they spent on the campaign trail but made sure they slept at their home in Chorley for several hours during the evening so that they could stay up to see some of the early results on the television channels.

Howard told Den that he would take control of everything in Chorley Town Hall that evening, as Den's Election Agent. He insisted that Den and his wife should arrive at the Town Hall at 10 pm, although the first large black metal boxes containing the voting papers would not arrive or be opened up until nearer midnight.

A large crowd of counting officials, Party workers, press and the public started to gather inside the Town Hall of Chorley from 10 pm. Howard knew that everyone would be in for a long night, and that there might well need to be a recount if the result was close. Between 11 pm and midnight all the black metal boxes containing the votes of the electors had been received at the Town Hall, tipped out over the long wooden counting tables, and the total numbers of the votes cast in each polling ward counted. Around the outside of the voting tables sat one hundred counting agents who bundled up the votes cast into hundreds, using rubber bands. Soon the total number of votes cast was ascertained, subject to correction when the number of spoilt papers was decided. Howard had gathered that the turnout was slightly higher than in the October 1974 General Election in Chorley (the final figure was indeed up by 1% to the very high figure of 82% turnout, one of the highest in the country).

A whole hour passed before the separation and counting of the votes for each of the candidates started. Howard could see that Den was looking rather concerned as he toured the tables and counted the number of bundles of 100 for each of the candidates on each of the tables. Howard told Den not to worry, but that was easier said than done. As all the bundles of votes cast were placed in large open boxes on top of the counting tables it was reasonably easy to see that the total number of votes for the Conservative and Labour candidates was close. Howard still told Den not to worry, then Den noticed a very large pile of votes being lifted from under one of the central counting tables. Den's heart jumped when he noticed that all of these votes were for him and not equally shared as all the other piles were. Howard's only comment was 'There you are, I told you not to worry.'

These separated and banded voting papers had all been votes for Den. They had been placed on the floor under the tables until the clerks had cleared sufficient space on top of the tables to allow the grouping of votes to continue.

*****

Unbelievably the final voting figures were not available, or announced until after 4 am, which was several hours after hundreds of other constituency voting results had been announced on the many radio sets in the Town Hall. It started to look good for the Conservatives, especially the longer the night went on.

At long last all the Parliamentary candidates and their Election agents were asked to join the Town Clerk, Brian Webster, up on the platform so that he could advise them of the final figures. The candidates were then asked to move towards the centre of the platform for the official announcement of the result.

The Town Clerk then announced that:-

'As the Returning Officer for the Chorley Constituency I hereby declare that the numbers of votes cast for each candidate are as follows:-

Den Dover Conservative 31,125
George Rodgers Labour 28,546
Mrs Neva Orrell Liberal 6,388
Michael Dean National Front 379

This was a resounding victory for the Conservatives and was seen as a significant result in one of the crucial marginal seats in the North West. Within an hour BBC TV had tracked Den down and recorded a five-minute interview for showing on the main TV coverage programme starting at 6 am.

As Den and his wife emerged from the Town Hall at nearly 5 am, there was a frost on the ground. Den was totally exhausted but at the same time on a real high. He had finally won a seat in Parliament as a Conservative MP. He had no idea what happened next but decided that he should quickly arrange a Thank You celebration event for the Saturday. This was an Open House at the Dover home a mile from Chorley Town Hall. Needless to say there was standing room only. Den reckoned that more than five hundred supporters and well-wishers passed through the front door. Fortunately it was a sunny dry day and most of the supporters, Party workers and friends were able to go out into the garden. It was a thoroughly enjoyable occasion for all concerned. Den made a very short speech, thanking everyone who had helped in his campaign, but especially his Election Agent, Howard Stirling.

*****

At the General Election of 1979 the Conservative Party, under the leadership of Mrs Margaret Thatcher, was returned to power with a majority of 44 over all other Parties.

Mrs Thatcher became Britain's first woman Prime Minister.

The Conservative Party won 339 seats compared to 276 seats in the October 1974 General Election. The Labour Party won 268 seats compared to 319 seats in the October 1974 General Election.

Chapter 53

The Dover family headed south on Sunday, 6 May 1979, after attending the local Methodist church service in their local village of Euxton. Den wanted to arrive at the Lambeth Head Office of the Housing Construction directorate early on the Monday morning in case anyone tried to object to him returning to his position as Director on a five year contract, which still had almost half that period to run.

Den's euphoria was very quickly deflated on the journey. When he stopped at a motorway service station he bought a Sunday Times and read the front page large print headline 'Tory MP told quit or risk the sack.' He wondered what all this was about, or rather which of his new colleagues the media was trying to destroy. He read every word carefully and only realised after the first few lines that the huge article referred to HIM.

The article had been written by a left wing journalist who was a Labour Councillor on the London Borough of Camden. It referred to the Report to the Housing Committee of the Greater London Council that had been satisfactorily dealt with by the Housing Committee and its Officers nearly a year earlier. It was clear to Den that this was a political attack on him and designed to cause maximum panic in Conservative circles.

This was character assassination of the worst kind, and no attempt had been made by the paper to contact him via his two homes, his Election Agent, the local Chorley press or the Conservative Party. Den was not wrong when he thought to himself 'Is this a taste of things to come?'

When Jack O'Brien called into his office early the next day he stated firmly to Den that he knew nothing about the article whatsoever. Jack thought that someone in the media must have been handed a copy of the Committee Report which had been marked with the words 'In Confidence.' However, he confirmed that the Report had been completely accepted by the Housing Committee of the GLC and all the matters referred to had been dealt with many months earlier. Den's defence mechanisms had been aroused and he resolved to toughen his stance against anyone who sought to damage his reputation, or perhaps try to force him to resign his Chief Officer position with the Greater London Council.

Initially Den had thought that the headline of the article was calling on him to resign as a Member of Parliament or risk the sack by his Party, presumably by them withdrawing the Conservative whip, and in effect disowning him. He later realised that the article was calling on him to resign his position as a Chief Officer with the Greater London Council—or risk the Council sacking him.

Den carried on as the Director of Housing Construction and decided that he would have to be very careful and be naturally suspicious of everyone around him—which was totally the opposite of his natural inclinations. Den received an urgent letter at his Borehamwood home from the Chief Whip of the Conservative Party in the House of Commons asking him to attend the Houses of Parliament on one of three days, to swear in. He decided he would do this outside the GLC normal working hours. He walked over to the Houses of Parliament during the hours specified and received another shock. He was walking up to the Main Gate to the car park when a policeman greeted him with the words:-

'Good afternoon Mr Dover. Can I help you with where you want to go?'

Den expressed his surprise that he had been recognised. He had no idea that all the policemen on duty within the Palace of Westminster had been using the Parliamentary recess during the Election Campaign period to swot up on all the potential new Members of Parliament. Den was massively impressed by this incident and the dedication of all those who worked within the Houses of Parliament.

One of the hardest jobs for a newly elected MP was to find an office to work in. Den eventually discovered that no new Conservative MP would be issued with an office, which would be shared with another MP, for at least six months, and possibly a year. This was a totally unacceptable situation and Den only coped by using his car boot as his office until the start of the year 1980. The one huge bonus was that every MP was entitled to a parking space in the underground car park situated below the large garden area between the Main Gate and Big Ben, the world famous clock tower.

One highlight of his early months in the House was the recommendation of his name for the Transport Select Committee. This was a wonderful gesture by a long-standing Conservative MP, Albert Costain who said that as the only civil engineer in the House of Commons, it was essential that he be appointed to this brand new Select Committee. He said that it was imperative that the good sense, technical knowledge and professional outlook of a civil engineer be made available to the new Committee. Albert had been a Director of the worldwide Costain civil engineering empire for decades and knew what he was talking about.

Chapter 54

The Official Opening of Parliament by the Queen was a stunning event. All road traffic in the surrounding area was prohibited and all Members of Parliament were required to be in the House of Commons chamber by 10.30 am prompt. All Members of the Upper Chamber, the House of Lords, were given a similar instruction. By 11 am, the Royal Procession arrived by road at the foot of the very tall square Victoria Tower, at the southern end of the Houses of Parliament. The Queen alighted from her State Coach, accompanied by her husband, the Duke of Edinburgh. They processed up the many steps to the Robing Room and then on towards the House of Lords, settling into their thrones in good time before the House of Lords was opened up to receive a very long procession of Members of Parliament who traditionally packed tight into the far end of the House of Lords to hear the Queen's Speech.

Finally, Den had arrived where he wanted to be. He felt that he had joined the most exclusive club in the world. He had had to struggle at all points along the road. He had very little knowledge about how the job of a Member of Parliament was carried out. He knew nothing of the detailed procedures involved, but he was certainly very keen indeed to learn everything he could about the role of a Member of Parliament—and as soon as possible.

It was clear that he was still surrounded by enemies of one kind or another but, like his father, he would fight on until victory was won. He gazed in awe at the wonderful architecture of the Palace of Westminster and found it difficult to realise that he was now working in the very same buildings where his two idols—Robert Hudson MP for Southport and Sir Winston Churchill—had paved the way for him, as Servants of the People.